VOLUME

Days of Blessing

Devotions for Wives and Mothers

NANCY CAMPBELL

100 Days of Blessing: Devotions for Wives and Mothers – Volume 2

Published by Welby Street Press, in association with Carpenter's Son Publishing, Franklin, Tennessee

Published in association with Larry Carpenter of Christian Book Services, LLC
www.christianbookservices.com

Cover and Interior Layout Design by Suzanne Lawing

Edited by Robert Irvin

Printed in the United States of America

978-1-940262-44-4

All Scriptures used in this book are from the King James Version or Revised Authorized Version. Other translations mentioned and abbreviated in the text are used with permission and are as follows:

CJB	Complete Jewish Bible
GNB	Good News Bible
JBP	The New Testament translated by J. B. Phillips
KNOX	The Holy Bible translated by Monsignor Knox
MSG	The Message
MLB	Modern Language Bible
NASB	New American Standard Bible
NEB	New English Bible
NIV	New International Version
NLT	New Living Translation
RSV	Revised Standard Version
TLB	The Living Bible

Dedicated to my daughters,
granddaughters,
great-granddaughters,
and to all wives and mothers
who are the builders of their nation.
You deserve affirmation and encouragement.

You are employed in the most
high-powered career in the nation.
And God Himself is your Employer.

Contents

Alphabetical Contents

Introduction

Strength for Nation Builders

I know you have been waiting for Volume 2. Once again, you will be encouraged each day with life-giving encouragement from God's Word. These devotions are written to strengthen you as a Nation Builder. Your task is huge and you need new courage for each day.

Many wives and mothers love to start the day with these devotions. However, many can't stop at one and want to keep reading. Once they get to the end of the book, they start again. There is too much to take in with one reading only, so feel free to read it over and over again.

You will be edified by reading the devotion, but when you get time, please check out all the Scriptures. There's nothing like delving into God's Word, is there? It is your life and sustenance. Many devotions have FURTHER STUDY at the end, with many more Scriptures to check out. As I mention in this book, the truth of a subject in God's Word cannot be found in one Scripture. It's what God says about the subject from Genesis to Revelation that gives us the balanced truth.

Can I remind you to take notice of the Affirmations at the end of each devotion? Don't just read them. Confess them out loud. There is such power in affirming and confessing. If one affirmation particularly speaks to you, write or type it out and pin it up in your kitchen.

May you be blessed beyond measure and may *"the God of our Lord Jesus Christ, the Father of glory, give unto you the spirit of wisdom and revelation in the knowledge of him: the eyes of your understanding being enlightened; that ye may know what is the hope of his calling, and what the riches of the glory of His inheritance in the saints, and what is the exceeding greatness of his power to us-ward who believe, according to the working of his mighty power"* (Ephesians 1:17-19).

In His love,
NANCY CAMPBELL
www.aboverubies.org

If you have not read Volume 1 of 100 Days of Blessing, go to www.aboverubies.org or www.facebook.com/AboveRubiesUS to order.

How would you like to start today with an "un" week? Why not try it? I will give you a different "un" for the next seven days.

1

Unhurried

"There remaineth therefore a rest to the people of God" (HEBREWS 4:9).

Why don't you slow down a little today? Create an "unhurried" atmosphere. "How can I do that?" you sigh. "I've got so much to do. I don't know how I can get through it all."

Dear mother, you don't have to do everything. If you are one who writes lists for each day, write down the most important things you have to do today, but don't be disappointed if you don't get them all done. With little ones all around, you accomplish an amazing feat if you only get one extra thing done in a day. Perhaps you may not even achieve one extra thing! However, if you have cared for your little ones, kept the home basically clean and tidy, and cooked nutritious meals for your family, you can pat yourself on the back!

You'll find your children will all be more relaxed and happier when you calm down and get out of your frenzied attitude. When my children were young, I found they had the most behavior problems when I was hurrying everyone to get this or that done, or getting ready to go here and there. When I got off my "high horse" and stopped the great hurry, the children were happier and easier to handle.

Of course, I'm not talking about laziness. You have to be industrious to accomplish your household chores. But you'll find you'll complete a lot more if you do them with an "unhurried" attitude, rather than a frenzied mind-set.

When your children are restless or irritable, stop what you are doing, sit down with them, and read them a story. This will calm you and the children. I love these lines from *The Reading Mother* by Strickland Gillilan . . .

"You may have tangible wealth untold,
Caskets of jewels and coffers of gold,
Richer than I you can never be,
I had a mother who read to me."

Take a few minutes out of each day to enjoy watching your children. Watch them play. It is more entertaining than TV. Take time for the special moments.

I remember reading about a man of God who used to sign his letters, "Restfully busy." Learn to be busy with a restful heart. This is your right as a child of God. God has provided a rest for you. Hebrews 4:9 says, *"There remaineth therefore a rest to the people of God."* God lives in rest and He is not in a hurry. Acknowledge this blessed truth and start living in the rest that God has ordained for you.

"Be still my soul! The waves and winds still know
His voice who ruled them while He dwelt below."
~ Kathrina von Schlegel

PRAYER:

"Thank you, dear Father, that You live in rest and You live in me and I live in You. Help me to embrace the rest that You have provided for me. Help me to live with an unhurried attitude today. Fill my heart with Your peace and my home with Your calm and serenity. Put an anointing of peace upon all the children. Thank you, Lord, for the rest and peace we are going to enjoy today. Amen."

AFFIRMATION:

I will enjoy a "restfully busy" day.

2

Unmovable

"Therefore, my beloved brethren, be ye steadfast, unmovable, always abounding in the work of the Lord"
(1 Corinthians 15:58).

Do you find that you are often swayed by what this or that person says? The answer is to get your roots deep down into the soil of God's truth. Search God's Word to find out what He says and stick to your convictions. The truth of any subject in God's Word cannot be found in one Scripture. It's what God says on the subject from Genesis to Revelation that gives us the balanced truth.

Paul says in Galatians 1:8, *"But though we, or an angel from heaven, preach any other gospel unto you than that which we have preached unto you, let him be accursed."*

As mothers, we need to be unmovable in our stand for Christ and His principles, especially as an example to our children. They need to see that we are not swayed or moved from truth because of persecution, because things don't work out according to how we think they should, or because of difficult circumstances. No matter what happens, we are unmoved and unshaken! This is the proof of our Christianity before the world.

We don't believe because everything is going nicely; we believe because it is God's eternal truth. His Word is always the final authority. Circumstances of life have nothing to do with it. You may be going through hard and difficult times, but don't give up. Stand strong. God is more interested in preparing you for eternity than giving you a joy ride along the way!

I am challenged by the confession of Shadrach, Meshach, and Abednego when faced with being thrown into the fiery furnace because they would not bow down to the image.

They were not ashamed to confess, *"Our God whom we serve is able to deliver us from the burning fiery furnace, and he will deliver us out of thy hand, O king. But if not, be it known unto thee, O king, that we will not serve thy gods, nor worship the golden image which thou hast set up*" (Daniel 3:17, 18, Emphasis Author's).

These young men did not only put their faith in God's deliverance, but in God Himself. They trusted God, not for what He would do for them, but for Who He is. Even if God did not deliver them, they were undaunted in their stand for righteousness. Their stand did not depend on the outcome, but in walking in their convictions.

I want to encourage you from Ephesians 6:13, 14: "*Wherefore take unto you the whole armor of God, that ye may be able to withstand in the evil day, and having done all, to stand. Stand therefore, having your loins girt about with truth, and having on the breastplate of righteousness.*"

As mothers, we also need to be immovable in our calling as a mother. A mother who knows the power of her God-given career and the power of her home to raise and nurture her children for God is a threat to the enemy. He does not want mothers in the home. He wants them out of the way so he can get his hands upon the children to infiltrate them with his deceptions. Therefore, the pressure upon mothers is great. It comes from society, the education system, the media, and even the church. But, we must be immovable!

When persecution and pressure comes at us, we must not cave in. We can confess as Nehemiah did when his persecutors tried to stop him rebuilding the wall and gates of Jerusalem, "*I am doing a GREAT WORK, SO THAT I CANNOT COME DOWN: why should the work cease, whilst I leave it, and come down to you?*" (Nehemiah 6:, Emphasis Author's).

PRAYER:

"Oh God, please help me to be unmovable—unmoved by the derogatory things that people say to me, unmoved by every sleight of doctrine, and unmoved from my convictions even when everything is going wrong. Help me to stand against the forces of evil. Help me to stand against the humanistic deceptions that are all around me. Help me to stand against every wind of adversity. Thank you, Lord, for Your strength and power, which strengthens me in my inner man. Amen."

AFFIRMATION:

"The braces within me shall be greater than the pressures upon me." ~ E. Stanley Jones

Untainted

"Pure religion and undefiled before God and the Father is this . . . to keep himself unspotted from the world" (James 1:27).

It's not hard to get tainted, is it? We listen to gossip, or gossip ourselves, and it taints our spirits and also distorts our view of the person spoken against.

We turn on the TV and it tarnishes our spirits with the filth and deception of the world. We give in to the flesh and "blow our cool!" We speak sharply to those we love. We covet and hanker for the material things of this world that we don't really even need. We become spotted and tainted.

James 1:27 encourages us to keep ourselves *"unspotted from the world."* Some other translations say, *"unstained from the world."*

Would you like to try for an untainted day today? Keep your mind and heart aware of anything that would grieve the Holy Spirit of God who lives in you. Say "No" to anything that would stain your heart that has been washed clean by the blood of Jesus.

Of course, you're human and you can still fall! But when you do, immediately ask God's forgiveness and claim the power of the blood of Jesus to cleanse you and make you pure again. This is the power of the Gospel. Jesus shed His pure blood to make you clean. No sin is too hard for Him to wash clean.

Just as we wash our physical bodies daily, so we should allow our spirits to be washed daily by the blood of Jesus, and by the Word of God. David prayed, *"Wash me thoroughly from mine iniquity, and cleanse me from my sin. Purge me with hyssop, and I shall be clean: wash me, and I shall be whiter than snow . . . Create in me a clean heart, O God; and renew a right spirit within me"* (Psalm 51:2, 7, 10).

Ezekiel 36:26 says, *"A new heart also will I give you, and a new spirit will I put within you, and I will take away the stony heart out of your flesh; and I will give you a heart of flesh."*

John 15:3 says, *"Now ye are clean through the word which I have spoken unto you."*

1 John 1:7, 9 says, *"The blood of Jesus Christ his Son cleanseth us from all sin. . . If we confess our sins, he is faithful and just to forgive us our sins, and to cleanse us from all unrighteousness."*

The secret of staying untainted is to keep short accounts with God. Ask your children to join you for a day with no spots!

PRAYER:

"Dear Jesus, You have washed me clean by Your precious blood. Help me to keep clean. Help me to be very sensitive to Your Holy Spirit who lives in me. Give me a hate for the things that You hate and a love for the things that You love. Save me from being tainted by the things of this world. Amen."

AFFIRMATION:

What can wash away my sin?
Nothing but the blood of Jesus!

4

Undaunted

"We are troubled on every side, yet not distressed; we are perplexed, but not in despair; persecuted, but not forsaken; cast down, but not destroyed" (2 Corinthians 4:8, 9).

Is everything coming against you? Do you feel you can't cope with all you have to do? Dear mother, don't give in. Remember, you are a child of God, and if a child of God, you are an heir of God. In fact, you are a joint-heir with Jesus Christ Himself (Romans 8:16, 17). God is for you. God is behind you. God is in you. God is with you all the way. He will never leave you or forsake you. Nothing, no nothing—neither persecutions, problems, heartaches, despair, nor even death—nothing can separate you from His love.

Don't give up. Don't be downhearted. Fix your gaze upon the Lord. Don't let anything deter you from finishing the race that is set before you.

Don't let society tell you that you are wasting your time at home with your children. You are in the perfect will of God. God has given you your precious children. They are gifts from Him. He has given them to YOU to train for Him. He has given you a big job and He doesn't want you to give up on it.

Stand undaunted—undaunted by problems and challenges, undaunted by what people say to you or about you, undaunted by discouragement, and even undaunted by lack of sleep.

What was Paul's confession in the midst of troubles, distresses, floggings, imprisonments, and even going without food and sleep? *"Nothing can daunt us"* he confessed (2 Corinthians 4:1, JBP). In fact, five times Paul confesses his undaunted trust in the Lord.

1. *"Therefore seeing we have this ministry, as we have received mercy,* ***we faint not****"* (2 Corinthians 4:1). This is the KJV of *"Nothing can daunt us."* The Greek word is *ekkakeo* and means "don't be cowardly, weary,

faint-hearted, or lose heart." You have received the wonderful ministry of motherhood from the Lord. Like Paul, you can confess, "I may feel overwhelmed, but I will not be faint-hearted or lose heart. I will not be daunted by the hugeness of my task."

2. *"For which cause **we faint not**; but though our outward man perish, yet the inward man is renewed day by day"* (2 Corinthians 4:16-18). Sometimes you may feel weary and worn out, but keep the right confession: "I will not be faint-hearted because I am looking past my difficulties to the eternal realm, which is the real world." I am challenged by the words of Alexander Maclaren (1826-1910): "In such a world as this, with such hearts as ours, weakness is wickedness in the long run. Whoever lets himself be shaped and guided by anything lower than an inflexible will, fixed in obedience to God, will in the end be shaped into a deformity, and guided to wreck and ruin."

3. *"Let us **not be weary** in well doing: for in due season we shall reap, if we faint not"* (Galatians 6:9-10). You are doing a great job as you faithfully and daily serve your husband and family. Sometimes you wonder if you can keep up. By God's grace you can, and you will. Don't give up before the reaping time. There is a reward coming.

4. *"Wherefore I desire that ye **faint not** at my tribulations for you"* (Ephesians 3:13). Sometimes we are more worried about our own tribulations than the tribulations of others.

5. *"**Be not weary** in well doing"* (2 Thessalonians 3:13). This Scripture is different from No. 3. In the context of verses 6-15 it actually means, as J. B. Phillips translates it, *"Don't get tired of honest work!"* In the context it speaks to the man working hard to provide for himself and his family. However, it also speaks to us who work in the home to not be weary of working hard as we mother and manage the home.

We also have the example of Jesus, who in the face of death and taking on Himself the sins of the world *"set his face like a flint"* (Isaiah 50:7 and Hebrews 12:2-4). He sweat drops of blood in anticipation of the agony, but He was still undaunted.

I love the affirmation of the psalmist who confessed, *"My heart is fixed, O God, my heart is fixed"* (Psalm 57:7; 108:1; and Psalm 112:7).

PRAYER:

"Oh Father, please help me to fix my heart and mind on You so that I will not be moved by the circumstances around me. Thank you that You are my Rock and my Fortress. You are my Hiding Place and my Strong Tower. I can lean on You. Thank you that You are my Strength for today. Amen."

AFFIRMATION:

Nothing can daunt me.

Uncomplaining

"Do all things without murmurings and disputings: that ye may be blameless and harmless, the sons of God without rebuke, in the midst of a crooked and perverse nation, among whom ye shine as lights in the world"
(PHILIPPIANS 2:14, 15).

Why is it so easy to grumble and complain? It comes naturally, doesn't it? I guess that's because it belongs to our fleshly nature. The trouble is that a complaining attitude can become a habit—a habit we need to break. You may need to practice this "un" for more than just today. They say it takes about three to four weeks to break a habit. But you can start today.

Why should we break the habit of complaining? Because it is a serious matter in the eyes of God. Thousands of the children of Israel were destroyed because they complained and murmured. A whole generation (apart from Joshua and Caleb) was prohibited from entering into the Promised Land because they grumbled!

God told the Israelites in Numbers 14:29, *"Your carcasses shall fall in this wilderness, and all that were numbered of you, according to your whole number, from twenty years old and upward, which have murmured against me."*

"They were complaining against Moses in the desert," you say. That's right. But God took it as complaining against Him. In Exodus 16:7 Moses said, *"He hears your murmurings against the Lord . . . that you murmur against us."* The Living Bible says, *"He has heard your complaints against Him (for you aren't really complaining against us—who are we?)"*

When we gripe and murmur in our homes, God hears it. He doesn't hear it as a gripe against your husband, your children, your circumstances, the home you live in, or your seeming lack of provision, but He hears it as a complaint against Him. He sees that you do not trust Him.

1 Corinthians 10:10: *"Neither murmur ye, as some of them also murmured, and were destroyed of the destroyer."*

Do you think you are ready to try an "uncomplaining" day? Each time you start to moan about something, try praising instead. Instead of complaining about the weaknesses of your children, encourage them. Instead of moaning about all the negatives you see in your husband, think of the good things about him—and tell him! Instead of groaning that you can't pay the bills, thank the Lord for His provision.

God hears prayer, but He answers faith!

It's amazing how things will change when you begin an "attitude of gratitude." Your circumstances may not always change, but you certainly will. And that's the most important. In Habakkuk 3:17 the prophet exclaims, *"Although the fig tree shall not blossom, neither shall fruit be in the vines; the labor of the olive shall fail, and the fields shall yield no meat; the flock shall be cut off from the fold, and there shall be no herd in the stalls: yet I will rejoice in the Lord, I will joy in the God of my salvation."*

You can always find things to complain about, but you can also always find things to be grateful about, too. Life is all in how you look at it. You will enjoy it if you are filled with gratitude and thankfulness. You will be miserable if you groan and complain.

You choose!

PRAYER:

"Dear Father God, I confess that I have been complaining and negative. I confess this sin of grumbling. Please cleanse me and forgive me with your precious blood. Fill me with an overflowing spirit of gratitude and thankfulness. Thank you for all your goodness to me. Thank you for my salvation. Thank you for the gift of life. Thank you for my husband, my children, my home, and the privilege of being a mother. Thank you that you have promised that you will never leave me or forsake me. Amen."

AFFIRMATION:

To grumble and complain is a miserable way;
I choose a thankful heart to enjoy my day!

6

Unresentful

"Looking diligently lest any man fail of the grace of God; lest any root of bitterness springing up trouble you, and thereby many be defiled" (Hebrews 12:15).

Do you feel resentful about the way your husband treats you? Do you feel resentful because you have to stay home with your children? Do you feel resentful because you feel like a "servant" in your home? Do you feel resentful about something someone has said against you?

Please don't harbor this spirit of resentfulness. I know you feel you don't deserve this treatment. You may feel you have a right to hang on to it. However, being resentful won't remedy the situation. It only makes it worse and will gradually destroy you. A resentful spirit poisons your spirit and even affects your health. It also affects the lives of your family and those around you. You can't afford to hang on to it any longer.

We must keep our spirits free from resentfulness, jealousy, anger, bitterness, and unforgiveness. What you harbor inside your heart will eventually infect your children and following generations. We must keep our spirits pure by being sensitive to the Holy Spirit who lives within us (Ephesians 4:30).

If you have any resentment in your heart, get rid of it. Confess it to the Lord and ask Him to cleanse you. Then start forgiving and blessing. 1 Peter 3:8, 9 tells us that when people say unkind things to us that we are to retaliate, not with bitterness and hurt, but with blessing.

Make this a habit of your life. When you feel resentful against someone for something they have said or done, bless them and pray for them. Speak good things about them and ask God to bless them with good blessings. You won't feel like it, but forget your feelings. Bless them anyway. Keep blessing them in your heart and in prayer until all the resentfulness and hurt is gone from your heart.

When you feel resentful against the circumstances you are facing, start praising and thanking the Lord instead. Once again, you won't feel like it. But, how do you want to live? In bondage to your feelings, or by God's kingdom principles that produce life and victory?

1 Thessalonians 5:18 (Emphasis Author's) says, *"In EVERYTHING give thanks: for this is the will of God in Christ Jesus concerning you."* God's perfect will for you is to give thanks, not only for the things you feel thankful about, but in every situation. Keep praising until all the hurt and resentfulness is gone. This is how you keep a free and pure spirit.

PRAYER:

"Dear Father, I confess to you all resentfulness and bitterness against (name the persons). I confess all resentfulness and self-pity about my circumstances. Wash my heart and make it pure. I thank you for (name persons) and for the situation in which you have placed me. I thank you that you are with me and working in me to make me more like your Son, the Lord Jesus Christ. Thank you that you are working all things out for my good. Amen."

AFFIRMATION:

I am walking in the joy of a free spirit.

Unworried

"Don't worry about anything; instead, pray about everything" (PHILIPPIANS 4:6, TLB).

Someone has said, "Why pray when you can worry?"

Worry, like complaining, seems to come naturally, doesn't it? And more often than not, we worry before praying! Why do we do this? The bottom line is that we don't really trust God. This is what makes worry a sin. The Bible is full of admonitions from the beginning to the end to "trust in the Lord." To trust God means to quit worrying and believe that God is in control of our lives and the situation and that He knows what He is doing. Yet, in light of the hundreds of exhortations to "trust," we keep on worrying.

In the early days of our marriage, when facing financial difficulties or other problems, my husband would put his trust in the Lord and be at peace. I was still learning how to trust the Lord and felt that somebody better do something in the situation. I would say, "If you're not going to worry about it, somebody's got to, so I'll just have to worry!" How disgusting! Did it ever help the situation? Never once!

Worry is not only a sin. It is a waste of valuable time. It is a waste of good energy. It gives you ulcers! And it doesn't accomplish one thing!

Worrying people always think of the negatives. Their cup is half empty. Those who trust the Lord think of the positives. Their cup is half full—or better, full to overflowing!

I believe that the antidote for worry is to trust the Lord. God can be trusted. He is faithful. He will not let you down. He will never leave you or forsake you. He is your Rock. He is your Fortress. He is your strong Deliverer.

Don't grumble about the fiery trial you are going through. Instead, thank the Lord that He is with you. Thank Him that He is working everything out for your good and for His glory. Rest in His love. Trust in His mercy and deliverance.

Throw all your burdens upon the Lord and leave them there. Trust Him to unravel your problems—you haven't been successful thus far. Trust Him to provide your needs—He is Jehovah Jireh. Trust Him to work in your husband—He will do a far greater job than you, and especially when you stop worrying and nagging. Trust him for your children.

Take to heart the words of Louisa M. R. Stead's hymn, which she wrote after her husband drowned while trying to save a drowning boy.

"'Tis so sweet to trust in Jesus,
And to take Him at His Word;
Just to rest upon His promise,
And to know, 'Thus says the Lord!'"

Do you think you could get through today without one worry? How would you like to go through today . . .

Unanxious
Undisturbed
Unflappable
Unflustered
Unfrowning
Unperturbed
Unruffled
Unstressed
Untroubled and
Unworried?

Your husband and children will be blessed out of their socks! And the atmosphere in your home will change.

PRAYER:

"Father, I confess that I have been trying to work out all my problems by myself. Cleanse me and deliver me from this worrying spirit. Today, I roll all my burdens upon you. I thank you that you are the Burden Bearer and have promised to sustain me. I rest in your unfailing love. Thank you, Lord. Amen."

AFFIRMATION:

Unworried and unflappable—my goal for today!

8

Up-To-Date as Tomorrow

"But from the beginning it was not so"
(MATTHEW 19:8).

We are the 21st-century generation, living more than six thousand years since God created man. Are we still walking in the ways God originally intended for mankind, or have we forgotten them after all these years? Someone said, "One generation is one generation away from degeneration." How far have we degenerated?

We hear some Christians saying, "What God said in the beginning is not relevant to this era of history." However, this kind of statement totally undermines the validity of God's Word. I believe God's Word is timeless. The psalmist proclaims that God's commandments *"stand fast forever and ever"* (Psalm 111:7, 8). We age and pass away, but God's principles stand forever. They don't have to be adjusted for each new generation. They are eternal laws that were designed and refined in the eternal realm to be workable for all generations.

This is why Genesis is such an important book of the Bible. Here God establishes His eternal laws on many subjects. Let's check to see if we are still walking in God's original intention in only two basic areas.

First, in our text in Matthew 19:7-9, the Pharisees challenged Jesus about Moses allowing divorce. What was His reply? *"For your hardness of heart Moses allowed you to divorce your wives, **but from the beginning it was not so.**"* Divorce has become part of our lives, nearly as much among those who say they are Christians as those in the world, but it is not God's original plan.

Why does marriage not work today? Because we try to do it our way! We think we have a better way than God. God intends the husband to be the head of the home, but most women run from this principle. It is true that many wives have been hurt by cruel and ungodly men, but this is far from God's heart. God's purpose is not to imprison a wife, but to protect her.

The husband's mandate from God is to cover his wife by caring for her needs: physically, emotionally, and spiritually. He covers her by caressing her with the same kind of love with which Christ loved the church. He provides for her so she doesn't have to leave her nest and her little ones to the mercy of others. He protects her from the deceptions of this world so she can walk in peace.

The wife's privilege is to submit to this covering and be blessed. Many women are more submitted to their employer than they are to their husband at home. They have to fit in to the dictates of their employer rather than the desires of their husband.

"But I can earn more than my husband," you reply. It doesn't matter whether you make three times as much as him; you have still strayed from God's original plan. God didn't create two Adams. He created an Adam and an Eve, each to fulfill a different task. We see God's plan for the husband to be the head of the home even in the order of creation. Man was created first, then the woman was created to be a helper to the man. She needs him, but he can't function without her.

Why does God hate divorce? Because it hurts the godly seed. You can read about this in Malachi 2:14-16. A child cannot avoid being hurt and tortured in his or her soul when parents divorce.

A woman shared at an *Above Rubies* retreat how she found it very difficult to mother the way she wanted to. She had built up hard walls around her. They started the day her father left when she was a child of four. She still remembers him driving down the road, even the color and kind of car. She hates that kind of car and that color today. From that moment she began to put up walls that she still finds hard to break down today. This is a typical story of children who are the victims of divorce.

Secondly, do we still take notice of the message God gave to the first wedded couple? Do you remember it? *"Be fruitful, and multiply, and replenish the earth, and subdue it: and have dominion over . . . every living thing that moves upon the earth"* (Genesis 1:28). These were the very first words that man ever heard from the mouth of God! Therefore, they must be very important to God!

Do we take any notice of God's original plan? Many couples would rather do anything than obey God's very first command. They would rather go to Siberia and "serve the Lord" than have another baby! They are so emphatic about it that they get sterilized to make sure that their reproductive cycle which God so amazingly designed can no longer function!

But it wasn't so at the beginning! They filled the earth. In fact, when God's people were in Egypt, they continued to be fruitful, even in the face of hard bondage andpersecution. They became *"more and mightier"* than the Egyptians (Exodus 1:7-12)!

When a husband and wife fulfill the specific tasks God ordained for them, they will accomplish far more together than both trying to do the same job. When both partners try to do Adam's job, the wife cannot truly fulfill her nurturing anointing of embracing children and training them for God's purposes. Conversely, I have seen husbands who have been badgered into doing much of the wife's work, and therefore they are hindered from accomplishing their task of providing adequately for the home.

The big question is: do we conduct our marriage according to the thinking of society today, or do we live according to what God stated at the very beginning?

PRAYER:

"Father, please forgive me for walking away from your original mandate. I want to live my life by your rules, not by the customs of this age. Give me courage to live in your light in the midst of darkness. Help me to stand strong and not give into the trends of society around me. Help me to walk the 'narrow way' rather than joining the throngs on the broad way that leads to destruction. Amen."

AFFIRMATION:

God's perfect will for my life will never contradict His original commandments.

9

Preparing for the Future

"David said, Solomon my son is young and tender, and the house that is to be builded for the Lord must be exceeding magnificent, of fame and of glory throughout all countries: I will therefore now make preparation for it. So David prepared abundantly before his death"
(1 Chronicles 22:5).

Although David had a vision to build God's house, God told him that he would not be the one to build it. Instead, his son, Solomon, who was maybe only 20 years of age when he came to the throne, would build the house. That didn't let David off the hook. He prepared everything that Solomon would need to build this *"exceeding magnificent"* house. In fact, the Bible says that *"he prepared abundantly before his death."* He prepared gold, silver, iron, brass, and cedar trees in *"abundance."* He organized *"workers of stone and timber"* and *"all manner of cunning men for every manner of work"* to enable him.

This also gives us a vision for the next generation. Young people can start preparing for the home they will build for the Lord while they are in their parents' household. This is where they learn to build as they see the way their parents build.

We should provide all we can to prepare them for their marriage and the family God will give to them. Some of this will be material things they will need for their home. I think it is a good idea to encourage our daughters to have a Hope Chest, or a Glory Box as we call it Down Under. This gives them an incentive to put things away for their home, rather than wasting their money on useless and unnecessary things.

However, we should provide more than material things. We should give opportunity for them to learn what is needed to build a marriage and home. This is one of the blessings of homeschooling. Because daughters are in the home, they learn how to manage a home. They learn how to cook for a big family, how to organize a home, the art of teaching as they teach younger siblings, and maybe how to begin a home business. They don't come into marriage unprepared, untrained, and confused. They come prepared and ready to embrace a family and establish a strong and godly home that will affect the nation.

I have young ladies who come to stay in our home to help with the ministry of *Above Rubies*. Most of them are girls who have graduated from homeschooling and are between the ages of 17 and 25. Colin and I constantly say that we have the "cream" of America come to us. What about the girls who are with us at the moment?

Mariah is the oldest of 11 children. At home she cooks all the meals for the family, learning how to shop economically and balance the family finances. She handles the laundry and helps school the younger children. She also works part time and here in Tennessee runs the very busy *Above Rubies* office, which she does very diligently and efficiently.

What about Lisa? She is the oldest of 10 children. She also does meal planning, grocery shopping, gardening, canning, and laundry. In addition, she has her own business of teaching piano to 33 students. They are a musical family and sing together at many functions.

Jackie is one of eight children. She helps keep the family running smoothly with grocery shopping, cooking, canning, and laundry. They have a big garden and she helps her sister in the spring; the sister who has a greenhouse business. She teaches her siblings science and history. Each summer she directs a musical drama in their community, including a live orchestra, which is a huge project. She has already directed *Seven Brides for Seven Brothers* and *Fiddler on the Roof*, among others. She is an excellent seamstress. They are also a singing family and perform at many different functions.

Daughters who are at school and then off to college and away from the home do not have the same opportunity for family training. Many of these young ladies come into marriage with no idea of how to cook, manage a home, and often without a vision for children. Instead they have been programmed with a humanistic and feministic mind-set which is negative to establishing a marriage and family.

What about our sons? Once again homeschooling is a great blessing as fathers can often include their sons in their daily business. Fathers have more responsibility than sending their children off to school. They need to teach them how to work hard and hopefully how to build their own home.

I love to see my sons-in-law periodically take their sons with them to their work so they can learn how to do a day's work and also learn how to run a business. Instead of being immature boys, they become *"plants grown up in their youth"* (Psalm 144:12).

Zadok, at 20 years, is already establishing his bio intensive garden business and doing very well. He is called "Zadok, the Natural Farmer" and we often hear the Rototiller still going at 2 a.m. in the morning! Sharar, 19 years, has invented a special shovel for finding gold (he has already been gold digging in the Yukon and hopes to go again). He is currently building a hyperbaric chamber as well as many other inventions and projects.

How can we prepare abundantly for our young sons and daughters to build strong families if they are not home? How can we prepare them to be parents if we stop babies coming into the home and they do not see their mother nursing and caring for little ones?

David made sure he provided everything that was needed for the building of the house before he died. We should also make sure we leave a legacy on how to build a great marriage and family to our children and grandchildren before we pass away.

PRAYER:

"Dear heavenly Father, please help me to see past the day-to-day and into the future. Show me how to abundantly prepare my sons and daughters to be adequately prepared for marriage, motherhood, fatherhood, and a successful future. Amen."

AFFIRMATION:

I am preparing abundantly for my children's futures.

10

God Shows the Way

"Thus saith the Lord, let not the wise man glory in his wisdom, neither let the mighty man glory in his might, let not the rich man glory in his riches: but let him that glorieth glory in this, that he understandeth and knoweth me, that I am the Lord which exercise lovingkindness, judgment, and righteousness, in the earth, for in these things I delight, saith the Lord"
(JEREMIAH 9:23, 24).

Isn't this the most wonderful Scripture? I memorized it recently. The more we know God, the more we know how to live. The more we understand of God, the more we understand how to parent, because He is the originator of parenting.

God is so vast, beyond the imagination of our finite minds, and not one name is enough to describe Him. In this Scripture we see three attributes of His character that are inseparable from Him.

LOVINGKINDNESS

This Hebrew word *chesed* is one of the most wonderful revelations of God in the entire Bible and is closely related to "grace" in the New Testament. It reveals His unfailing love even when we don't deserve it, His mercy, forgiveness, loyalty, goodness, and kindness.

But it is not speaking of a general kindness; it is a kindness which involves two parties. It speaks of God's covenant with Israel, which is an everlasting covenant. His dealings with Israel show how He deals with us. Because of their waywardness and rebellion, God had to continually judge and punish His people. Because He is God, He cannot let go His justice and righteousness, and must execute judgment on sin. Eventually, He could not tolerate the evil of the Israelites any longer and scattered them to the four corners of the earth.

Nevertheless, God had made a covenant. He is lovingkindness (*chesed*). His lovingkindness will not let go. He will not wash His hands of Israel, nor of us. He judges, but never gives up. Rebellion cannot destroy His love. It is the essence of that lovely old hymn, "O love that will not let me go."

After vomiting the Israelites out of the land because of their sin, God sends hundreds of promises through His prophets to tell them that He will one day bring them back to the land again. We are now seeing these prophecies come to pass. We saw the miracle of Israel become a nation again on 14 May 1948, and now Jews are pouring back to the land from all over the world. This is God revealing Himself as *chesed.*

It is also related to the old English word "troth." Have you heard this word before? At the end of their vows, the bridal couple says, *"And thereto I give thee my troth."* Our children used these original wedding vows on their wedding day. I was so pleased that our grand-daughter also used the same vows. It was quite fun to hear Ben and Chanel practicing to say "troth" on their wedding rehearsal night. It's not an easy word to pronounce! It means that the couple is confessing publically that they will be faithful to their marriage covenant.

JUSTICE AND RIGHTEOUSNESS

The Hebrew word for "judgment" is *mishpat* and should be translated justice. Justice is the use of authority to uphold and execute what is right. It is acting as a judge and rendering the proper verdict—God's verdict.

The Hebrew word for "righteousness" is *ts'daqh* and very similar to justice. It is a legal term and is also related to two parties keeping their covenant. God is the ultimate law-giver and He abides by His own standards.

WHAT ABOUT ME?

How does this all relate to us? If we want to know God, we must come to understand God on these terms, for He delights in these attributes. If we are going to teach our children what God is like, we must learn to parent with these three attributes. How can we do it? It seems beyond us, doesn't it? But, the more we press into God, the more we will understand and the more He will teach us.

We must uphold the standard of God's righteousness in our home. We must execute justice when our children rebel and refuse to obey. We must execute discipline. We cannot let these things go and think it is insignificant, for in doing so, we refuse to know God and refuse to show our children what God is like.

Conversely, God's *chesed* will overpower our every motive in dealing with our children. It is related to the New Testament *agape* love which is God's love. Our love can give up and wane, but God's love never gives up.

PRAYER:

"Oh God, please help me. I want to know you more and more. I want to know you in your lovingkindness, justice, and righteousness. Please teach me and help me to parent the way you parent us. Thank you, Father. Amen."

AFFIRMATION:

God's way is not only the best way, it is the only way.

FURTHER READING:

http://aboverubies.org/JusticeintheHome

http://aboverubies.org/LoveintheHome

http://aboverubies.org/EverlastingPossession

11

The Banquet

"He brought me to the banqueting house, and his banner over me was love" (SONG OF SONGS 2:4).

Did you know that God loves feasts and banquets? And He invites us to come to His table of food, feasting, and fellowship?

Actually, the word "banqueting house" in this Scripture is *yayin* and means "effervescence, fermented wine, intoxication." The NEB translates it, *"He took me into the wine garden."* Isaiah 25:6 tells of a great feast that God is one day going to prepare for all His people in Jerusalem: *"And in this mountain shall the Lord of hosts make unto all people a feast of fat things, a feast of wines on the lees, of fat things full of marrow, of wines on the lees well refined."* Who is going to make this feast? The Lord of hosts himself! Does this sound like the God that you know? Yes, this is your God. God's house is a house of nourishment and His table is laden with abundant food and intoxicating joy. Moffat's translation describes it, *"a banquet of rich food and of rare wines, of marrowy dainties and of choice old wines . . ."* Read the description of Solomon's table (who was a type of Christ) in 2 Chronicles 9:4, 5.

Not only does the Bible describe God as a chef preparing delectable delicacies to nourish our bodies and delight our taste buds, but also sharing rich food to nurture our souls and spirits. Proverbs 9:1-6 says, *"Wisdom has built her house, she has hewn out her seven pillars; she has slaughtered her meat, she has mixed her wine, she has also furnished her table."* Do you lack wisdom? God's table is filled with wisdom. Do you seek after knowledge? All knowledge, understanding, and revelation are in God and Christ and He lavishly spreads His table for you.

But you have to come. I have to come. We don't automatically receive without coming to dine at His table. Let's feel God's heart as we read Proverbs 9:2-6 (The Message): *"The banquet meal is ready to be served, lamb roasted, wine poured out, table set with silver and flowers . . . Are you con-*

fused about life, don't know what's going on? ***Come with me, oh come, have dinner with me!*** *I've prepared a wonderful spread—fresh-baked bread, roast lamb, carefully selected wines. Leave your impoverished confusion and live."*

We read the same invitation in Isaiah 55:1, 2: *"Ho, every one that thirsteth,* ***come*** *ye to the waters, and he that hath no money,* ***come*** *ye, buy and eat, yea,* ***come*** *buy wine and milk without money and without price . . . hearken diligently unto me, and eat ye that which is good, and let your soul delight itself in fatness."*

When I come to God's table, the table of His rich Word, I can delight myself in fatness. I don't have to be impoverished. I don't have to be hungry and thirsty in my soul. I don't have to be malnourished in my spirit. I can eat until I'm full. There's more than I need. The table is laden! This table is not for fast food grazers. We have to **sit** at this table. We have to linger. How sad to live an impoverished life when God has provided a table that is dripping with all we need. Will you come and feast each day?

God's table is also an example for the way we should spread our table. Food is to be eaten at a table, not in front of the TV, on the sofa, or in the car looking at the back of someone's head. God planned for us to **sit** at a table where we can not only eat leisurely, but look at one another and communicate.

God sets His table. Do you set your table? Proverbs 9:2 (NLT) says, *"Wisdom has* ***prepared*** *a great banquet, mixed the wines, and* ***set the table*** *. . ."* If the God of Wisdom takes time to prepare delicious food and set His table, don't you think it would be wise for us to do the same? Preparing food for our families and setting the table beautifully is not a chore. It's a God thing. It's a ministry. When we sit at the table together as a family, not only do we feed our physical bodies, but we provide opportunity to feed the soul and the spirit too. Especially, as we crown the meal with the Family Altar—reading God's Word, worshipping, and praying together.

As God furnishes a delightful table for you, will you prepare and set a delightful table for your family?

PRAYER:

"Oh God, please save me from passing by your bountiful table of wisdom and knowledge. I don't want to be an impoverished soul. I want to be filled to overflowing so I can bless others too. Amen."

AFFIRMATION:

I'm setting the table for my wonderful brood,
I'm furnishing it with love and nourishing food,
I'm making it a place where they all love to be,
A place of enrichment and a lasting legacy!

12

Your Reward Is Coming

"He which soweth sparingly shall reap also sparingly; and he which soweth bountifully shall reap also bountifully" (2 CORINTHIANS 9:6).

My heart overflows with thankfulness each morning as I enter my garden to pick another harvest. And it grows overnight! I pick a huge basket of cucumbers, tomatoes, peppers, okra, and more each morning, and there's another huge basket to pick the next morning. I am in awe of God. I can't help exclaiming every morning,"Thank you, Lord for your amazing bounty."

I remember springtime when it was time to plant. I had just arrived home from Europe, where Colin and I were ministering, with a debilitating cough and was quite ill. I had to get out the next issue of *Above Rubies,* proofread and edit Serene and Pearl's book, *Trim Healthy Mama,* and the garden was waiting to plant. I didn't know how I could gather up the energy to plant the garden. I was tempted to forget about it. But I knew if I didn't do it, we wouldn't reap a harvest in the summer. And of course, you know my favorite affirmation: "Things don't just happen; you have to make them happen." So I went out, and in my weakness and continual coughing, planted anyway.

Now, every day I am amazed at the bounty and glory of my garden. And I am humbled to realize that I can't take any credit for it. All I did was plant. My dear husband watered and God caused it to grow. He gives the increase. 1 Corinthians 3:6, 7 says: *"I have planted, Apollos watered; but God gave the increase. So then neither is he that planteth any thing, neither he that watereth; but God that giveth the increase."*

My 21-year-old grandson, Zadok, who works very hard market gardening, shared with me yesterday how every vegetable he picks, he looks upon it as a gift from God. He knows he can't make one plant grow. It is all God.

Dear mother, it is the same in your high calling of motherhood. All you have to do is sow and water and God will do the rest. There are times when you feel weak, you feel overwhelmingly tired, you may even be sick, or you feel the job is too big for you. Can I encourage you to keep planting anyway? Even in your weakness and inadequacy, don't give up.

There will be times that you will sow with tears—tears of tiredness, sadness, and heartache. Keep sowing. Be encouraged with God's promise: *"They that sow in tears shall reap in joy. He that goeth forth and weepeth, bearing precious seed, shall doubtless come again with rejoicing, bringing his sheaves with him"* (Psalm 126:5, 6).

Be faithful to plant the *"precious"* seeds of God's truth into the hearts of your children every day. Be faithful with Family Devotions morning and evening. As you are faithful to plant God's Word into their lives and water it with prayer, God will do the rest. You don't make it grow. Only God can do that. He will work His harvest in their lives. Without a doubt, you will reap your harvest and give God the glory.

The Word is able to save their souls (Psalm 19:7; 2 Timothy 3:15; and James 1:21), keep them from sin (Psalm 119:9, 11), teach them wisdom (Psalm 19:7), conform them to the image of His Son (Romans 8:29 and 2 Corinthians 3:18), and guide them in the way God wants them to go (Psalm 119:105 and Proverbs 6:20-23).

Also, plant seeds in your children of love, patience, encouragement, and affirmation and watch them grow.

PRAYER:

"Dear Father, please help me to be faithful to sow into the hearts of my children. I thank you for your eternal promise that tells me that I will reap a precious harvest as I sow your precious truths. Amen."

AFFIRMATION:

Even when I feel tired and weak, I will keep sowing.

13

In Your Mouth
Part 1

"As for me, this is my covenant with them, saith the Lord; My spirit that is upon thee, and my words which I have put in thy mouth, shall not depart out of thy mouth, nor out of the mouth of thy seed, nor out of the mouth of thy seed's seed, saith the Lord, from henceforth and forever"
(ISAIAH 59:21).

What a wonderful promise to claim for our children and our children's children. But these words will not be fulfilled without our participating.

Where does God want His Words to be in our lives? In our hearts? Yes, we must hide God's Word in our hearts. In our minds? Yes, His Word should fill our minds. In our spirits? Yes, God's Word should richly fill our spirit.

But, God wants something more. He wants His Word to be in our MOUTHS! He wants His Word to be in the mouths of our children, their children, and their children forever. And yet, it is a strange phenomenon today, that the mouths of children and teenagers of Christian families are filled more with the names of actors, music stars, and the latest movies than the Word of God!

Did you know that our walk with God is all to do with the mouth? We are born again into God's family by believing in our heart and confessing with our mouth, and that's how we continue our walk with God.

Romans 10:9, 10 says: *"That if thou shalt confess with thy mouth the Lord Jesus, and shalt believe in thine heart that God hath raised him from the dead, thou shalt be saved. For with the heart man believeth unto righteousness; and with the mouth confession is made unto salvation."* A person is only half saved if they do not confess with their mouth.

Everything we believe in God's Word will only be truly effective in our lives as we confess it. God wants His Word to be constantly popping out of our mouths. Can you repeat a Scripture right now without having to run for your Bible? What about your children? Can they spontaneously speak Scriptures from their mouths? Is God's Word so drilled into your children that it easily drips from their mouths?

I believe this is why it is so very important to establish Family Devotions every evening and morning where we read God's Word to our children and take time to memorize it together. It won't just happen; you have to make it happen!

God never wants His words to depart from our mouths. The real Hebrew meaning is that they "will not withdraw from your mouth." From generation to generation, they must continue in the hearts and mouths of our children.

Joshua 1:8 says, *"This book of the law shall not depart out of thy mouth; but thou shalt meditate therein day and night, that thou mayest observe to do according to all that is written therein: for then thou shalt make thy way prosperous, and then thou shalt have good success."*

Once again, we get the same message. It must not depart out of our mouths. How can this happen? By meditating day and night. The word "meditate" has a larger meaning in the Hebrew that we would think. It means . . .

1. To ponder and meditate.
2. To mutter, to whisper, to speak the Word to yourself.
3. To speak the Word out loud.

Mother, if the Word is not coming out of your mouth, it will not become part of your children's lives. If it is not coming out of their mouths, how will they pass it on to the next generation?

God's plan is *"from henceforth and forever."* What is your vision? What can you start doing today to make this happen in your family and the coming generations?

PRAYER:

"I thank you, dear Father, for the power of your Word. It is life and truth. I want your Word to be flesh and blood in my life. I want your Words to drip from my mouth. Please help me to be diligent in my own life and in imparting the Word into the mouths of my children. Amen."

AFFIRMATION:

I am raising children whose mouths are filled with God's Word.

14

In Your Mouth (Diligently)
Part 2

"And these words, which I command thee this day, shall be in thine heart: and thou shalt teach them diligently unto thy children, and shalt talk of them when thou sittest in thine house, and when thou walkest by the way, and when thou liest down, and when thou risest up"
(Deuteronomy 6:6, 7).

We know this Scripture back to front, don't we? But are we actually doing it? In the last devotion we found that God wants His words to be in our mouths and in the mouths of our children. How will that happen? By our diligently teaching them.

The word "diligently" in the Hebrew is *shanan* and means "to pierce through, to sharpen, to whet, to engrave, to enforce, to inculcate, and to teach incisively." This is far more than passive reading, isn't it?

When we had Family Devotions together this morning, my husband not only read the Word to us, but he pierced it into our lives. As he read from *The Daily Light on the Daily Path*, which is a compilation of Scriptures on a certain theme, he asked questions. Sometimes he would stop halfway through the Scripture he was reading to see if we could quote the rest of the verse from memory. Some Scriptures were very significant and we repeated them out loud together.

Let's look at some other translations of the above Scripture, which will help us to really get the message.

The Amplified Bible: *"You shall whet and sharpen them so as to make them penetrate, and teach and impress them diligently upon the minds and hearts of your children."*

Century English Version: *"Memorize his laws and tell them to your children over and over again. Talk about them all the time, whether you're at home or walking along the road or going to bed at night, or getting up in the morning."* God's words certainly have to be in our hearts in order to talk to our children about them all the time, don't they?

New Living Translation: *"Repeat them again and again to your children."*

The Message: *"Get them inside of you and then get them inside your children."*

Modern Language Bible: *"You shall impress them deeply upon your children."*

Have you got it? Now, dear sweet mother, what are you going to do about it? We can't be passive about it, can we? We must be faithful to not only read the Word to our children, but to what? Engrave, teach incisively, impress deeply and diligently, pierce through, sharpen, whet, enforce, inculcate, repeat them again and again, and get them inside your children. Am I like a broken record? Perhaps we need it until this really becomes our lifestyle.

May we become mothers whose mouths are filled with God's Word and who train children to have mouths filled with God's Word.

PRAYER:

"Oh Father, please save me from 'mouthing off' to my children, but instead I want to have a mouth filled with your Word. Amen."

AFFIRMATION:

I am training children to overcome by "the word of their testimony."

15

Ear Trainers
Part 1

"The ear that hears the reproof of life abideth among the wise. He that refuseth instruction despises his own soul: but he that hears reproof gets understanding" (PROVERBS 15:31, 32).

What is the first thing we should teach our children? When I ask women this question at seminars they give me lots of very good answers, but usually not the one I am looking for. What is my answer? I believe that the first thing we teach our children is how to listen.

If children do not learn how to hear, they will not learn to obey. If they do not learn to listen, they will not learn to hear the voice of God speaking to them. If they do not learn the art of listening, they will not learn to acquire knowledge. If they do not learn how to hear, they will not come to faith, because *"faith comes by hearing, and hearing by the Word of God"* (Romans 10:17). How you train your children to hear will determine their relationship with God!

It is possible to hear but not really hear. That's why Jesus constantly reiterated, "He that has ears to hear, let him hear." We have to learn to listen with our ears, but this takes training.

All parents are ear trainers. Our parenting determines whether our children will have obedient ears—or disobedient ears, lazy ears, dull ears, defiant ears, resistant ears, gullible ears, or even forgetful ears. What kind of ears are you training your children to have? When you ask them to do something but they take no notice of you, you are training them to have defiant ears. When you ask them to do something and they delay doing it, they have dull ears. When you ask them to do something, but they don't bother doing it until you have asked for the sixth time (and by now you are shouting), you are telling them that they do not have to obey until the sixth time! You are producing lazy ears.

What kind of ears does God want our children to have?

ATTENTIVE AND OBEDIENT EARS (SHAMA)

When God told Solomon that he could ask God for anything he liked, Solomon responded by asking for "an understanding heart" (1 Kings 3:9). The Hebrew word is *shama* and means, "to hear with attention and obedience, to give undivided listening attention." What did Solomon want more than riches and fame? A hearing heart. May God give us wisdom to teach our children how to have hearing hearts.

The word *shama* is synonymous with obedience. Proverbs 25:12 says, *"As an earring of gold and an ornament of fine gold is a wise reprover to an obedient (shama) ear."*

Proverbs 1:5 says, *"A wise man will hear, and will increase learning."* There is no way we can teach our children to be wise without teaching them to hear with undivided attention.

This Hebrew word is used 1,159 times in the Old Testament. That's how much hearing with obedience means to God.

SHARP EARS (QASHAV)

When King Saul disobeyed the word of the Lord, the prophet Samuel came to him and said, *"Hath the Lord as great delight in burnt offerings and sacrifices, as in obeying the voice of the Lord? Behold, to obey is better than sacrifice, and to hearken (qashav) than the fat of rams. For rebellion is as the sin of witchcraft, and stubbornness is as iniquity and idolatry"* (1 Samuel 15:22, 23).

The word *qashav* describes acute hearing. It means "to prick up the ears, sharpening them like an alert animal." Children with qashav ears will be ready for God to use as soldiers in His army.

QUICK EARS (TACHUS)

James 1:19 says, *"Let every man be swift (tachus) to hear."* This Greek word means "prompt or ready." Most Bibles translate it as "quick to hear." It describes instant obedience. True hearing results in immediate action. I used to say to my children, "Delayed obedience is disobedience."

How do we teach our children this kind of hearing? As soon as they can understand a command, we teach them to obey that command. But before they can obey, we must make sure that they have heard us. Sometimes, you may have to get your little child to repeat your command to make sure they have heard you. Don't yell commands from another room. Always give commands eye to eye and face to face so that you know your children hear what you ask them to do. When you know that they have heard, teach them how to obey straight away. Don't accept anything less. This takes time and effort, but remember, mother, you are an ear trainer! This is one of your most important tasks as a parent!

May God help us to train our children to be prompt and obedient hearers.

PRAYER:

"Oh God, please forgive me for not diligently training the ears of my children. Please help me to train children who have obedient ears. Amen."

AFFIRMATION:

I am a diligent ear trainer!

16

Ear Trainers
Part 2

"Received ye the Spirit by the works of the law, or by the hearing of faith?" (Galatians 3:2, 5).

Have you ever thought of the words, "the hearing of faith?" Before we have faith, we must hear first. Faith is not an airy fairy thing that is based on nothing! It is only true faith if it is based on the Word of God. Romans 10:17 says, *"So then faith comes by hearing, and hearing by the word of God."*

This is why it is so important for mothers to be ear trainers. We must train our children to hear and obey us so they can hear and obey the Word of God. We must train our children not just to hear words, but to get into the habit of listening with their heart and inner ears.

Not only do we train them to have obedient and prompt ears, but we train them how to listen to the voice of the Holy Spirit as He speaks through His Word. Timothy came to faith by listening to the Scriptures as a child. 2 Timothy 3:15 says, *"From a child thou hast known the holy Scriptures, which are able to make thee wise unto salvation through faith which is in Christ Jesus."* We don't wait until our children are older to read them God's Word. We start when they are babies. The little babe nursing at the breast can hear God's words at Family Devotions every evening and morning. The little toddler rocking on his mother's or father's knee at Family Devotions is being prepared for salvation as he listens to the living words of God.

In his book, *How to Have a Family Altar*, Norman V. Williams states, "Babies have ears to hear with! They have hearts to believe with! The Holy Spirit who holds the reins of that child's mind and heart is mightily present to bless when you give the Word of God! . . . It is your duty to exhort your child daily with the blessed Word of God. If you do that, you will be amazed to see what the Holy Spirit will do in that little heart! . . . This is the family altar—bringing our children to Christ in His Word that He might touch them!"

Paul also speaks to Timothy about being *"nourished up in the words of faith"* (1Timothy 4:6). We will nourish our children in the words of faith as we teach them how to listen. The more they hear (listening beyond words to the voice of the Holy Spirit illuminating the Word), the more they will walk in faith. We don't want our children to know "the letter of the law," but the anointing of the Spirit of God upon the Word, because *"the letter kills, but the Spirit gives life"* (2 Corinthians 3:6).

Jesus reprimanded the people for having *"dull ears"* (Matthew 13:15, 16). The writer of Hebrews could not reveal the *"strong meat"* to his readers because they were *"dull of hearing"* (Hebrews 5:11-14). May God save us from having dull ears. May He save us from raising children who have dull ears.

"The hearing of faith" also shows us how important it is to encourage one another with God's Word. This is why we should not forsake *"the assembling of ourselves together, as the manner of some is; but exhorting one another: and so much the more as ye see the day approaching"* (Hebrews 10:25). When we confess the truths of the Word of God to one another's ears we build one another up. The more we come together and affirm the truth to one another, the more we increase each other's faith. That's why we need one another.

Hebrews 12:25 says, *"See that you do not refuse him who speaketh. For if they did not escape who refused him who spoke on earth, much more shall we not escape if we turn away from him who speaks from heaven."*

PRAYER:

"Dear Father, please help me to nourish my children up in the Word of God by reading it to them daily. Help me to teach them how to listen to me so they will know how to hear words from Heaven. In Jesus' name, Amen."

AFFIRMATION:

I am teaching my children how to listen to the One who speaks from Heaven!

17

Folding Your Flock

"Feed the flock of God which is among you . . . being examples to the flock. And when the chief Shepherd shall appear, ye shall receive a crown of glory that fadeth not away"
(1 PETER 5:1, 2).

One of the most beautiful revelations of God is that He is our Shepherd. He is our personal Shepherd and He is the Great Shepherd of His flock—His people of Israel, and the church. Not only is He our Shepherd, but of all the animals God created, He chose to call us His sheep—and sheep cannot survive without a shepherd.

The Chief Shepherd wants to shepherd His precious flock through His under-shepherds. He raises up shepherds to watch over His flock, the church.

Acts 20:28 says, *"Feed the church of God, which he hath purchased with his own blood."* The word "feed" means a lot more than giving food to eat. The word is *poimaino*, which involves the full responsibility of the shepherd—leading them to nourishment, but also guiding, guarding, tending, and **folding the flock**.

When Jesus spoke to Peter after His resurrection, He exhorted him three times: *"Feed my lambs . . . Feed my sheep . . . Feed my sheep"* (John 21:15-17). The first and last exhortation to "feed" literally means to nourish with food. However, the second time Jesus said these words he used *poimaino*, the word that means the fullness of shepherding.

I love the term: "folding the flock," don't you? In biblical times, the shepherd folded his flock each night. He counted each one and made sure they were all in the fold, safe and secure from any wild predators. He often slept at the door of the fold to protect his sheep. During the day, he watched over them constantly with his rod and staff, and led them to green pastures.

God also wants you, as a shepherding mother, to fold your flock. One of the biggest things you do as a shepherdess is feed your children. That's what sheep do all day long—eat! They rarely lift their heads from eating grass! Now do you wonder why God calls us sheep? Don't think you are wasting your time when you seem to be preparing meals all day! This is a huge part of your shepherding.

But, you do more than prepare meals. You reveal the shepherding heart of God as you tenderly nurture your flock. You walk in God's likeness as you nurse your baby, gently lead, and lovingly teach and train your little ones (Isaiah 40:11).

However, you are not only a sweet, caring mother. You are also courageous! You have the enormous task of protecting the minds, souls, and spirits of your children (1 Thessalonians 5:23).You are guarding them from evil—from all deceptions, delusions, and detours from God's paths that are everywhere in this society.

When the enemy comes stalking your children, you are like a wild watchwoman as you grab your child from the jaws of the Destroyer. That's what David, the shepherd of Israel, did. Such was his courage that He grabbed a ferocious lion by the beard and rescued his lamb from its mouth (I Samuel 17:34-36).

This protecting anointing is very much part of your mothering, because shepherding is both tender and powerful. The prophetic words concerning Christ the Messiah say, *"And you, O Bethlehem, in the land of Judah, are by no means least among the rulers of Judah; for from you shall come a ruler who will shepherd my people Israel"* (Matthew 2:6). The Messiah who will rule the nations with a rod of iron is also the tender Shepherd (Revelation 2:27).

Shepherding is so much part of who God is that He continues to shepherd us even in the eternal realm. Revelation 7:15-17 says, *"He that sitteth on the throne shall dwell among them. They shall hunger no more, neither thirst any more; neither shall the sun light on them, nor any heat. For the Lamb which is in the midst of the throne shall feed (poimaino) them, and shall lead them unto living fountains of waters and God shall wipe away all tears from their eyes."*

God will never stop folding His flock. He is the Chief Shepherd and will continue folding us throughout all eternity, leading us continually to greener and greener pastures and fountains of living waters. We will be totally satisfied and contented sheep, yet always being led to more and more delightful pastures.

Do you notice that He is not only the Shepherd, but also the Lamb? He is the Lamb that was slain and who bears the marks of our salvation in His body. And, although He sits on the throne, He also dwells with us and enjoys the eternal days with us. He is now, and always will be, the "dwelling" Shepherd who loves to dwell with us and be part of our lives.

You also, as a shepherdess, will always want to be with your sheep, to dwell with them, and to be part of their lives. Even an earthly shepherd would not take a lamb away from its mother or take the lamb out of the family flock. In the same way, a shepherd mother cannot part with her little lamb, even for a few hours. As they continue to grow, she still wants them around her, to enjoy them and teach them in God's ways.

Don't only observe your flock. Fold them into your heart. Fold them into your secure and godly home. Fold them into your dreams. Fold them into your daily prayers.

PRAYER:

"Dear Shepherd of Israel, please anoint me to shepherd my little flock in the same way you shepherd your flock. Show me how to be a tender and loving shepherdess and yet warlike against the prowling enemy that seeks to steal my children. Amen."

AFFIRMATION:

I am folding my flock, day and night.

18

God's Practical Plan
Part 1

"Build houses and live in them; and plant gardens and eat their produce" (JEREMIAH 29:5, NASB).

I am always amazed as I read God's Word to find how practical it is for our daily lives. God comes down to our "nitty gritty" and leaves us without a doubt as to how He wants us to live.

In Jeremiah 29:5-11 (NASB), God sent a charge through the prophet to the Jews who were taken captive to Babylon. It was a practical message, reminding them of His original plan. Remember, they were commands to people living in captivity! He told them that even though they were now living in captivity, He still wanted them to continue in His plan, the plan He gave them from the very beginning. God's plans and purposes do not change according to our circumstances. His eternal principles work in every situation and for every generation.

God gives seven commands . . .

1. BUILD HOUSES

"Build houses and live in them" (verse 5). It is God's blessing for us to be settled in a home. God made sure He had the home ready and waiting before He formed His female creation. The home is our sanctuary—a solace from the outside world where we make a haven of peace for our husband to return each evening and a place where we nurture and train our children. God's plan is for children to be raised in the home.

2. PLANT GARDENS

"Plant gardens and eat their produce" (verse 5). You may be thinking that it's nice to hear about gardens, but you don't have any room to make a garden where you live. Even if you have very little land, I would encourage

you to prepare a small garden, or even grow a few lettuces, herbs, or tomatoes in pots on your deck. A little garden is better than no garden at all. Many have forgotten in this modern society in which we live that gardening is part of homemaking. The first home was called the *Garden* of Eden and God established the first home as the prototype for all future homes.

God intends us to grow produce to help feed our families. In years gone by this was necessary for survival. If you didn't have a garden, you didn't eat! Today we can get by without a garden, but I wonder if we really get away with it? If we want to eat healthy produce, we need to grow it ourselves! Most commercial produce is heavily sprayed with chemicals and a high percentage is genetically modified. Of course, you can purchase organically grown produce from a farmer's market, but your own garden saves heaps of money.

This is so much part of God's plan that He commanded the Jews to plant gardens even in captivity! Gardens don't just appear! You have to work at them. That's what God told Adam to do in the very beginning. Genesis 2:15 (GNT) says, *"Then the Lord God placed the man in the garden of Eden to cultivate it and guard it."* The Hebrew word "cultivate" is *avad* and means "to toil, to serve, to make weary, to be fatigued."

It's not always easy to start a garden. Some people say, "It's okay for you because you live in the country and have plenty of room." Actually, on our hill there is no suitable soil. We had to purchase soil to fill our 13 long raised beds.

Evangeline, our daughter, has the most magnificent vegetable garden to feed their large family of 10 children. I have to concede that her garden is now better and much bigger than mine! Her garden didn't suddenly appear either. I am amazed every time I look at this huge garden space knowing that it was hewed out of trees and bramble—a jungle that looked impossible. But, Evangeline had a dream which she made happen. It reminds me of my favorite saying, "Things don't just happen: you have to MAKE THEM HAPPEN." They got "stuck in." They cut down the trees, dug out the roots, and with back-breaking effort broke up the soil.

This morning I read to my granddaughter one of Edgar Guest's poems, "Results and Roses." Here's an excerpt . . .

The man who wants a garden fair,
Or small or very big,

With flowers growing here and there,
Must bend his back and dig.

The things are mighty few on earth
That wishes can attain,
Whate'er we want of any worth
We've got to work to gain.

PRAYER:

"Dear Father, I thank you so much that you show me the way you want me to live. Help me to walk in your ways. Amen."

AFFIRMATION:

I am creatively dreaming of my garden and I will put arms and legs to my dream.

SCRIPTURES ABOUT GARDENS:

Genesis 1:29; Proverbs 6:6-11; 12:11; 24:27; 27:18; 28:19; 31:16; and 2 Corinthians 9:6.

19

God's Practical Plan
Part 2

"Take wives and become the fathers of sons and daughters, and take wives for your sons and give your daughters to husbands, that they may bear sons and daughters" (Jeremiah 29:6, NASB).

We continue to look at the seven points which God commanded the Jews to do while they were in captivity.

3. GET MARRIED AND HAVE CHILDREN

"Take wives and become the fathers of sons and daughters" (verse 6). Even in captivity God wanted His people to continue the original command He gave to them in Genesis 1:28: *"Be fruitful and multiply, and fill the earth."* This command is reiterated over and over again in the Bible and has never been rescinded. The adverse circumstances of the captives didn't change God's command. We notice the same thing happened while the children of Israel were suffering under great affliction in Egypt. Even though the Egyptians put hard taskmasters over them and made their lives bitter with hard labor, they continued to be fruitful. They had all the excuses they needed to stop having children in such difficult circumstances but *"the more they afflicted them, the more they multiplied and the more they spread out, so that they were in dread of the sons of Israel"* (Exodus 1:12, NASB).

4. ENCOURAGE YOUR CHILDREN TO GET MARRIED AND HAVE CHILDREN

"Take wives for your sons and give your daughters to husbands, that they may bear sons and daughters" (verse 6). It's not hard to realize as we read these words that God loves weddings and babies! It's all His idea! God delighted in bringing the first couple together and He delights in doing it

today. Every wedding gives the hope of new life—life from God Himself!

God's judgment was to take away the joy and celebration of weddings (Jeremiah 7:34, 9:16, and 25:10). God's blessing was to restore weddings. Jeremiah 33:10, 11 says, *"Thus saith the Lord; again there shall be heard in this place . . . the voice of joy, and the voice of gladness, the voice of the bridegroom, and the voice of the bride."* Weddings are the blessing of God. We should encourage our children who get married to embrace children rather than waiting a few years. In fact, if a couple is not ready to take on the responsibility of embracing children, they are not ready for marriage.

5. DO NOT DIMINISH

"Multiply there and do not decrease" (verse 6). God specifically commands them not to decrease! Isn't it sad that many believers in God are set on doing the opposite to His plan? They would much rather decrease than increase. They would rather follow the devil's plan to eliminate life than to multiply life. Consequently, there is a whole army of God's people who are missing today!

6. PRAY FOR YOUR CITY

"Seek the welfare of the city where I have sent you into exile, and pray to the Lord on its behalf; for in its welfare you will have welfare" (verse 7). God wants us to pray for the city or area where we live. We have a responsibility to pray for God's peace to come to our cities and in doing so we will reap peace. Pray together as a family for your city and nation each day.

7. DON'T BE DECEIVED

"'Do not let your prophets who are in your midst and your diviners deceive you, and do not listen to the dreams which they dream. For they prophesy falsely to you in My name; I have not sent them,' declares the Lord" (verses 8, 9). God didn't tell them to watch out for being deceived by the Babylonians. He knew they would not be tempted by their evil and liberal lifestyle. But He warned them about being deceived by those *"who are in your midst"* (check out Lamentations 4:12). Because we live in a society that is steeped in a humanistic agenda, we must constantly line up our beliefs and worldview in keeping with God's eternal Word! If what we are thinking and doing does not line up with God's Word, we must walk away from it, no matter who proclaims it. Our responsibility as parents is to watch that our

children are not deceived by the society in which they live.

As we seek to obey God's plan for us, we will walk in the blessings of God. These reminders from God are all for our blessing. Verse 11 says, *"For I know the plans that I have for you, declares the Lord, plans for welfare and not for calamity to give you a future and a hope."* The majority of God's people know this Scripture and claim it for their own. What they often forget is that it comes after the seven points we have been talking about. It is these principles that will give us a blessed future and hope!

PRAYER:

"Dear Father, please save me from being gullible and duped by the humanistic propaganda all around me. Give me eyes to see through deceptions and to know the witness of your truth in my heart. Amen."

AFFIRMATION:

I now know the answer to having a future and a hope!

SCRIPTURES ABOUT FILLING THE EARTH:

Genesis 1:28; 9:1-7; Exodus 7:7; Numbers 14:21; 22:5; Psalm 80:8-9; 127:3-5; Isaiah 27:6; Ezekiel 36:38; Zechariah 8:4, 5; and Luke 14:23.

20

Carry Them in Your Arms

"Save thy people, and bless thine inheritance: feed them also, and lift them up forever" (PSALM 28:9).

How many times have you exclaimed, "This baby won't let me put him down. He wants me to carry him all the time!" You feel frustrated, and sometimes even angry. You have so many other pressing things to do.

But have you stopped to think what you are really doing when you carry your baby? You are revealing a glimpse of what God is like. You couldn't do anything more powerful than that, could you? He is the tender Shepherd who loves to hold us in His arms. Isaiah 40:11 describes Him: *"He shall feed his flock like a shepherd: he shall gather the lambs with his arm, and carry them in his bosom, and shall gently lead those that are with young."*

There is not a person who doesn't love Psalm 23. We love to own God as our Shepherd for He doesn't leave us isolated to cry on our own, but gathers us in His arms and carries us close. Not even a burly, rough shepherd leaves a little lamb to fend for itself.

When you carry your baby in your arms, you are like the Great Shepherd of the sheep. It is not a nuisance. It is not time-wasting. It is God-like. It is so much part of the character of God that He not only carries us when we are helpless babies, but right through our lives, even into our golden years. Isaiah 46:3, 4 says: *"Listen to me, O house of Jacob . . . who have been upheld by me from birth, who have been carried from the womb: even to your old age, I am he, and even to gray hairs I will carry you! I have made, and I will bear; even I will carry and will deliver you."*

And let's read Isaiah 63:9 also: *"In all their affliction he was afflicted, and the angel of his presence saved them: in his love and in his pity he redeemed them; and he bare them, and carried them all the days of old."*

Have you noticed that babies, toddlers, and even little children love to be lifted up and held? The baby cries and cries, but the moment you lift him up, he stops crying. Why? Because he is meant to be lifted up and held close to you. Babies love to be up at our level. I remember staying with a family in Canada years ago. Like all little ones, their little boy loved to be held and would say, "Uppie, Campbell . . . Uppie, Campbell" until I lifted him up.

Talking about the nursing mother, Isaiah 66:11-13 (NIV) says, "*You will nurse and be carried on her arm and dandled on her knees. As a mother comforts her child, so will I comfort you.*"

Of course, I know that your arms get tired. We are not like our Great Shepherd whose arms never get tired and of whom the Scriptures says, "*Underneath are the everlasting arms*" (Deuteronomy 33:27). But why not get a baby carrier? I think a baby carrier is indispensable for a mother. My daughter Serene's baby carrier is like another limb of her body! It's amazing what you can accomplish in the home while wearing your baby in the carrier.

I find it sad that studies reveal that western mothers spend more time physically separated from their babies than mothers in non-western societies.[1] Another study in Africa tells of babies who sleep with their parents and are held and touched 99 percent of the time in a 24-hour period in contrast to European/American babies who are only held and touched 18 percent of the time.[2] Another interesting finding is that colicky babies are not found in non-western societies where babies are constantly close to their mothers and where the mother responds at the first sign of discomfort or unhappiness in her baby.[3]

However, I love the sentiments of some American mothers who have written to me . . .

"I hold my babies close to 22 hours a day. I sleep with the baby in my arms and when I can't hold them another family member holds them. My babies do not cry very often because their needs are met so quickly by mama, daddy, or a brother or sister." This is the blessing of larger families. It is a big job for a mother of her first baby to constantly hold her baby, but as the family grows there are more arms to hold the baby. Contrary to public opinion, babies in large families receive far more attention and are held much more than babies in smaller families.

"There is nothing like having your baby in your arms (or your sling) all day, always in your world, always learning and enjoying your closeness—and you don't miss a smile or a laugh!"

"I am guilty of carrying all my children more than many people think

I should and nursing longer than some. However, I believe they are only small once and by the time they are two to three years old, they are running and playing and want less of you. I believe in carrying them and enjoying them while I can."

A grandmother writes, "Some people think it spoils children to constantly hold them, and there are obviously times when it's not possible. However, I've yet to hear a parent of grown children say they wish they'd held their children less."

My thoughts for this devotion are from our text, Psalm 28:9. The words "lifts them up" mean "to support, sustain, carry."

I think that King David, the great warrior, must have been constantly mothered as a baby. His understanding of God comes from his own experience as he prays for Israel, *"Lead them like a shepherd, and carry them in your arms forever"* (NLT). I love the CEV translation which personalizes it, "Be our shepherd always and carry us in your arms."

Enjoy being like your Great Shepherd as you mother your little ones.

PRAYER:

"Thank you for showing me, dear Shepherd, that I am revealing your likeness when I carry my baby. Help me to realize that it is not a time-wasting chore, but a godly attribute.

AFFIRMATION:

I will shepherd my little ones like God shepherds His sheep and lambs.

FURTHER STUDY:

Read also Exodus 19:4; Deuteronomy 1:31; 32:10-12; and Psalm 71:6.

Studies cited in "Putting the Baby Down: The Roles of Physical Proximity in Mother Infant Vocal Communication" by Alanna K. McLeod

1. *(Barr, 199; Hewlett & Lamb 2002; Konner, 1976, 1977; Le Vine et al., 1994; Lummaa, Vurorisalo, Barr & Tehtonen 1988; Small 1988).*
2. *Hewlett & Lamb, 2002.*
3. *Barr, 1999; Lummaa et al., 1998; Small 1998.*

21

A Meal or a Snack?

"Jesus saith unto them, My meat is to do the will of him that sent me and to finish his work"
(John 4:34).

Jesus' life-work, which was food to Him, was to accomplish His Father's will. Our food should also be to fulfill the Father's will. His perfect will for our lives as mothers is to embrace the high calling of motherhood which He has given to us and to make it our "food," not a "little snack"!

Not only was it Jesus' food and life to do the Father's will, but it was also His delight. Psalm 40:6-8 says, *"Sacrifice and offering thou dist not desire . . . burnt offering and sin offering hast thou not required. Then said I, Lo, I come: in the volume of the book it is written of me, I delight to do thy will, O my God: yea, thy law is within my heart."* Jesus came as the Lamb of God to be the ultimate sacrifice for our sins and to offer His life. He delighted to do His Father's will, even though, in the flesh, He would rather this "cup" was taken away from Him (Matthew 26:39, 42). Do we also delight in our calling?

Do you notice that Jesus did not hide His life purpose in His heart, but affirmed it, confessed it, and made it known! It is important to confess our purpose. It becomes "life and food" far more when we confess it than if we only hide it in our hearts. Confessing releases action. Confessing keeps you on target. Confessing your purpose keeps you going when everything goes against your purpose!

The following is a statement of purpose for you as a mother. You may like to type or print it out and pin it up in your kitchen to encourage you each day. Don't only read it. Remember to confess it out loud and affirm your purpose, even as Jesus did.

I AM A MOTHER AND I HAVE A PURPOSE!

I am not languishing. I am not floundering. I am not deceived.

I have a vision. I know who I am and who God created me to be.
I know my purpose. I have direction. I know God's mandate for my life.
I am walking in the perfect will of God.
I know it's not easy. I know it's hard.
But I've counted the cost. My goal is set.
How could my career be easy when I am impacting this nation for God?
Also the generations to come! And eternity!
How can it be easy when I am destroying the plans of the devil?
Such is the power of my God-ordained career,
the highest calling ever given to women—motherhood!
I have embraced my calling. I am not intimidated by antagonists.
I will not be moved. My heart is fixed.
I may be hidden in my home, but look out, world!
I am sharpening and polishing my arrows.
I am getting them ready to shoot forth and destroy the works of the enemy.
In the power and anointing of God I am advancing His kingdom!

Here is another affirmation to write out and affirm.

MY GOAL AND PURPOSE

P Passionately mothering!
U Unflinchingly keeping my eyes on the goal!
R Regularly and richly imparting God's Word to my children!
P Praying constantly with my heart always looking to the Lord!
O Ordering and managing my home with diligence!
S Saturating my husband and children with love and encouragement.
E Embracing and nurturing the children God is giving to me.

PRAYER:

"Dear Father, please help me to not only do and delight in your high calling for my life, but to finish my task. I want to daily affirm it before you, my family, and others. Amen."

AFFIRMATION:

I am no longer floundering, for I have a purpose!

22

I Beg Your Pardon!

"Whosoever will come after me, let him deny himself, and take up his cross, and follow me, for whosoever will save his life shall lose it; but whosoever shall lose his life for my sake and the gospel's, the same shall save it" (MARK 8:34, 35).

I wish I had a life!"

"I beg your pardon? Did I hear you correctly?"

What kind of a life are you looking for, dear mother? A life that serves your own interests? A life of working for an earthly employer when you could be employed by the God of the universe? Do you realize that God has employed you to raise your children for Him? How sad God must be when mothers go AWOL and leave their high calling for some lesser career.

You say you don't have a life! Do you realize this is a lie? Did you know that you create your own world right where you are? You have the power to make your marriage, mothering, and home pulsate with life. It all depends on your attitude. If you think that mothering is insignificant, you'll be frustrated. But when you realize you were born for this task, embrace it, and put your whole heart into it, you'll never have another boring moment!

Are you nursing your young baby? What could be more powerful than giving life and nourishment to a God-given child and watching this child grow? When you nurse your baby at your breast you give more than milk; you nourish your child's soul and spirit too. God says to you as He spoke to Moses' mother, *"Take this child and nurse him for me and I will give you your wages"* (Exodus 2:9).

Do you have little ones you are seeking to train in the right direction? Are you homeschooling? Of course, you'll face problems and frustrations, but this is all part of the reality of life. You'll face challenges anywhere and in whatever career you choose. However, in this great task of mothering, you are impacting a nation! You are molding children for eternity.

Are you still bored? Reach out in hospitality. You can be in full-time work for God in your home. The home is the most exciting place. You can change the world from the heart of your home. All you have to do is forget about yourself and pour your life out for others.

Can I give you a challenge? Each day, think of something new to make life exciting for your husband and for your children. Come on now! Don't read any more until you stop and think about it. What are you going to do? Let your imagination run wild . . . Have you got the plan yet? Keep thinking until you get one. Now think about how you are going to put it into operation.

Are you already anticipating an exciting evening with your husband? My, you certainly have a life! It is exciting! Your husband will be mesmerized! Your children are going to be happy all day. They won't get bored and cranky because you will constantly be thinking of creative ideas. And you, well, you are never going to be bored again. You will tell the world about your great life in your home!

Think about other people you can encourage, too. There are other mothers who often feel discouraged like you do. Ask a mother and her children for lunch and think of a way you can do something special for her. In reaching out to her, you will forget about your own problems. I have always found that the best antidote to self-pity is to do something for someone else. It's amazing how your own problems (or boredom) pale into insignificance.

Perhaps you may like to organize a picnic with some other mothers who live near you. Or, invite an older lonely person for a meal. Encourage your children to memorize some poems or Scriptures that they can recite to her with animation. Or, they could practice some songs to sing to her. You will bless her, and your children will get blessed at the same time, too.

You do not find your life in trying to find yourself. You find your life in pouring it out for others. This is when you find abundant life! Philippians 2:4 says, *"Look not every man on his own things, but every man also on the things of others."*

PRAYER:

"Lord, help me live from day to day
In such a self-forgetful way
That even when I kneel to pray
My prayer shall be for others.

Others, Lord, yes others,
Let this my motto be,
Help me to live for others,
That I may live like Thee."

AFFIRMATION:

I've got a life, it's exciting and free,
I've found the secret, it's not about me!

23

I Was Wrong

"Therefore shall a man leave his father and his mother, and shall cleave unto his wife: and they shall be one flesh" (Genesis 2:24).

I have always taught that Oneness is the first principle of marriage. However, I was wrong. Before God speaks about becoming "one flesh," He first introduces three basic principles for marriage. How could I not see that before?

THE FRUITFUL ANOINTING

The first one, of course, is mandated in the very first words that God ever spoke into the ears of man, *"Be fruitful, and multiply, and replenish (fill) the earth, and subdue it: and have dominion. . ."* (Genesis 1:28).

Fruitfulness is the overriding blessing God has given to marriage. God is a God who loves fruitfulness, and He looks for fruitfulness in each marriage. It is the first blessing that He gave to man, for these words were not only a mandate from God, but His blessing. Genesis 1:28 says, *"And **God blessed them**, and God said unto them, Be fruitful. . ."* This blessing is reiterated all through the Bible. Psalm 107:38 (NASB) says, *"**He blesses them** and they multiply greatly."*

The divine plan of "one flesh" marriage is to embrace the spirit of fruitfulness.

THE HELPING WIFE

The next thing we read about God's plan for marriage is in Genesis 2:18: *"And the Lord God said, It is not good that the man should be alone; I will make him an help meet for him."*

The Hebrew word for helpmeet is *ezer* and means "helper, to come to one's aid." Although the husband and wife work together in their powerful directive to take dominion on this earth for God, He specifically gave the ministry of helping to the wife. Is this insignificant? No, it is powerful. This is the first time *ezer* is used in the Bible, and yet it is the same word that is used to describe God, who is our *"Help and deliverer"* (Psalm 40:17). The spirit of helping, in the same way God comes to our aid to help us, is also the backdrop of "one flesh" marriage.

THE CLEAVING HUSBAND

We read in Genesis 2:24: *"Therefore shall a man leave his father and his mother, and shall cleave unto his wife."* The word cleave in the Hebrew is *dabaq* and means "to cling or adhere to, abide, follow hard after, be joined together, to stick to." A husband is to be totally faithful to his wife. He is to be glued to his wife. He has no other rival than his wife.

It is also true that the wife is to cleave to her husband, but this characteristic is particularly pinned on the husband. God never intended a man and woman to become "one flesh" except in the confines of a faithful and covenantal marriage. It is not an independent act. Fruitfulness, faithfulness, and helpfulness are the basis of this godly institution.

THE ONE FLESH ANOINTING

With God's full understanding of faithfulness and fruitfulness, we embrace the "one flesh" marriage. It means that we are to be one in spirit, purpose, and vision. But, it is physical "one flesh." We are to embrace this wholly as it is the heat of the marriage relationship. Oops. I just made a typing error! I meant to type, "the heart of the marriage," but I think we could also call it the "heat of the marriage."

God reiterates this vision in the New Testament in Matthew 19:4, 5 and again in 1 Corinthians 7:3-5: *"Let the husband render unto the wife due benevolence: and likewise also the wife unto the husband. The wife hath not power of her own body, but the husband: and likewise also the husband hath not power of his own body, but the wife. Defraud ye not one the other, except it be with consent for a time, that ye may give yourselves to fasting and prayer; and come together again, that Satan tempt you not."*

Because God said, *"they shall be one flesh,"* it should be a familiar part of marriage. He did not say that they would occasionally be one flesh, but "they shall be one flesh." That sounds to me like quite a consistent lifestyle.

Dr. Reuven P. Bulka writes, "Marriage is not simply living the same as before but with someone else. Nor is it simply a change of lifestyle with added benefits and duties. Marriage is, and should be lived, as a higher dimension of existence. All that goes on prior to marriage ideally prepares for marriage, but marriage itself is a fresh start in the way life was meant to be."

We should not expect to live our marriage according to the status quo of couples who choose their own way for marriage. We must embrace a higher way, a way that transcends the natural, for it is God-planned. Embrace God's way and all that He has planned for you in your marriage.

PRAYER:

"Thank you, Father, for showing me the way you want me to live my marriage. I thank you that your way is the way that brings joy, blessing, and peace. Amen."

AFFIRMATION:

I am embracing all that God has designed for my marriage.

24

Not Ashamed
Part 1

"In nothing terrified by your adversaries"
(PHILIPPIANS 1:28).

Why is it that we are often so fearful to witness for Christ? Or, to stand up for the truths of God's Word even though they are counter-culture to society around us? I guess it is because we don't like being scorned at, laughed at, or even persecuted.

God knows that we are fearful, and therefore He strengthens us with His living words. Read the following different translations of Philippians 1:28:

"Not for a moment intimidated by your antagonists" (MLB).

"Never be scared for a second by your opponents; your fearlessness is a clear omen of ruin for them" (Moffat).

"Never for a moment quail before your antagonists" (Weymouth).

"Not flinching or dodging in the slightest before the opposition" (MSG).

Are you encouraged now? I think it's time to rise up and not be ashamed, don't you?

WE MUST NOT BE ASHAMED OF THE GOSPEL OF CHRIST

Paul confesses in Romans 1:16, *"For I am not ashamed of the gospel of Christ: for it is the power of God unto salvation to every one that believeth."*

It was impossible to shut up the early Christians, even when they were put in prison. When the authorities commanded them not to speak in the name of Jesus, what did they answer? *"We ought to obey God rather than men!"* And then Peter immediately starting preaching about Jesus again! Read Acts 5:27-33; Philippians 1:20, 21; and 2 Timothy 1:8, 12.

It is important to remember that our Christianity is a CONFESSION! We are born again into God's family when we believe that God raised Jesus from the dead and also when we CONFESS with our mouth that Jesus is Lord (Romans 10:9-11).We begin by confessing, and we continue by confessing! We confess everything we believe. 2 Corinthians 4:13 says, *"According as it is written, I believed, and therefore have I spoken; we also believe, and therefore SPEAK."* (also: Psalm 116:10 and Hebrews 10:23). Our walk with Christ is not a "silent faith" but a "speaking faith."

Psalm 107:2 says, *"Let the redeemed of the Lord SAY SO, whom he hath redeemed from the hand of the enemy."*

Never be ashamed of truth. Always counteract the deceptions!

WE MUST NOT BE ASHAMED OF SPEAKING BEFORE AUTHORITIES

Psalm 119:46 says, *"I will speak of thy testimonies also before kings, and will not be ashamed."*

WE MUST NOT BE ASHAMED OF GOD'S WORD AND HIS TRUTH

Do you take your Bible with you everywhere you go? I am amazed how few believers carry Bibles these days. The majority of them don't even bring them to church! No wonder we are not impacting this nation. We are no longer people of the Book! And because we are no longer people of the Book, we don't know the truth. And because we are ignorant of the truth, we are easily deceived. Of course, I must concede that many people have the Bible on their iPhones and iPads today. However, there is something about carrying a Bible. Non-believers are scared of Bibles, not iPhones.

It's time to not only be believers, but BIBLE believers—and BIBLE carriers! What would happen if every believer starting carrying their Bible with them? They wouldn't think of going to church without it? After church, they get out their Bibles at a restaurant as they discuss the morning sermon with friends.

Maybe the reason that many believers don't take their Bibles with them everywhere is that they don't read them at home. Do we read the Bible daily to our children? If not, maybe our children think we are ashamed of the Bible and that it is not the most important book in the world, after all!

It is a good idea to teach your children to get into the habit of taking their Bible with them to church. Sit as a family in the front seats. Encourage the children to open to the Scriptures as the preacher speaks, and to take notes! Start them studying for their A.U.G. degree at an early age. (Check which degree it is in 2 Timothy 2:15 [KJV]). You could start a revival in your church!

Mark 8:38 says, "*Whosoever therefore shall be ashamed of me and of my words in this adulterous and sinful generation; of him also shall the Son of man be ashamed, when he cometh in the glory of his Father with the holy angels.*" Read also Psalm 119:6, 80.

We are blessed to have freedom to read God's Word in our western countries. We must "hold fast" that which we have, lest it be taken away (Revelation 3:11). Recently I watched the movie of William Tyndale, who was burned at the stake because of his passion to get the Bible into the hands of the people. Now we have it in our hands and don't appreciate it!

PRAYER:

"Oh God, I live in a sinful generation who disdains your Word. Please help me not to be ashamed, but to be faithful to speak your truth in every situation, 'in season and out of season.' Amen."

AFFIRMATION:

"I'm not ashamed to own my Lord,
Or to defend His cause,
Maintain the honor of His Word,
The glory of His cross."
~ Isaac Watts

P.S.
Did you check out the degree you should all be studying together?

25

Not Ashamed
Part 2

"O come, let us worship and bow down: let us kneel before the Lord our maker" (Psalm 95:6).

WE MUST NOT BE ASHAMED OF PRAYING IN PUBLIC

If prayer is part of our lives, we'll pray anywhere. We'll pray with people in shops, in restaurants, and in the street if they are in need of prayer. Paul tells about the believers in Tyre who *"brought us on our way, with wives and children, till we were out of the city: and we kneeled down on the shore, and prayed"* (Acts 21:5). This was not in church, but in public. They not only prayed together, but kneeled down and prayed. It is easy to pray in your heart in public when no one knows what you are doing, but if you kneel down and pray, they certainly will. I'm not talking about making a show of praying, but there are times when the situation calls for prayer and that could mean kneeling!

My sister, Kate, was burdened by the Lord to pray for the city of Franklin. God impressed upon her to not only pray at home, but to pray in the city square. She has now been praying every Friday lunch time in the Franklin City Square for the last 10 years, along with others who join her. One day, no one came to join her. While she was standing alone praying in her heart, she felt the Holy Spirit ask her to kneel down and pray. Although feeling very embarrassed, she did not want to quench the Holy Spirit and therefore kneeled to pray. Oh, for hundreds of believers to kneel in the streets of our cities to pray for them.

Jeremiah 29:7 tells us to pray for the peace of the city in which we live. It's not just a good idea, it's a command from *"The Lord of hosts,"* who is the Great Warrior, the Lord of the armies of Heaven. This command was given to the Jews in Babylon. Daniel was one of them and he obeyed the word of the Lord and *"kneeled upon his knees three times a day, and prayed, and gave thanks before his God"* (Daniel 6:10). He continued to do this even when there was a law against it and his life was at stake (Daniel 6:11-13)!

Recently in Tennessee the ACLU came against a school where the football team and coach bowed their heads for one minute of silent prayer. They didn't even pray out loud, but received flack for it. What a blessing to see people rise up in response to the accusations. Thousands came to the next game (more than ever before). Before the game, once again they gave time for a minute of silent prayer. As the crowd bowed their heads in silence, one person began to speak the Lord's Prayer OUT LOUD. Soon the whole crowd joined in! It only takes one person to stand up. Will you be one who takes the first step? Will I?

WE MUST NOT BE ASHAMED OF HAVING CHILDREN

Psalm 127:4, 5 says: *"As arrows are in the hand of a mighty man; so are children of the youth. Happy is the man that hath his quiver full of them: they shall* ***not be ashamed****, but they shall speak with the enemies in the gate."*

Society tries to shame families who have more than the "status quo"of two children. But who is really unusual? It's families who deliberately limit their families! I'm not talking about those who are physically unable to have children, but to intentionally stop having children is contrary to anything written in God's Word. In fact, God says that the families who are blessed with many children will not be ashamed!

They are raising children to bring more of God and His ways into this world. They are raising mighty warriors who will know the truth and know how to speak the truth. They are raising arrows to attack the enemy's kingdom. They are molding children for eternity. They need never be ashamed. They can lift their heads high, for they are walking in the perfect will of God. No matter what anyone says, they will not be intimidated by their antagonists!

PRAYER:

"Thank you, Father, that I do not need to be ashamed when I am walking in Your will. I know that Your thoughts are higher than my thoughts, and Your ways are higher than my ways. Please help me to walk in Your ways, even when they are counter-culture. Amen."

AFFIRMATION:

"Ashamed of thee, of that blest Name
Which speaks of mercy full and free?
Nay, Lord, I would my only shame
Might be to be ashamed of thee."
~ Isaac Watts

SCRIPTURES ABOUT KNEELING:

God wants us to kneel before Him: Psalm 95:6.

Jesus kneeled to pray: Luke 22:41.

Examples of people kneeling before the Lord: 1 Kings 8:54; 2 Chronicles 6:13; Daniel 6:10; Luke 5:8; Acts 7:59-60; 20:36; 21:5; and Ephesians 3:14.

26

Not Ashamed
Part 3

"My people shall never be ashamed. And ye shall know that I am in the midst of Israel, and that I am the Lord your God and none else" (JOEL 2:26, 27).

WE MUST NOT BE ASHAMED OF TRUSTING THE LORD

What can you do when you cannot see any solution to your problem? There's only one thing to do, and that's trust the Lord. It's not the only thing to do; it's the best thing to do. When you trust the Lord, you will never be ashamed, for God is faithful. He cannot go against His promises and it is impossible for God to lie!

I will have to admit that God often keeps you waiting. And He often answers differently than what you expect. You wonder why you don't get your answer immediately. God is doing more than bringing deliverance. He is working in our hearts at the same time. He is teaching us patience and how to trust Him more and more, even when we cannot see any light in the tunnel.

David confessed in Psalm 25:2, 3, 20: *"O my God, I trust in thee: let me not be ashamed, let not mine enemies triumph over me. Yea let none that wait on thee be ashamed. . . O keep my soul, and deliver me: let me not be ashamed; for I put my trust in thee."* Read also Psalm 31:1, 17 and 69:6. David also states in Psalm 34:5, *"They looked unto him, and were lightened: and their faces were not ashamed."*

WE MUST NOT BE ASHAMED OF HOPE

The word "hope" means to be expectant, to believe that God is going to do something good. If we do not hope, we do not understand who God is, for He is a good God and everything He does is good.

Romans 5:3-5 says: *"We glory in tribulations also: knowing that tribula-*

tion worketh patience; and patience, experience; and experience, hope: and hope maketh not ashamed." What teaches us to have hope? Tribulations! It is in our hardships that we experience that God works everything out for good. Each experience gives us more hope in God so that we can eventually be full of hope. We will not be ashamed, even when people think we are crazy for trusting God (Romans 9:33; 10:11; and Philippians 1:20).

When Abraham believed God's promise to receive a son in his old age, Romans 4:18 tells us, *"Who against hope, believed in hope, that he might become the father of many nations, according that which was spoken, So shall thy seed be."*

WE MUST NOT BE ASHAMED OF SUFFERING FOR CHRIST

Paul confesses in 2 Timothy 1:12, *"For the which cause I also suffer these things: nevertheless I am not ashamed: for I know whom I have believed, and am persuaded that he is able to keep that which I have committed unto him against that day."*

1 Peter 4:16 says, *"If any man suffer as a Christian, let him not be ashamed; but let him glorify God on this behalf."*

WE MUST NOT BE ASHAMED OF THE SAINTS WHO ARE SUFFERING FOR CHRIST

2 Timothy 1:8 says, *"Be not thou therefore ashamed of the testimony of our Lord, nor of me his prisoner: but be thou partaker of the afflictions of the gospel according to the power of God."*

2 Timothy 1:16, 17: *"Onesiphorus . . . was not ashamed of my chains . . . but sought me out very diligently, and found me."*

Rather than being ashamed, we should feel their pain as though we were suffering. Hebrews 13:2 (NLT) says, *"Remember those in prison, as if you were there yourself. Remember also those being mistreated, as if you felt their pain in your own bodies."*

WE MUST NOT BE ASHAMED OF THE BLOOD OF CHRIST

We have no salvation except through the blood of Christ. We have no access to the promises of God except through the blood of Christ. We cannot overcome the enemy apart from the blood of Christ. Let's never be ashamed of the precious, pure, powerful blood of Jesus that was poured out on the cross for our sins.

Revelation 12:11 says, *"And they overcame him by the blood of the Lamb, and by the word of their testimony, and they loved not their lives unto the death."*

WE MUST NOT BE ASHAMED IN HARD TIMES

Psalm 37:18, 19 says: *"The Lord knoweth the days of the upright: and their inheritance shall be forever. They shall not be ashamed in the evil time: and in the days of famine they shall be satisfied."* The NLT translates it, *"They will survive through hard times, even in famine they will have more than enough."*

What a wonderful promise. We do not know what lies ahead in the coming days, but we have this promise that if we walk uprightly (the word is *tamim* meaning "free from blemishes and spots, faultless, blameless") we will never have to be ashamed.

PRAYER:

"I thank you, Father, that when I trust you I will never be ashamed. When I lean on my own strength, it will not hold me; but you are my Rock on which I can lean all my weight. Amen."

AFFIRMATION:

In good times or bad times, I will not be ashamed!

27

Possess the Gates
Part 1

"Be thou the mother of thousands of millions, and let thy seed possess the gate of those which hate them"
(GENESIS 24:60).

Why will parents not be ashamed who have many children? They are training their children to know how to fight enemies. They are preparing them for war. But, rather than teaching them how to use swords and spears, they are teaching them to speak words of truth and wisdom.

We don't have children for the sake of having children. We have a purpose to raise children who know how to combat the enemies of darkness and who know how to contend for their faith. We raise children who will know the truth, who will stand for truth, and who will keep on standing for truth even when everyone is trying to knock them down! We teach them to not only know the truth, but to speak the truth knowledgably and articulately.

1. SPEAK IN THE GATES

Where will our children speak? Some will speak one on one and others will speak to crowds, but all must be prepared to speak in the gates (Psalm 127:4, 5). What are the gates? In biblical times they were the most important part of the city, where the elders sat to administer judicial matters and kings met with their subjects. The judges and officers judged the daily matters of the people and the prophets proclaimed warnings from God. Today, it relates to the city councils, the state capitals, and the White House in Washington, D.C., where decisions and laws are made. Are we preparing children who will know how to speak with legislators and governors?

The Bible has a lot more to say about the gates of our cities and nations. Not only are we to train children to speak in the gates, but to also:

2. POSSESS THE GATES

Who are to possess the gates? God's people! The word "possess" in the Hebrew means "to seize, take possession of, to occupy." In the Bible, to *"possess the gates"* means to take authority over the entire city. Don't you think it is time the righteous occupied the gates of our cities and nation? We can't have righteous laws without righteous men in government. We can't have peace in the land unless the godly rule.

Why do we languish in mediocrity when we are meant to be possessing? *"Righteousness exalteth a nation, but sin is a reproach to any people"* (Proverbs 14:34). Also read Proverbs 11:10, 11 and 29:2.

God promised Abraham that *"thy seed shall possess the gate of his enemies"* (Genesis 22:17). Because we are the children of Abraham by faith, it should be our vision, and the vision for our children, to possess the gates of our enemies. Rebekah's family had this vision when they gave the blessing to her as they sent her forth to be Isaac's bride: *"Be thou the mother of thousands of millions, and let thy seed possess the gate of those which hate them"* (Genesis 24:60).

3. PROCLAIM WISDOM IN THE GATES

We are not to hide the wisdom of God's truth behind closed doors, or even in the church. We must proclaim wisdom and drop little seeds of truth wherever we go—when we get talking to someone in the supermarket, on the sports field, or at any function. Proverbs 1:20, 21 (NKJV) says, *"Wisdom cries in the chief place of concourse, in the openings of the gates: in the city she utters her words."* The wise will speak in the gates; the fool will be too afraid to speak in the gates (Proverbs 8:1-7 and 24:7).

4. ESTABLISH JUSTICE IN THE GATES

The prophet cried out in Amos 5:15, *"Hate evil, love good; establish justice in the gate. It may be that the Lord God of hosts will be gracious to the remnant of Joseph."* It is because we have tolerance in the gates that our nation is declining and the light of God's truth is dimming.

As God's people we are to hate evil, not tolerate it. We are to abhor what is an abomination in God's sight, not trifle with it. We must hate it enough that it will cause us to take action and establish justice in our courts and in our land. We must loathe it enough that we will pray and intercede. Ezekiel 9:4-6 states that God told Ezekiel to *"Go through the midst of the city, through the midst of Jerusalem, and set a mark upon the foreheads of the men that sigh and that cry for all the abominations that be done in the midst.*" They were the only people who escaped judgment. Are you one who sighs and cries for the evil in the land?

PRAYER:

"Oh God, please save me from assimilating into this world system and help me to intercede on behalf of my nation. Strengthen me to raise children who are filled with your Word and who will be bold to speak your Word, even in the face of opposition. Amen."

AFFIRMATION:

I am preparing children to speak in the gates!

FURTHER STUDY:

Go to page 279.

28

Possess the Gates
Part 2

"When the righteous are in authority, the people rejoice: but when the wicked beareth rule, the people mourn"
(PROVERBS 29:2).

We continue to discover what God says about "gates" in His Word.

5. DEFEND JUSTICE IN THE GATES

Proverbs 17:15 says, *"He that justifieth the wicked, and he that condemneth the just, even they both are abomination to the Lord."* We are tired of this state of affairs, and God says it is an abomination. We see it happening all around us, and even in our courts. Because of lies and warped judgment, innocent parents are in jail. The humanist media loves to trap and ridicule the righteous. Justice is distorted (Isaiah 59:14, 15 and Amos 5:10).

There will come a day when all this will change. The Bible tells us about *"the defender of justice in the gate."* How we need men today who will defend justice in the gates. We need to train up young men in our homes who know how to defend and battle in the gates for truth and justice. Isaiah 29:20, 21 (MLB) speaks of the day when *"the tyrant shall have vanished; the scoffer shall have ceased; and all those intent on doing evil shall be cut off, who for a word declare a person guilty, and entrap the* ***defender of justice in the gate****, and with empty arguments turn aside the person who is in the right."*

God has also promised that He will give a *"spirit of justice to him who executes justice, and of valor to those who turn back the battle to the gate"* (Isaiah 28:6, MLB).

6. ESTABLISH TRUTH AND PEACE IN THE GATES

Zechariah 8:16 says, *"Speak ye every man the truth to his neighbor; ex-*

ecute the justice of truth and peace in your gates." Justice demands truth. "*Lying lips are abomination to the Lord*" (Proverbs 12:22).

Truth and justice are the foundation for ordering our home. There will be no peace unless we first have truth and justice. We will not find men to execute justice and truth in the gates if it has not become ingrained in their lives from early childhood. Because Daniel was trained in a God-fearing home, he was ready and prepared to stand in the gates and influence a heathen nation (Daniel 2:49).

What is the result of truth and righteousness in the gates? Peace. This is what we long for, isn't it? Sadly, we have war in the gates when we turn from God's ways. Judges 5:8 says, "*They chose new gods; then was war in the gates.*"

7. CHALLENGE EVIL IN THE GATES

After being with God for 40 days and nights and receiving the divine tablets of stone which were written with the hand of God, Moses came down from Mt. Sinai to find the children of Israel had already turned from God and were worshipping a golden calf and defiling themselves with pagan revelry. Did Moses show a spirit of tolerance? No way. He was so furious he threw the tablets to the ground; he ground the golden calf into powder, mixed it with water, and made the people drink it! "*Then Moses stood in the gate of the camp, and said, 'Who is on the Lord's side? Let him come unto me*'" (Exodus 32:26).

It is time to challenge the evil that is going on in the gates of our cities and our land! The Bible also talks about challenging evil in the gates of the Lord's house. Where are the men who are unafraid to challenge the compromise and deception in the church? God told Jeremiah to "*Stand in the gate of the Lord's house, and proclaim there this word, and say, Hear the word of the Lord, all ye of Judah, that enter in at these gates to worship the Lord. Thus saith the Lord of hosts, the God of Israel, Amend your ways and your doings*" (Jeremiah 7:2, 3). Also read Jeremiah 17:19-21.

May God raise up men like Moses, Jeremiah, and Elijah who will not be afraid to challenge evil in the gates. May God raise up true watchmen who will guard the adversary from coming into the gates of the church. Lamentations 4:12 says, "*The kings of the earth, and all the inhabitants of the world, would not have believed that the adversary and the enemy should have entered into the gates of Jerusalem.*" What about the gates of the church?

8. GUARD THE GATES

Nehemiah 11:19 talks about 172 men who guarded the gates of Jerusalem. God has appointed 12 angels to guard each gate of the New Jerusalem (Revelation 21:12). If the gates of God's city are to be guarded, what about the gates of our homes, our cities, and our nation?

We need watchmen in the gates of our land, but it starts in the home. We must guard the gates of our homes from all break-ins of the adversary—sin, deception, worldliness, and mediocrity. It starts with parents who command their household in the ways of justice, and who do not allow disobedience, rebellion, lies, and deceit to go undisciplined. It will take parents who abhor evil, love righteousness, and who teach their children to do the same.

If every God-fearing family carefully guarded the gates of their home, it would filter up to the gates of our nation. It all starts with the family, which is God's original plan. God established the family before the church and before government. Every individual family must take their responsibility to execute justice in their home gates.

Isaiah 3:26 says, *"Her gates shall lament and mourn"* and Jeremiah 14:2 says, *"Judah mourneth, and the gates thereof languish."* Will we have mourning in our gates or rejoicing?

PRAYER:

"Great God and Father, I cry out to you for 'defenders of justice' to be raised up in our midst. Help me, as a mother, to begin training 'defenders of justice' in my home. Teach me how to execute justice in my home. Amen."

AFFIRMATION:

I have a vision to train "defenders of justice" for the nation!

29

Lovingkindnesses

"I shall make mention of the lovingkindnesses of the Lord, the praises of the Lord, according to all that the Lord has granted us, and the great goodness toward the house of Israel, which He has granted them according to His compassion and according to the abundance of His lovingkindnesses"
(Isaiah 63:7, NASB).

On a shopping day at Aldi, our daughter, Serene, began to load a big cart of groceries onto the counter. Unexpectedly, a lady came up to her and said, "Let me help you," and proceeded to place all her groceries on the counter for her. Serene felt very blessed, especially when she did not even have all the other children tagging on, but only Breeze in the Ergo baby carrier. She went through the checkout, and as she began to put her big pile of groceries into bags with one hand, a man came up and said, "I'll bag that for you." He put all her frozen foods in her freezer bags and everything else into other bags and boxes.

As she walked her cart through the door, another lady came out of nowhere and said, "I'll push your cart for you," and pushed it all the way to her car. The lady left and, before she knew it, another lady came up and said, "I'll pack these groceries in the car for you" and proceeded to pack all her groceries away—better than she had ever seen them packed!

Serene could hardly believe what was happening and felt God pouring out His love upon her! But, if that wasn't enough, a young girl came up to her and said, "Can I take the cart back for you?" This is where the story fails because Serene said, "Oh no, it's OK, I can do it." She realized that she deprived this young girl of a blessing.

Five people, each unknown to one another, reached out to help a young mother. Can you imagine what this world would be like if each person reached out to help and bless someone like this each day?

Our daughter Mercy came home from work the other day with a happy smile on her face all because a customer took time to speak kind words to her. It made her day. We can make someone's day every day.

Proverbs 19:22 (NASB) says, *"What is desirable in a man (or woman) is his kindness."* This is the same Hebrew word as "lovingkindnessess." And the same word is used in Proverbs 31:26 describing the virtuous woman: *"In her tongue is the law of kindness."*

Everyone is looking for kindness. Our husbands long for us to speak kind words to them. Our children long for us to be kind to them. A hurting world is desperate for kindness.

Do you notice that our Scripture text does not only speak of one lovingkindness, but many? It is a plural word. God is a God of lovingkindness who wants to abundantly and continually pour out lovingkindnesses upon us. However, the only way He can tangibly do this is by doing it through us.

Wouldn't it be great if we could make it our aspiration to do something kind or say something kind to someone every day? Of course, we'll start with those closest to us—our husband and children. It's not much use saying kind words to those outside the home if we can't say them to those inside the home! But, when our home is filled with lovingkindnesses, we'll begin pouring them out on everyone around us, too.

PRAYER:

"Oh God, and Father, I thank you so much for all your lovingkindnesses to me. I am overwhelmed by your love and faithfulness. Please anoint me to pour out your love and kindness to others so I can show them what you are like. Amen."

AFFIRMATION:

I am a kindness spreader!

30

God's Word in Your Life
Part 1

"The Word that God speaks is alive and active; it cuts more keenly than any two-edged sword: it strikes through to the place where soul and spirit meet, to the innermost intimacies of a man's being: it exposes the very thoughts and motives of a man's heart"
(Hebrews 4:12, JBP).

As I read through Psalm 119 recently, I noticed eight things that happen ***"according to the Word of God."*** Shall we look at them together?

1. CLEANSING

Psalm 119:9 says, *"How can a young man cleanse his way? By taking heed **according to your word.**"*

We are exhorted in James 1:27 *"to keep ourselves unspotted from the world."* Do you want to keep your life pure and cleansed? Come daily to God's Word. Jesus said, *"Now you are clean through the word which I have spoken unto you"* (John 15:3). It is as important to wash our souls and spirits in the Word as it is to wash our bodies. God's Word will also keep our homes cleansed. Read it personally. Read it together as a family at the dinner table. The Word washes us from the deceptions of this world and the spots of sin that tarnish our souls and the atmosphere of our homes.

2. REVIVING

Psalm 119:107 (NKJV) says, *"Revive me, O Lord, **according to your word.**"* Read also verses 25, 50, 93, 149, 154, and 156.

The Hebrew word "revive" is *chayah*. It is a "re" word. It means, "to rebuild, recover, restore, relive, repair, refresh, and revive." The Word of God will renew you, recreate you, revitalize you, replenish you, and refine you. It will also reform, rearrange, redirect, retrain, and yes, reprove you.

Do you feel as though you are losing strength, losing the joy of life, and becoming stale? Do you need re-ing? The Word of God will "re" you! It is animating. It is life-giving. In fact, it is your very life. Jesus counteracted the devil with these words: *"Man shall not live by bread alone, but by every word that proceedeth out of the mouth of God"* (Matthew 4:4 and Deuteronomy 8:3).

Jesus also said: *"It is the Spirit who gives life; the flesh profits nothing. The words that I speak to you are spirit, and they are LIFE"* (John 6:63).

Every mother needs refreshing. She dreams of having some time on her own, taking a relaxing bath, going out to dinner, or watching a wholesome movie. But the greatest way to get refreshed is often our last resort! It is opening God's Word. It will refresh, restore, and revive you.

Over 50 years ago, when Colin and I were newly married, we had the privilege of living in a home owned by the China Inland Mission in Whangarei, New Zealand. The only people who had ever lived in this home were missionaries. We ourselves were waiting on the Lord and preparing to go to the mission field in the Philippines. When we left, a dear old couple (in their eighties) came to live in the home. They had served the Lord in China for 40 years and later in Formosa (which is now Taiwan) after China had closed. At last they were retiring.

Arthur Beard was such an inspiration to us. He loved God's Word. It was his life. Every day he read *The Daily Light*, and without glasses, mind you! This book is a compilation of Scriptures for each day on a certain theme, which we also read every day at Family Devotions in our home. The Scripture references are listed at the end of the page. As he read the Scriptures for each day, he would check to see if he could remember where each verse was found. He remembered correctly nearly 100 percent of the time.

At one stage, while on the mission field, Arthur Beard got cancer. However, it didn't stay in his body long. He read God's Word out loud daily, and he was healed. His body was revived and made anew by the living Word of God (Psalm 107:20)!

Let the life-giving Word of God "re" you!

PRAYER:

"Father God, I thank you that your Word is life to my soul. Teach me how to read it in faith to receive your refreshing and reviving into my tired soul and body. Amen."

AFFIRMATION:

By the power of God's Word, I am "re-ing" to go!

31

God's Word in Your Life
Part 2

"The salvation of the righteous is from the Lord;
He is their strength in the time of trouble"
(Psalm 37:39).

God's Word is your life-source, today and every day.

3. STRENGTHENING

The psalmist cries out in Psalm 119:28, *"My soul melts from heaviness; strengthen me* ***according to your word."***

The Psalmist is grieving. Tears pour down his face and his chest heaves with weeping. He feels his soul dissolving and dropping away. The Hebrew word "melts"actually means "to drop away." It is the poetical way to express weeping.

Are you going through a time of grieving? Are you overcome with sorrow? Do you feel your soul dropping away because your heart is broken? You don't have to continue this way. Even in his anguish, the psalmist knows there is an answer. It is God's living words. He knows its power to strengthen his soul and his emotions.

Dear grieving one, get down on your knees, open God's Word, and ask Him to speak to you. His Word has the power to strengthen your heart. Claim His promises. Start speaking them out loud. They will restore and strengthen your innermost soul and emotions.

God not only has the power to strengthen you physically, but to strengthen you inwardly. His strengthening Word will put a song in your heart. Read Psalm 27:14; 31:24; 73:26; 118:14; 138:3; and Ephesians 3:16.

4. MERCIES AND SALVATION

Psalm 119: 41 says, *"Let your mercies come also to me, O Lord, your sal-*

vation according to your word." Read also verses 58 and 76.

God's mercies are very great and line up with His everlasting Word. We cannot expect mercy when we violate God's written laws because mercy does not compromise truth. Mercy and truth are twins. Psalm 25:10 says, *"All the paths of the Lord are mercy and truth unto such as keep his covenant and his testimonies."* Read also Psalm 85:10 and 89:14.

We receive mercy when we repent and appropriate the precious blood of Jesus, because this promise is written in the Word. The Word is filled with precious promises, but most are preceded by a commandment. When we obey His commandments we will receive the bountiful mercies of the Lord.

It is through the mercies of the Lord and the living Word of God that we are saved from sin and born again. 1 Peter 1:23 (NKJV) says, *"Having been born again, not of corruptible seed but incorruptible, through the Word of God which lives and abides for ever."* And Titus 3:5 says, *"Not by works of righteousness which we have done, but according to His mercy He saved us."*

PRAYER:

"Oh thank you, Father, for your great mercies, for your great salvation, and for your great and powerful living Word. Thank you with all my heart. Amen."

AFFIRMATION:

I bask in God's mercies today.

32

God's Word in Your Life
Part 3

"You know in all your hearts and in all your souls that not one thing has failed of all the good things which the Lord your God spoke concerning you. All have come to pass for you, and not one word of them has failed" (Joshua 23:14). Read also Joshua 21:45 and 1 Kings 8:56.

Everything else around you may fail, but God's Word will never fail you. You can count on it.

5. GOD'S GOOD WORKINGS

Psalm 119:65 says, *"You have dealt well with your servant, O Lord,* ***according to your word.****"*

The Hebrew word for "dealt well" is *asah,* which actually means "to do, to work, to make, to create, to build."

God's ultimate plan for us is to transform us into the image of His Son. He wants many sons in the likeness of His Son. He works in us by His Holy Spirit and by the power of His Word to change us into His likeness. The more we allow the Word to dwell in our hearts, the more we are transformed into the way God wants us to think and live.

God's Word doesn't always suit our circumstances, but if we know what's good for us, we'll put aside our desires and embrace the transforming principles of God's Word. We will resist our humanistic reasonings and allow God to fill our minds with His life-changing thoughts that He has given us in His Word.

Everything that God has written is for our good; God's ways are for our best. Deuteronomy 6:24 says, *"And the Lord commanded us to observe all these statutes, to fear the Lord our God, for our good always"* (Deuteronomy 10:12, 13).

The psalmist experienced God's words changing him for good. In Psalm

119:67 he confesses, *"Before I was afflicted I went astray. But now I keep your word."* Again in verse 71 he says, *"It is good for me that I have been afflicted, that I may learn your statutes."*

Allowing God to change us can be painful. It pricks our nest. It is uncomfortable. But who wants to stay the same for the rest of their lives? How boring. God loves us too much to leave us in our shallow, sinful state. He wants to take us on to victory. He wants to lift us up to the overcoming life. He wants to transform our thinking into His thinking.

There can be times in our lives when God's *rhema* word comes to us and yet we do not see the fulfillment of it. This happened in Joseph's life. God revealed Joseph's destiny to him in two dreams. He was going to be a ruler and his father and brothers would bow down to him. This sounded pretty exciting. But things didn't turn out like the dream. His brothers who were supposed to serve him turned against him. They would have killed him except for the intervention of Judah. Instead, they banished him from their sight and sold him off to merchantmen on their way to Egypt. He was torn away from his beloved father, his family, his country, and everything familiar.

Down in Egypt things went from bad to worse. Although he walked in integrity and refused to give into the seducing of Potiphar's wife, he was falsely accused and thrown in prison. Even when he sought to do the right thing, it turned against him and he was doomed to a dungeon.

Was God's Word false? No. God, who lives in the eternal and who is not bound by time, was working and setting the stage for Joseph's destiny. In His perfect timing, He delivered Joseph from the prison. Joseph miraculously becomes second-in-command to the Pharaoh of Egypt. Then comes the day, in fulfillment to God's promise and word, that Joseph's brothers bow to him.

In that poignant moment, when Joseph reveals himself to his brothers and they are reconciled together, he says these words: *"God sent me before you to preserve a posterity for you in the earth, and to save your lives by a great deliverance. So now it was not you who sent me here, but God"* (Genesis 45:7, 8).

Again, at the death of his father, he reminds his brothers again, "*But as for you, you meant evil against me; but **God meant it for good**, in order to bring it about as it is this day, to save many people alive.*" Read these words again . . . ***"God meant it for good"***!

All the suffering that Joseph endured was ultimately for his good, and not only for his good, but also for his family and for the nations.

Have you received a word from God? Yet, everything is turning out the opposite! Don't give up on God's promise to you. God does not work in your time. He works in His time. He sees the future. You can count on Him to work everything out for your good! His whole purpose is to do a good work in you. Philippians 1:6 says, *"Being confident of this very thing, that he who has begun a good work in you will complete it until the day of Jesus Christ."*

PRAYER:

"Oh Lord, I thank you that you are a good God. I thank you that I can trust your timing to fulfill your purposes in my life. I yield my life to you and to the principles of your good Word. I thank you that you will complete the good work that you have started in me. Amen."

AFFIRMATION:

I trust in the unfailing goodness of God.

33

God's Word in Your Life
Part 4

"Let the word of Christ dwell in you richly in all wisdom; teaching and admonishing one another in psalms and hymns and spiritual songs, singing with grace in your hearts to the Lord"
(Colossians 3:16).

As a mother, every day you are desperate for wisdom. God's Word is your wisdom. It will even give wisdom to the simple (Psalm 19:7).

6. UNDERSTANDING

Psalm 119:169 says, *"Let my cry come before you, O Lord: give me understanding* ***according to your word****."*

"Give me understanding, Lord." Is this the cry of your heart? We need understanding each moment of the day. At least I do. Proverbs 24:3 tells us that it is by wisdom and understanding that we build and establish our homes. That means that we can't accomplish our great task of mothering without the anointing of understanding.

What is the middle letter of the word *truth*? It is U, which stands for understanding. Understanding is the heart of truth. You can't have understanding without truth. And you can't have truth without God's Word.

There is worldly understanding and there is godly understanding and they can be poles apart. Don't be content with humanistic understanding and what seems good to you. Make sure it lines up with God's eternal Word. Add an extra sentence to your prayer, "O Lord, give me understanding **according to your word**." You will be filled with understanding when you immerse yourself in God's Word.

Now when you get God's understanding, you might find yourself out of step with the rest of the world. I am always challenged by the Scripture Romans 3:4: *"Let God be true but every man a liar."* Are we prepared to stand with God's truth even if everyone else is doing something different?

How can we receive understanding from the Word?

1) By Asking God

Each time you open God's Word, pray, "O Lord, give me understanding according to your Word. Open my eyes to behold wondrous things in your law."

2) By Digging

We need to get below the surface to hear the heart of God. It's not enough to read the Word. We have to think about it, meditate upon it, and chew it over and over. I love to check out the Hebrew and Greek words. I use a wonderful Bible which helps me to do this. It is the *Hebrew-Greek Key Word Study Bible* edited by Spiros Zodhiates. I read the King James translation, but enjoy checking other translations.

There is one thing that is very important to remember. The truth of a particular subject is not found in one Scripture, but in what God says about the subject from Genesis to Revelation. When we check out every Scripture in God's Word on a particular subject, we can then have a full understanding of what God is saying.

3) By Divine Insight

I love it when God comes to my spirit with a flash of enlightenment. But, mostly, I have to dig. Read Ephesians 1:18 and Colossians 1:9.

4) By Discussing

Whenever I am meditating on a certain Scripture or thinking about a specific subject, I talk to my husband or daughters about it. "What are your thoughts about this?" I ask. We always discuss our latest thoughts and revelations when we get together. It's our favorite thing to do. It's a great way to fine-tune your understanding. As we discuss together, we adjust one another, and are spared from getting on a tangent. Our thoughts are also deepened and expanded. There is nothing more satisfying than discussing the Scriptures and sharing insight and revelation with fellow believers. The only sad thing is that so few believers really want to do it.

Get into the habit of asking your husband for understanding. "But he's not walking with the Lord," you exclaim. That doesn't matter. God has made him your covering, whether he walks with the Lord or not. Ask him for his insight on all matters. Ask him for his understanding about Scriptures, too. There's nothing like asking him to get him searching. And because God has ordained for him to be your head, you'll be amazed at what insight God will give him.

PRAYER:

"Oh God, I long for your understanding. I can't adequately mother without it. Please give me insight and understanding according to your word. Amen."

AFFIRMATION:

Rather than the world's way, I'm looking to God for understanding on how to mother my children.

34

God's Word in Your Life
Part 5

"And the Lord shall deliver me from every evil work, and will preserve me unto his heavenly kingdom. To him be glory for ever and ever. Amen" (2 Timothy 4:18). Read also 2 Peter 2:9.

Never use God's Word as a last resort. Daily fill your heart and mind with His life-giving words. Daily read it to your children and fill their minds with His powerful, delivering words.

7. UPHOLDING

Psalm 119:116 says, *"Uphold me* ***according to your word,*** *that I may live."*

God's Word is able to hold you up. When you feel as though you are sinking, resort to the Word. It will bear you up. It will bear you up above your circumstances. You'll still face them each day, but you will walk in the power of God's Word that will carry you above the difficulties.

I teach my grandchildren these lines . . .

"When my foot begins to slip
God will hold me with His grip!"

8. DELIVERING

Psalm 119:170 says, *"Let my supplication come before you; deliver me* ***according to your word.****"*

God is a God of deliverance. He has promised to deliver us when we cry out to Him. Psalm 22:5 and Romans 10:13 say, *"For whosoever shall call upon the name of the Lord shall be saved."* There is no pit too deep, no problem too insurmountable, and no predicament too difficult from which God cannot deliver you! Are you bound by fears, anger, self-pity, or negative habits? God does not want you to live in this state. He waits to deliver you. Cry out to Him and use the power of His Word.

What about fears? David confessed in Psalm 34:4, *"I sought the Lord, and he heard me, and delivered me from all my fears."* You don't have to live with one fear! Find antidote Scriptures about fear. Memorize them. Confess them out loud constantly. Use them against the enemy every time fear begins to take hold. Here are some suggestions for you: Deuteronomy 31:6, 8; Psalm 91; Isaiah 41:11, 13; 2 Timothy 1:7; and Hebrews 13:5, 6.

Do you have a problem with spouting out angry words? Fill your mind and heart with Scriptures like these: Leviticus 19:18; Psalm 119:165; Proverbs 15:1; 16:24; 31:26; Matthew 5:44; Ephesians 4:1-2, 32; and Colossians 3:12, 13. Whenever you feel anger rising up, speak one of these Scriptures out loud.

Are you in the habit of always complaining? Check out these Scriptures: Psalm 34:1; 35:28; 44:8; 71:8; Proverbs 17:22; Ephesians 5:20; Philippians 2:14, 15; Colossians 2:7c and 1 Thessalonians 5:18. Memorize them so that you can quote them out loud every time you begin to grumble and moan.

One of the worst habits we tend to fall into is selfishness! It's easy to make a lifestyle of this habit, but it destroys our marriage and family life. If you tend toward this one, use these Scriptures: 1 Corinthians 10:24, 33; 13:5; 2 Corinthians 5:15; Philippians 2:3, 4 and 6, 8.

What about evil or immoral thoughts? You can be delivered from these as you wield the sword of the Word of the Lord. Every time an evil thought enters your mind, don't receive it. Don't dwell on it. Instead, quote the Word of God, even as Jesus did when Satan came to tempt him. This was Jesus' way to overcome the enemy. It's your way too. Start the new habit of saying, "It is written" (Matthew 4:1-11). Read Philippians 4:8 and James 4:7, too.

God's powerful, living words are able to deliver you from your habits. A habit is "a tendency to act constantly in a certain manner." God's Word can help you change that tendency to a different tendency. Thomas à Kempis said, "Habit is overcome by habit."

What negative habit do you want to be rid of in your life? Here's an answer. Search for the antidote Scriptures. Memorize them. Each time you start to get in the groove of your habitual tendency, stop and recite the appropriate Scriptures OUT LOUD! I am sure that if you do this for at least three weeks, you will be delivered. You will begin walking in a new and positive habit instead of the negative one.

PRAYER:

"Oh God, I thank you that you sent your only Son to die to deliver me from my sins, from my habits, and from my selfishness. I thank you that you have also given me your Word to change me and deliver me. Help me to live in the power of your life-changing Word. Amen."

AFFIRMATION:

I am no longer chained to my habits because I live in the delivering power of God's Word.

35

Full-Time Service

"Not that we are sufficient of ourselves to think any thing as of ourselves; but our sufficiency is of God; who also hath made us able ministers of the new testament" (2 Corinthians 3:5, 6).

What a great privilege to be in full-time service for the Lord. Mother, do you realize that you are in full-time ministry? You are engaged in the most powerful career in the nation—mothering, nurturing, educating, and training the next generation. You are determining the destiny of our nation.

What do you answer when someone asks you your occupation? Have you ever thought of answering, "I'm in full-time ministry"? "What is the area of your ministry?" they may ask. "I'm a children's pastor," you reply. "Oh, in what church are you serving?" "The church of (give your family name)." Of course, being in full-time ministry for God, you'll be serving the Lord with all your heart, *"Not lagging in diligence, fervent in spirit, serving the Lord"* (Romans 12:11).

Apart from the greatest title of Mother, which we are all proud to wear, you also carry the following titles:

Accountant, Arbitrator, Art Appreciator, Arrow Polisher, and Ambassador for the King of Kings.

Bodyguard, Bookkeeper, Bible Teacher, and Bulk Buyer.

Career Consultant, Chauffeur, CEO of your Family Clan, Cheerleader, Children's Pastor, Children's Best Friend, Childhood Psychologist, Creative Designer, Cultivator of "Olive Plants," Customer Service Representative, Coach and Child Development Specialist, and Counselor.

Dietitian, Discipler, Director of Home Affairs, Driving Instructor, and Domestic Engineer.

Encourager, Entrepreneur, Entertainer, and Educator.

First Lady of the Home, Fashion Consultant, Finance Manager, and Food Tester.

Gardener, Generation Builder, and Guidance Counselor.

Hairdresser, Happy Homemaker, Historian, Home Builder, Home Executive, Home Manager, Hostess, and Hygienist.

Influencer of Nations and Future Generations, Intercessor, Interior Decorator, and Investigator.

Janitor, Judge.

Lapidary (polisher of precious stones), Librarian, Life Giver, and Launderer.

Master Story-Teller, Memory Maker, Mender of Hearts (and Knees), Mentor, Missionary, Molder of Children for Heaven, and Movie Critic.

Nation Changer, Nurse, Nutritionist, and Nurturer.

Personnel Manager, Professional Baker, Professional Chef, Professional Cleaner, Pediatrician, Photographer, Project Manager, Protector, and Purchasing Agent.

Queen of Your Home.

Recreation Director, Referee, Repairer of Breaches (and Britches!), and Restorer of Peace.

Safety Instructor, Schedule Coordinator, Sculptor, Seamstress, Security Guard, Social Coordinator, Speech Therapist, Shepherdess of Your Flock, and Switchboard Operator.

Taxi Driver, Teacher, and Time Management Expert.

Vacation Coordinator, Visionary.

Walking Encyclopedia, and of course, you are a WONDER WOMAN!

Lift your head high, dear mother. You have the greatest career in the nation.

PRAYER:

"Thank you, Father, for giving me such an amazing career. I know it is enormous and I can't do it in my own strength. I thank you that in my weakness, you are strong and you are constantly with me, empowering and anointing me to fulfill this great task. Amen."

AFFIRMATION:

I'm in full-time ministry for God as I nurture and train my children.

36

Mothering Attitudes

"And whatsoever ye do, do it heartily, as to the Lord, and not unto men; knowing that of the Lord ye shall receive the reward of the inheritance; for ye serve the Lord Christ" (Colossians 3:23, 24).

Yesterday I wrote about serving the Lord in motherhood. How does God want us to do this? The following 21 points from the Bible tells us exactly the way God wants us to mother.

1. ABOUNDINGLY (1 CORINTHIANS 15:58)

To "abound" in the work of the Lord is the Greek word *perisseuo* and actually means "to be excessive, over the top, going beyond what is necessary, superabundant." Are you only doing what you have to do to get through the day? Or are you mothering "over the top"? What a fun way to live! What a great way to serve the Lord as you mother each day. When you change a diaper, laugh and smile at your baby. When you are doing mundane tasks, do them with exuberance. When you are preparing a meal, make it a beautiful meal to bless your family.

The same Greek word is used when it describes the twelve extra baskets which were *"over and above"* what was eaten by the five thousand (John 6:13). It is the same word that is used when the prodigal son came to himself and remembered that in his father's house there was *"enough and to spare"* (Luke 15:17).

2. AS TO THE LORD, AND NOT UNTO MEN (COLOSSIANS 3:23)

When we seek to do every big or little task for the Lord, it changes our whole attitude.

3. FAITHFULLY (MATTHEW 25:21, 23)

4. FERVENTLY (ROMANS 12:11)

5. FOR THE GLORY OF GOD (1 CORINTHIANS 10:31)

6. HEARTILY (COLOSSIANS 3:23)

The Greek word for "heartily" is *psuche* and means "soul." That means we are to not only do our mothering tasks physically, just because we have to do them, but we put our whole heart and soul into them.

7. HUMBLY (MATTHEW 20:26-28)

8. IN THE FEAR OF THE LORD (HEBREWS 12:28 AND PSALM 2:11)

9. IN THE NAME OF THE LORD JESUS (COLOSSIANS 3:17)

As we do each task in the name of Jesus, it becomes a sacred task.

10. JOYFULLY (DEUTERONOMY 28:47)

Wipe off the frown. Put a smile on your face. Don't worry about whether you feel like it or not. Smile and your attitude will change.

11. LOVINGLY (GALATIANS 5:13)

12. NEVER GIVING UP (ACTS 20:24 AND 2 TIMOTHY 4:7)

13. RELYING ON GOD (PHILIPPIANS 4:13)

You'll never make it in your own strength!

14. THANKFULLY (COLOSSIANS 3:17)

No more groaning and complaining. Thank and praise the Lord instead.

15. WILLINGLY (PROVERBS 31:13)

No more excuses!

16. WITH ALL OUR MIGHT (ECCLESIASTES 9:10)

17. WITH ZEAL (JOHN 2:17)

Forget moping around the house. Forget apathy. You are involved in the greatest career in the nation. You are influencing this nation and generations to come. Do it with zeal.

18. WITHOUT BEING SIDETRACKED (NEHEMIAH 6:3)

19. WITHOUT EXPECTING ANYTHING IN RETURN (LUKE 17:7-10)

20. WITHOUT GRUMBLING (PHILIPPIANS 2:14, 15)

21. WITHOUT SEEKING RECOGNITION (EPHESIANS 6:6)

Which attitude spoke to you? It's just about too much to take them in all at once, isn't it? You may want to work on one attitude each week.

Isn't it wonderful that God does not leave us in doubt? He shows us the way. He wants us to mother. When we do it our own way, especially giving in to our own moods and feelings, we reap discontent and misery. When we do it His way, we reap the blessings of peace and joy. And we reap the rewards. Mothering is never in vain. It is never wasted. It is an eternal career and lasts forever (1 Corinthians 15:58).

Mother with your eye on the finish line (1 Corinthians 9:24; Galatians 6:9; and Philippians 2:12-14)!

PRAYER:

"Oh God, please forgive me. I so easily succumb to self-pity and the 'poor me' attitude. Help me to live beyond thinking of myself and to mother with a free and overflowing attitude of joy. Amen."

AFFIRMATION:

Hallelujah! I am in the most high-powered career in the nation, and I am employed by God Himself!

37

Training Royalty
Part 1

"Instead of thy fathers shall be thy children, whom thou mayest make princes in all the earth"
(PSALM 45:16).

What an amazing vision for parents, to prepare children to be princes and princesses in all the earth. The Hebrew word for prince is *sar*. It is used to describe our Savior, the Messiah. He is called *Sar Shalom* in Isaiah 9:6, *"The Prince of Peace."* God wants His children to also walk with princely character. *Sar* has a number of meanings.

TO BE A HEAD

God wants us to raise our children . . .

1. To be the head and not the tail (Deuteronomy 28:13).
2. To not be defeated by the temptations of the devil and this world, but to overcome. We must remind our children that they should not be surprised when trouble and difficulties come their way. If we did not have trials, we would have nothing to overcome. God's rewards are only for the overcomers; therefore, we can rejoice that we have obstacles to overcome! Read Numbers 13:30; John 16:33; Romans 12:21; 1 John 4:4, 5; Revelation 2:11, 17, 26; 3:5, 12, 21; and 21:7.
3. To not be subservient to the lusts of this world but to reign in life with Christ. Read Galatians 5:16; 2 Timothy 2:12; 1 John 2:15-17; and Revelation 5:10.

TO BE A RULER

God wants us to teach our children to rule over their own spirits. It is a powerful thing to rule the spirit, and this gift belongs to princes. Proverbs 16:32 tells us that the one who rules his spirit is better than one who captures a city! We have to teach this principle to our children. Instead, many children are trained by their parents to have no control over their spirit. From an early age they are gratified with every whim and fancy. When they whine for something, they get it. When they pester their parents for something, they get it. This does not train them to rule over the lusts of the flesh nor prepare them to rule in adult life.

A disciple of Christ learns to deny his own lusts and desires. Titus 2:11, 12 says: *"For the grace of God that brings salvation has appeared to all men, teaching us that,* ***denying*** *ungodliness and worldly lusts, we should live soberly, righteously, and godly in this present world."* Did you notice the word "deny"? Jesus also said, *"If any man will come after me, let him deny himself, and take up his cross and follow me"* (Matthew 16:24).

The Message version of the Bible puts it this way, to kill off the tendency of *"doing whatever you feel like whenever you feel like it, and grabbing whatever attracts your fancy. That's a life shaped by things and feelings instead of by God"* (Colossians 3:5, 6).

TO BE A MASTER

God wants us to teach our children to master their emotions, to live by the truth of the Word of God rather than their feelings. A wimpy person lives by their feelings, and feelings are deceiving. They change from day to day and come and go, whereas God's eternal truth is absolute. We should teach our children to keep a good spirit and trust in the Lord even when things are going bad. Rather than give in to their feelings, we teach them to thank the Lord for His goodness and that He is a faithful God. We teach them to confess their trust in the Lord. We teach them to confess the joy of the Lord even when they feel unhappy. We teach them to put a smile on their face instead of a grumpy face. These daily habits will help them to be masters of their fickle feelings and to be men and women who will trust God and stand strong even when everything is going wrong.

TO BE A LEADER

A person of princely character is not easily led into devious ways by others. Instead, he is one who knows what he believes, stands true to what he believes, and leads others into truth. We must soak our children in the Word of God. We must impart the understanding of God's truth to them so that they are rooted in truth and are confident to lead others in the ways of God (1 Corinthians 9:24-27 and 2 Timothy 2:2).

TO BE A PRINCE OR A NOBLEMAN

We must raise our children to know that they are sons and daughters of the King of kings and Lord of lords. They belong to royalty, the greatest kingdom on earth. This does not mean that they are proud, for pride has no part of God's kingdom. He looks for subjects of his kingdom who are meek, humble, and tremble at His Word.

However, we teach them to walk with dignity as true representatives of the King of kings. We should bear the image of royalty because we are His children. We as mothers should walk, speak, dress, and act as subjects of the heavenly kingdom and teach our children to do the same. We should have about us a heavenly aristocracy. Because we belong to the One who owns the cattle on a thousand hills, we can walk with stateliness even though we may not have a penny to bless ourselves! *"Penniless, we own the world,"* confessed Paul (2 Corinthians 6:10, NEB).

TO BE A PRIEST

God has made us kings and priests to God (Revelation 1:6; 5:10; and 20:6). Not only has He made us kings and priests, but He says we will reign on the earth. If we are going to reign, we should start practicing now.

We will teach our sons to be priests in their homes, taking their leadership to provide and protect their families and to lead them into the ways of God. They will take up their responsibility to rule in godliness and not give in to wimpiness. As priests, we all have a responsibility to intercede on the behalf of others and to bless others in His name (Deuteronomy 10:8; 18:5; and Numbers 6:23-27).

PRAYER:

"Father, please teach me how to train my children to walk as subjects of the King of kings and Lord of lords. Amen."

AFFIRMATION:

I am training royal subjects!

FURTHER READING:

http://aboverubies.org/selfindulgent

38

Training Royalty
Part 2

"Josiah took away all the abominations out of all the countries that pertained to the children of Israel, and made all that were present in Israel . . . to serve the Lord their God. And all his days they departed not from following the Lord, the God oftheir fathers"
(2 Chronicles 34:33).

While Josiah reigned as king of Israel, the whole nation of Judah did not depart from following the Lord. What a marvelous testimony for the leader of the nation. The amazing thing is that this was not the testimony of an older experienced man, but of a young man.

The Bible tells us in 2 Chronicles 34:2, 3: *"He did right in the sight of the Lord, and walked in the ways of his father David and did not turn aside to the right or to the left. For in the eighth year of his reign* ***while he was still a youth,*** *he began to seek the God of his father."* Josiah was only 16 years old when he began to seek the Lord with all his heart. This is the most opportune time for young people to seek God—the time when they are filled with energy, passion, and vision. The greatest way they can exert this energy is toward God and His kingdom.

ZEALOUSLY SEEK GOD

How do we get our young people to seek God? We can't make them do it. No law can make them do it. It has to come from their heart. Therefore, how can we influence their hearts?

1. Inspire them to a life of serving God and others. Encourage them to get involved with missions and helping the needy. A selfish mentality where everything revolves around "me" is a destructive attitude.
2. Make sure they are raised on God's Word. Conduct Family Devotions together every morning and every evening, not in legality, but with

vitality, asking questions, and promoting discussion. God's Word has power to change their lives and draw them closer to the Lord. Encourage them to have their own daily quiet time.

3. Train them in character. Don't allow petty attitudes and self-pity trips. Don't allow grumbling and complaining. Prepare them to be able to face all situations in life, to minister equally to the poor and to the rich. Everyone born of royalty is consistently, systematically, and extensively trained for kingship and queenship. They will not live like children of the King of kings without our faithful training.
4. Pray for them. Our greatest weapon is prayer. When we pray, the Holy Spirit will work in their lives in answer to our earnest and fervent prayers. Prayer was our greatest weapon as we raised our teenagers.

It saddens me to see so many so-called "Christian" young people who are taken up with the worldly pursuits of this life. Instead of seeking God and shining with His light, they are more interested in looking at the opposite sex, talking immaturely with their friends, chewing gum, and dressing immodestly. "Cleavage" seems to be "in" thing, with adult women as well as teenage girls. Where is the example for our youth? Do young ladies and women not realize that this relegates them to the "common" instead of belonging to royalty—princes and princesses of the King of kings?

A DIFFERENT SPIRIT

It's time to earnestly cry out to God for our young people. Pray that they will not be interested in living the status quo life of the other young people around them, but they, like Caleb, will have a different spirit than everyone else. I love the description of Caleb in Numbers 14:24: *"But my servant Caleb, because he had another spirit with him, and hath followed me fully him will I bring into the land . . . and his seed shall possess it."*

When young people become filled with the zeal of God they can change a nation. That's what Josiah did. We read in 2 Chronicles 34:3, *"And in the twelfth year he began to purge Judah and Jerusalem."* Josiah was now 20 years of age, still a young man. At this age he began to clean up the nation. He rose up in boldness to expose the works of darkness. He was not only concerned about the evil, he did something about it. He purged the land of evil, tore down the altars of Baal, chopped down the incense altars, broke them in pieces, ground them to powder, and scattered them. He burned the bones of the priests of Baal and tore down the Asherim altars and beat them to powder. This was radical stuff! There was no half-heartedness here, but absolute passion and zeal for the Lord. Let's pray for a nation of young people with this passion.

THROUGHOUT THE WHOLE EARTH

Psalm 45:16 tells us we are training princes for all the earth. We are getting them ready to send forth across the earth. We are getting them ready to go into the nations to take the gospel, to rise up against evil and deception, and do something about it! These young people are not the "ordinary" who try to fit in with the "in" crowd. They are living like royalty as they represent their King of kings.

PRAYER:

"Father, please help me to prepare children who will seek after you with all their hearts and be zealous for God. Amen."

AFFIRMATION:

I will not give up my vision to train children who will resist and oppose all evil.

39

Training Royalty
Part 3

"Jehoiachin was eight years old when he became king, and he reigned three months and ten days in Jerusalem, and he did evil in the sight of the Lord" (2 Chronicles 36:9, NASB).

We noticed in *Training Royalty, Part 2* that Josiah sought the Lord while he was still a youth. His son is now made king while a child, but the Bible says that he did that which was evil before the Lord. And yet he was only eight years old (although different translations give varying ages). Even at an early age children can follow after evil or follow after the Lord.

I am sure it depends on their training. This is why we must be faithful to fill our children with God's Word even while they are small. Satan wants the minds and hearts of our young children. That is why we must be diligent to train them from a very young age. We want them for God, not for the devil's kingdom. I remember at nine years of age wanting to ask Jesus Christ into my life. Even at that age I struggled and felt the power of the enemy holding me back. It was a spiritual battle.

My daughter Evangeline experienced the same thing when she gave her life to Jesus as a young child. Evangeline shares her testimony: "God saved me at four years of age. Even today, it is still the most vivid and powerful experience of my life. I was lying in bed. I still remember the orange bedspread cover. My mother came into my room and said, 'Stephen (my twin) has just asked Jesus to come into his life. Would you like to also?' At that moment the world stopped and the fight between the powers of darkness and heaven began. My whole body was shaking. With all my heart I wanted to ask Jesus into my life, but the pull from Satan was so strong. "No, no, no" the voice of Satan pulled at my heart. The struggle was powerful.

Eventually I said "Yes" with all my heart. I followed my mother in prayer asking Jesus to come into my life. At that moment I knew God. I experienced the reality of God. He came into my life and filled me. He opened my mind to Him. I was saved for life—no turning back! I have known His powerful presence in my life ever since. Instantly, I felt peace. Instantly, I was not afraid of the big owl outside my room—or of anything. I have never been afraid of anything from that day."

I often wonder why God-fearing parents allow their children to go into the public school system to be subtly indoctrinated with humanism, socialism, and progressivism. I wonder why it doesn't bother them that they will be trained to think like socialists and become more and more conformed to the spirit of the world.

Psalm 1:1, 2 says: *"Blessed is the man who walks not in the counsel of the ungodly, nor stands in the path of sinners, nor sits in the seat of the scornful; but his delight is in the law of the Lord, and in His law he meditates day and night."* Many of our children, especially at college, sit under professors who scorn the Bible and the ways of God. God's blessing is on those who do not sit in the seat of the scornful and the counsel of the ungodly. Just imagine if every God-fearing parent took their children out of *"the counsel of the ungodly"* and brought them home to teach them in the ways of God! We would have a revolution in the country—and we certainly need one!

Back in the days of Israel when they were training princes and mighty men to fight for their country, they didn't train ones and twos; they trained thousands of them. Look at just some of the numbers that came to help David to make him king, in 1 Chronicles 12:24-36.

"The children of Judah . . . ready armed to the war (6,800)."

"The children of Simeon, mighty men of valor for the war (7,100)."

"The children of Zebulun . . . expert in war (50,000)."

"The children of Dan, expert in war (28,600)."

"The children of Asher, expert in war (40,000)."

As I read through the Word of God I don't see any commandments to send our children to Bible-hating colleges where they are brainwashed to think like humanists. Instead, I see God wanting to pour out His Holy Spirit on our children. Acts 2:17, 18 says: *"And it shall come to pass in the last days, saith God, I will pour out of my Spirit upon all flesh: and your sons and your daughters shall prophesy, and your young men shall see visions, and your old men shall dream dreams: and on my servants and on my handmaidens I will pour out in those days of my Spirit; and they shall prophesy."*

Do you want your children and teens to be worldly, humanistic thinkers? Or, do you want them to be filled with the Holy Spirit, boldly speaking forth God's truth in this deceived world? This won't happen unless they are in an environment where God can pour His Spirit upon them. That environment is not in a godless education system. Who do you think has the best idea? God? Or man with his own ideas?

PRAYER:

"Oh God, please help me to raise my children in an environment where you can fill them with your Holy Spirit and prepare them to be mouthpieces for you in the land. Amen."

AFFIRMATION:

I'm taking God's side rather than man's!

40

Training Royalty
Part 4

"Rescue me and deliver me from the hand of foreigners, whose mouth speaks vain words, and whose right hand is a right hand of falsehood—that our sons may be as plants grown up in their youth; that our daughters may be as pillars, sculptured in the style of a palace"
(Psalm 144:11, 12).

Once again,the Bible talks about our children in the context of royalty. The NASB calls them, *"Our daughters as corner pillars, fashioned as for a palace."*

There are two purposes for pillars:

1. TO SUPPORT A BUILDING

You would think the Bible would refer to our sons as pillars, as they denote strength, but God chose to liken our daughters to pillars. He wants them to be strong, too. Our daughters will one day bear the responsibility of raising a family, which is a huge task. They must be physically strong, prepared and ready to bear children. They must also be mentally, emotionally, and spiritually strong. They must be strong in their commitment to purity, holiness, faith, truth, and strong in standing against the deceptions of this age. We notice that our daughters are likened to pillars of a *palace*, not some insignificant building. They are extra strong pillars to hold up a magnificent building.

The word "virtuous" in Proverbs 31:10 is *chayil* and means "a force, strength, valor, an army." It is interesting that the virtues of strength and valor are also related to a woman!

2. TO BEAUTIFY THE PALACE

The pillars of a palace were not only to support the upper story, but to beautify the building. Let's look at other translations:

"Daughters of graceful beauty like the pillars of a palace wall" (TLB).

"Our daughters like carved columns, shapely as those of the temple" (NAB).

We are not only to raise our daughters to be strong, but to be beautiful. Did you notice the descriptions? "Shapely"—not out of shape! *"Graceful beauty"*—daughters who walk like royalty with head high and open face; who act with dignity, speak like royalty, and dress like royalty (not necessarily with expensive clothes but with clothes that glorify the King of kings).

Fide's Translation says, *"Our daughters like upright pillars, fine-wrought for a palace."* They do not slouch, but sit and walk uprightly—both physically and spiritually.

WHAT ABOUT OUR SONS?

The NEB says, *"Happy are we whose sons in their early prime stand like tall towers."* There is nothing bowed down about sons and daughters of royalty.

I love how the young men of Asher were described as *"choice and mighty men of valor"* (1 Chronicles 7:40). The word "choice" is *barar* in the Hebrew and means "singled out, chosen, cleansed, purified, polished, and proved." What a powerful career to raise "choice" young men for God's glory.

However, before we can reap the harvest of choice young men and women, we have to do something. Before the promise comes the command: *"Rid me, and deliver me from the hand of strange (alien) children, whose mouth speak vanity, and their right hand is a right hand of falsehood"* (Psalm 144:11). They will not become sons that grow tall in godly stature and daughters who are like the pillars of a palace while we allow them to be educated by the falsehoods of humanism and secularism. We must search for colleges that have a godly foundation.

Our children will not automatically become princes and princesses. Psalm 45:16 says, *"Instead of thy fathers shall be thy children, whom* ***you will make*** *princes in all the earth."* They don't suddenly turn out like princes. We have to make them into princes and princesses. This takes committed, full-time training. May God anoint us for this great task! Read Psalm 112:1, 2.

PRAYER:

"Oh God and Father, please help me to see that I have the privileged task of training royalty. Help me to get rid of every obstacle that would deter my sons and daughters from the destiny you have determined for them. Amen."

AFFIRMATION:

I am training my sons and daughters for royalty.

41

God Affirms: You Affirm

Part 1

"I AM THE LORD: that is my name:
and my glory will I not give to another"
(Isaiah 42:8).

Do you notice that throughout the whole Bible, God continually affirms who He is? He doesn't explain who He is, He just plainly and unashamedly states who He is. *"I AM THAT I AM"* God unequivocally announces in Exodus 3:14. Again, in Isaiah 48:12, He states without explanation, *"I AM HE."*

Jesus Christ, the Son of God, also stated *"I AM HE"* (John 8:24 and 28; 13:19). When Jesus said *"I AM HE"* in John 18:3-8, the band of officers "fell backwards." Again, He says in John 8:58, *"Before Abraham was, I AM."* Throughout the gospels and in Revelation He continually affirms that He is *"I AM."*

"I AM the bread of life" (John 6:35, 48, 51).
"I AM the light of the world" (John 8:12; 12:46).
"I AM from above" (John 8:23).
"I AM the door of the sheep" (John 10:7).
"I AM the good shepherd" (John 10:11, 14).
"I AM the resurrection and the life" (John 11:25).
"I AM Master and Lord" (John 13:13).
"I AM the way, the truth, and the life" (John 14:6).
"I AM the true vine" (John 15:5).
"I AM Alpha and Omega, the beginning and the ending" (Revelation 1:8, 11, 17; 22:13).
"I AM He that liveth, and was dead, and behold I am alive forevermore" (Revelation 1:18).

"I AM the root and the offspring of David" (Revelation 22:16).
"I AM the bright and morning star" (Revelation 22:16).

We read in Hebrews 1:3 that Jesus Christ is the *"express image of His person."* The word "person" in the Greek means "substance, assurance, confidence." This same word, *hupostasis,* is translated "confident boasting" in the following Scriptures: 2 Corinthians 9:4; 11:17; and Hebrews 3:14. God and Christ confidently affirm who they are.

Because we are created in the image of God, we are a little "I am" of God's creation. In being so, we also should confirm, as God does, who He created us to be. I believe we need to confirm this in three areas of our lives.

1. EMBRACE THE UNIQUENESS OF YOUR PERSONALITY AND THE GIFTS GOD HAS GIVEN TO YOU

There is no one like you in the whole world. There never has been and never will be again. You are unique. Your gifts, coupled with your personality, are one of a kind. Someone else may have similar gifts, but not your personality.

You don't have to aspire to have someone else's gifts. You don't have to try and have a personality like someone else. To do so is to waste your time and the life God has given you. Claim who you are. This is how you will glorify God in your life.

A. W. Tozer says, "Deep inside every man there is a private sanctum where dwells the mysterious essence of his being . . . It is man's 'I am,' a gift from the I AM who created him."

Also embrace the limitation of your gifts. When you embrace the gifts God has given you and use them fully for His glory, they are limitless. When you don't hanker after gifts you don't have, you are set free. There are so many things that I know I am not good at, but I don't worry about it. I am too busy doing what I can do to worry about what I can't do.

It is the same with your children. Don't expect them to have the same gifts as you, or as their siblings. Every one of our children are incredibly different in gifts and personalities and we encouraged them to go after what God put in their hearts. It makes life fulfilling and exciting.

PRAYER:

"Dear Father God, the I AM of the universe. Thank you for making me who you planned me to be. I accept my gifts, and my limitations, and yield my life to glorify you as the little 'I am' you created in your image. Amen."

AFFIRMATION:

I will not be embarrassed by my uniqueness, but "be" it with all my heart.

42

God Affirms: You Affirm
Part 2

"And Adam said, This is now bone of my bones, and flesh of my flesh: she shall be called Woman, because she was taken out of Man" (Genesis 2:24).

We continue to look at what God wants us to confirm in our lives.

2. EMBRACE WHO GOD TRANSCENDENTALLY CREATED YOU TO BE

God sent Jesus into the world to show the world what He is really like. However, now that Jesus has ascended, He sends us into the world to reveal the image of God (John 20:21). Because we are created in the image of the I AM THAT I AM, we should also unashamedly affirm who God created us to be.

Why are so many women ashamed of being female? I believe that the devil, who hates the image of God, wants to deny God's creation. He wants to distort the image of God in this world.

It is not enough to know who God created us to be. It is not enough to believe who we are. As God does, we should also embrace, affirm, and live to the full who we are. To do anything less is to waste the life that God intends for you.

To get you started, here is an affirmation for you to confess:

I am a woman, therefore I am feminine. I will glory in my femininity in order to give glory to God. I will dress, speak, walk, and act femininely.

I am a woman, therefore I am a "womb man." My womb is my most distinguishing characteristic as a woman. God chose to create me with a womb, therefore I embrace the function of my womb for the glory of God.

I am a woman, therefore I am a "life-giver." The first woman was named Eve, meaning life-giver. She was the prototype of all women to come. I delight to bring life to the world, through my womb, my words, and my actions.

I am a woman, therefore I am a nurturing mother. God has put this anointing innately in my very being. I am also created with breasts to nurse babies. I embrace my womanly nurturing anointing to bring glory to God.

I am a woman, therefore I am different than men. I have my own particular function and calling that God purposed for me. I will embrace it and walk in it, and resist all temptation to take my husband's role.

I am a woman, therefore I find my greatest joy in my home. God has given me the blessing of a home to be a nestbuilder. I have the privilege of making a sanctuary for the glory of God and to raise my children in this safe nest.

I am a woman, therefore I have been chosen to be a helper to my husband and an heir together with him as we advance God's kingdom together.

I am a woman, therefore my price is worth more than rubies and pearls. My divine calling, commissioned from the beginning of the world to guard my marriage, my children, and my home, is worth more than all the jewels in the world.

When I embrace who God created me to be, I bring honor and glory to Him. When I deny my femaleness, I dishonor God, who created me and His plan for my life.

It is true that you may be scorned for affirming who you are. People didn't understand Jesus, nor will they understand you. The humanistic mind cannot comprehend the things of God.

PRAYER:

"I thank you, dear Father, that I do not have to doubt who you are. You are the God of the universe, and You are my God. You are God alone and there is none else. Please save me from doubting who you made me to be. I want to bring honor and glory to your name. Amen."

AFFIRMATION:

I am daily and unashamedly affirming who God created me to be.

43

God Affirms: You Affirm
Part 3

"I am crucified with Christ: nevertheless I live: yet not I, but CHRIST LIVETH IN ME: and the life which I now live in the flesh I live by the faith of the Son of God, who loved me and gave himself for me"
(Galatians 2:20).

Yesterday we talked about affirming who God created us to be physically. However, even more importantly, we must also affirm God's character in us.

3. EMBRACE WHO YOUR LIFE IS IN CHRIST

Jesus Christ, the Son of God, not only died to save us from the punishment of our sins, but to live in us in order to reveal the image of God to the world. The apex of Christianity is *"Christ in you, the hope of glory"* (Colossians 1:27 and 2 Corinthians 3:18).

God does not intend for you to live according to the dictates of your fleshly nature, but to yield to His life that dwells in you (Galatians 2:20). In fact, you do not owe one tiny bit of debt to your fleshly feelings (Romans 8:12-14). The understanding of this truth changes the way we live. It changes the atmosphere of our homes.

As a young mother, I started off living according to my feelings. Sometimes I was up. Sometimes I was down. What an inferior way to live! Then I discovered the truth of Philemon 6, *"That the communication of thy faith may become effectual by the acknowledging of every good thing which is in you in Christ Jesus."*

What does this really mean? When you invite Jesus Christ to be your Savior and Lord and to come and dwell in you by His Holy Spirit, He comes in (Revelation 3:20)! He doesn't come in as half of who He is, but all of who He is! He comes into your life as if there was no one else in the world. He comes in the fullness of the Godhead. Jesus said in John 14:23, *"If a man love me, he will keep my words: and my Father will love him, and WE WILL COME UNTO HIM, and make our abode with him."* Jesus didn't say, "I will come," but, *"WE WILL COME."* Isn't that amazing?

When Christ comes into your life, you have *"every good thing"* in you that is in Jesus. He doesn't give His patience to some people, but leave it out of you! He doesn't give His joy to some people, but leave it out of you. He is who He is and can be nothing less, and He lives in you!

This truth is astounding. It is life-changing. However, you will not experience it until you acknowledge it. Perhaps you have had a sleepless night with the baby or young children. You feel tired and lousy. If you make this your confession, you'll feel even worse. Instead, acknowledge that God is the strength of your life. "Thank you, Lord, that you live in me. I thank you for your divine strength, which is strengthening me today." You'll be amazed how God will enable you to get through the day when you didn't think you could make it. (Of course, you'll try to take a little nap in the afternoon, if you can!)

There are times when the children get out of hand, you get angry with them, and start shouting. What are you doing? Giving into your frustration and fleshly anger. You don't have to do that—you are the most patient mother living in your city!

"I beg your pardon," you reply! Yes, Christ lives in you, and there is no one filled with more patience and longsuffering than Him. Acknowledge His longsuffering in you. "Thank you for your patience, Lord. Thank you that I'm filled with patience because you live in me."

What will happen? You can now deal with the situation in a calm spirit. You can only do either of two things—scream and yell at your children, or acknowledge His longsuffering that is in you! One or the other! Which do you choose?

What about when you feel down in the dumps and full of self-pity? Is Christ full of self-pity? Is He disgruntled, complaining, and morose? No. Joy is His character. Hebrews 1:9 tells us that He is filled with joy more than anyone else. And He lives in you. Start thanking Him for His joy that fills your life. Don't listen to those feelings. Keep confessing the joy and your feelings will soon catch up with your confession.

You must acknowledge Christ's life in you for it to become effectual. The word "effectual" is *energes,* meaning, "active, operative, powerful." It is the same word, "*powerful,*" that is used to describe God's Word in Hebrews 4:12.

We don't have these wonderful attributes in our own flesh. We only have them in the life of Christ that dwells in us. I think the saddest indictment to Christianity today is that we do not embrace the fullness of Christ's death upon the cross for us. He died to not only save us from our sins, but from our day-to-day fleshly nature by dwelling IN US! He wants us to exchange our fleshly life for His divine life.

Which way are you living in your home today?

PRAYER:

"I thank you so much, dear Lord, for the indwelling Holy Spirit in me. I thank you for your life and character in me. Please help me to yield to your life and not my fleshly lusts. Amen."

AFFIRMATION:

Today I will say "No" to my fleshly feelings and "Yes" to the life of Christ in me!

44

Shine Like Stars

"Do all things without murmurings and disputings: that ye may be blameless and harmless, the sons of God, without rebuke, in the midst of a crooked and perverse nation, among whom ye shine as lights in the world; holding forth the word of life"
(PHILIPPIANS 2:14-16).

The other morning I rose early to spend time with the Lord and in His Word. I walked outside to take out the dog. It was still dark but the sky was lit up with shimmering stars. In all my life I have never seen so many stars in the sky. It was like a dazzling canopy over the whole earth. I was in awe.

It must have been such a clear night (without competition of city lights) when God took Abraham outside to behold the night sky and said to him, *"'Look up into the sky and count the stars if you can. Your descendants will be like that—too many to count!' And Abram believed the Lord, and the Lord declared him righteous because of his faith"* (Genesis 15:4-6, NLT).

God promised Abraham descendants as many as the stars in the heavens shining on a clear night. God has kept His promise and millions of children have come forth from the loins of Abraham—not only from his loins, but also all the children of Abraham by faith. Galatians 3:6, 7 says, *"Even as Abraham believed God, and it was accounted to him for righteousness. Know ye therefore that they which are of faith, the same are the children of Abraham."*

God does not want a sprinkling of His people in the earth; He wants them to fill the earth, as the stars fill the sky.

SHINING STARS

He does not want them to only fill the earth, but to shine with His glory. God's purpose for His people is for them to reveal His image in the earth. We are His lights to shine in this dark, deceived, and depraved world. We are to shine like stars on a clear night when there are no clouds. We must dispel all sin and murkiness in our lives that would obscure the revelation of God to the world.

Philippians 2:15, 16 (Way) says, "*That you may show yourselves blameless, uncontaminated, irreproachable children of God, in the midst of a society morally warped, spiritually perverted, amongst whom you* ***shine out clearly, like stars in the world's sky,*** *holding out to it the light of the Word of Life.*" The GNT says, "*You must* ***shine like stars lighting up the sky.***"

The word "shine" is *phaino* and means "to be conspicuous, to be seen, to lighten, to show, to shine." We must not hide our light. We are to be conspicuous. Matthew 5:14-16 says, "*Ye are the light of the world. A city that is set on a hill cannot be hid... Let your light so shine before men, that they may see your good works, and glorify your Father which is in heaven.*"

BEACON LIGHTS

Paul confessed that God "*kindled a flame in my heart to make me* ***a world's beacon*** *of the knowledge of the glory of God as revealed in the face of Jesus the Messiah*" (2 Corinthians 4:6, Way). Often you cannot see the brilliance of the stars when you live in the city. Therefore, you may have to think of yourself as a beacon light! Don't dim your light, but put your headlights on full and expose all the darkness of evil and depravity around you.

We are living in an hour when we need to be more conspicuous than ever. Evil is encroaching over the earth, but the more evil intrudes, the more we must shine the light of God's truth and righteousness. It is time for the fulfillment of Isaiah 60:1, 2, a word that God originally spoke to Israel, but is also a word to us who are Abraham's children by faith in Christ: "*Arise, shine; for thy light is come, and the glory of the Lord is risen upon thee. For, behold the darkness shall cover the earth, and gross darkness the people: but the Lord shall arise upon thee, and His glory shall be seen upon thee.*" The darker the days, the more conspicuous we must become. The greater the evil, the more we must shine (Matthew 13:43).

Daniel 12:3 says, "*And they that be wise shall shine as the brightness of the firmament; and they that turn many to righteousness as the stars forever and ever.*"

PRAYER:

"Thank you, dear Jesus, that you are the light of the world. You now light the world through me. Please save me from being a foggy light that blurs the vision of your life in me. Amen."

AFFIRMATION:

I'm shining God's light into the dark places of my home and society!

45

Peaceful Dwellings
Part 1

"My people shall dwell in a peaceable habitation" (Isaiah 32:18).

One evening, a few years ago, when Pearl's children were younger, she put them all to bed and decided to come for a walk and join us for Family Devotions. The above Scripture was one of the Scriptures we read.

"How does this work?" she exclaimed. "My home was not very peaceful today!"

In the morning her son, Rocklyn, put too much paper in the toilet. To try and flush the toilet paper down he kept flushing and flushing. Of course, it overflowed—all over the bathroom and out onto the lounge carpet, poops and poopy paper included! Pearl used 20 towels to clean up the mess, but managed to keep her cool! She disinfected the bathroom and did several loads of laundry.

By afternoon, peace reigned again. All towels were dried and folded when Noble went to the toilet! He also put too much paper in the toilet and so Rocklyn, the expert toilet flusher, came to his rescue! Another flood! This time it was worse and even grosser! It took more than 20 towels to clean up! Pearl didn't keep her cool this time! "Get out!" she screamed to her children as she started the huge cleanup all over again!

So how do you have a peaceful home when you constantly face upsetting incidents? God knows that when you have children life is not perfect. They do foolish things. They break things. They make messes. They squabble. Help! The only way to keep things perfect is to have no children. But that's boring! And what do you accomplish by having a perfect house with no upsets? All you gain is a perfect house! That doesn't change the world. That doesn't raise godly children who will do mighty exploits for God. Proverbs 14:4 says, *"Where no oxen are, the crib is clean; but much increase is by the strength of the ox.*" Children bring work—and messes, but also joy, increase, riches, and growth in character.

And, in the midst of it all, we can have peace. This is God's plan for our dwellings. It doesn't mean that we won't face interruptions, upsets, messes, and heartaches. But we can have God's peace in the midst of trials. Anyone can have peace when everything is going perfectly. But the "*peace that passes all understanding*" is peace that we experience in the midst of difficulties and trials. It's the peace we experience even when we are upset (Philippians 4:7).

God wants us to enjoy this peace. And He enables us to enjoy it. He lives in us and He is Peace! When Christ Jesus came into your life by His Holy Spirit, He did not leave His peace out of you. In the midst of problems, thank God for His peace. Thank Him that His peace overflows your heart. Are you kidding yourself? No. It is truth. You can choose to live by your feelings or by the life of Christ who lives in you. And His life is peace!

Don't despair. God understands your frustrations. He is right there with you. I am sure that He was having a little laugh as He watched the shenanigans at Pearl's home. Even as Pearl laughed about it later—and apologized to her children for screaming at them.

PRAYER:

"Thank you, Lord, that you are the God of peace. Wherever you are, there is peace, even when everything is going wrong. Help me to acknowledge your peace in every circumstance. Amen."

AFFIRMATION:

I will be a peacemaker today, speaking peace in the midst of chaos and trauma!

46

Sure Dwellings
Part 2

"My people shall dwell in . . . sure dwellings"
(Isaiah 32:18).

God uses three descriptions to describe the homes of His people. Not only does He want them to be homes of peace, but to be secure dwellings, secure from danger and enemy attack. The word "secure" is *mibtach* and it is usually translated "confidence," such as Psalm 65:5, *"O God of our salvation; who art the* ***confidence*** *of all the ends of the earth."*

We can be confident that our homes will be safe when we put our trust in the living God and fulfill the prerequisite, which is to walk in righteousness. The preceding Scripture before Isaiah 32:18 says, *"And the work of righteousness shall be peace; and the effect of righteousness quietness and assurance forever"* (v. 17). Righteousness and peace are twins! You can't have peace without righteousness. Psalm 85:10 says, *"Righteousness and peace have kissed each other."* What a beautiful picture.

I love the Scripture in Proverbs 14:19, which says, *"The evil bow before the good; and the wicked at the gates of the righteous."* The wicked come to a screeching halt at the gates of a righteous home. They want nothing to do with righteousness. But they must be uncompromisingly righteous gates. The enemy will detect any compromise, any crack, or any hesitation of standing absolutely on the side of right.

In Ezekiel 14:12-20 it tells about the coming judgment of famine, devastation, and war, but the only people who would be saved (in the midst of the judgment) would be Noah, Daniel, and Job. Why these three men? Because of their righteousness. We will never avoid tough times, but we can have confidence of God's preservation even in the midst of them. After the promise of *"secure dwellings"* God promises in the next verse, *"even if the forest is destroyed and the city is annihilated"* (Isaiah 32:19, NET). When we walk in righteousness we can have peace even when everything is falling down around us.

There is something even more wonderful to see in this phrase, *"sure dwellings."* The word "dwelling" that is used here is mostly used of the tabernacle in the wilderness (119 times), the place where God's presence dwelt. More than anything else, God wants to live in your dwelling place.

PRAYER:

"Oh Father, please fill our dwelling place with your presence. When you are in the midst we will experience security, no matter what is happening around us. Amen."

AFFIRMATION:

God is my Salvation, my Security, my Sanctuary, and my Sufficiency!

47

Quiet Resting Places

Part 3

"My people shall dwell in . . . quiet resting places"
(Isaiah 30:15).

We come to the third description of the home God wants us to enjoy. Here is the Scripture again: "*And my people shall dwell in a peaceable habitation, and in sure dwellings, and in quiet resting places*" (Isaiah 32:18). A quiet resting place! Doesn't that sound idyllic? It sounds like a wonderful vacation to me. But, let's get back to the real life. It's not always quiet when you have lots of children around you. There is often so much to do that life doesn't seem like a rest! I know that I would have to go away for a vacation to have a rest from my busy life around here.

And yet this is what God calls our homes—resting places (Proverbs 24:15). I don't think it is necessarily a rest from noise and activity (although we need these respites from time to time). I believe it is a rest from fear. A rest from tension and strife. A rest from anger, bickering, and fighting. A rest from complaining and grouching. These are the things that put strain on you and your home. It's not the noise of children, it's not the hard work—it is the wrong attitudes! They cause frustration and vexation of soul more than outward circumstances.

Jesus gave us a wonderful invitation to rest: *"Come unto me, all ye that labor and are heavy laden, and I will give you rest. Take my yoke upon you, and learn of me; for I am meek and lowly in heart: and you shall find rest unto your souls. For my yoke is easy, and my burden is light"* (Matthew 11:28-30).

Do you notice there are two rests He calls us into? First, the rest of sins forgiven when the burden of the guilt of sin is rolled away. Second, you can experience a deeper rest in your soul as you take His yoke upon you and learn of Him. As the ocean is calm underneath even though the violent storm tosses the waves above, so you can experience a deep rest in your soul even when the waves of turmoil billow over you. You can have a rest of spirit in your home even in the midst of noise and the bustle of activity.

Of course, God also wants us to have times of literal rest, too. The evenings should be quieter times of family togetherness. Our daughter Evangeline's home is not always quiet with her ten children (and she is the rowdiest of them all!) but when they come in for supper, she expects them to change from being cowboys, Indians, pirates, or army guys, etc. and welcomes them into "twilight" zone. She dims the lights and lights the candles in the wintertime to promote the quieter atmosphere.

God also gives us one day a week to rest from our work and the busyness of the week. This also helps to make our homes a resting place.

Another Scripture where God calls our homes a resting place is Proverbs 24:15: *"Lay not wait, O wicked man, against the dwelling of the righteous, spoil not his resting place."* Deal severely with anything that spoils the rest in your home. Are you harboring a bad attitude toward someone? Forgive, and put it right. Are you mad with your husband? Forgive, and take a humble attitude. Are you complaining about anything and everything? Get your attitude right. It's not worth spoiling the rest in your home. 2 Chronicles 23:21 tells us how the land of Israel was quiet when they got rid of evil.

Isaiah 30:15 says, *"In returning and rest shall you be saved, in quietness and confidence shall be your strength: and ye would not."* Don't be like the Israelites. God called them to rest but they would not receive it. Perhaps you are too busy doing things out of the home that you have no time to create peace in your home. When you return home you will find rest. Hosea 11:11 (Knox) says, *"**In their own home**, says the Lord, I will give them rest."*

PRAYER:

"Dear Father, please show me the attitudes in my heart and in my home that spoil rest. Give me strength to get rid of them for I want my home to be a resting place for everyone in my home and all who come to visit. Amen."

AFFIRMATION:

In the midst of lots of noise, I will never lose my poise,
Although my work may never cease, I will never lose my peace!

48

Walk Through the Land

"How long are ye slack to go to possess the land, which the Lord God of your fathers hath given you?"
(Joshua 18:3).

It was a new day for the Israelites. They had subdued the land. And now, because they were settled, they set up the tabernacle in Shiloh. Instead of carrying the tabernacle from place to place, they made it permanent. But there were still seven tribes who had not received their inheritance.

Joshua therefore commanded them to choose three men from each of the seven tribes to *"Go and walk through the land, and describe it"* (Joshua 18:8). These scouts had to survey the land and map the entire territory, listing the towns in each section. They had to bring back a thorough, written report to Joshua, who would cast sacred lots in the presence of the Lord to determine which tribe would have each section.

This reminds me of a land that we have waiting for us. It is a vast spiritual land that has already been given to us—God's precious Word, filled with promises and principles of God's plan for us and how to walk in victory—and all that has been given to us in Christ. We can read about these riches in 2 Peter 1:3, 4: *"According as his divine power hath given unto us all things that pertain unto life and godliness, through the knowledge of him that hath called us to glory and virtue: whereby are given unto us exceeding great and precious promises: that by these ye might be partakers of the divine nature, having escaped the corruption that is in the world through lust."* It is a land that "flows with milk and honey," but we have to go in and take it.

But how can we take it if we don't know what we have? We have to walk through the land, survey it, and find out what belongs to us. We must know what we have to possess before we can possess it! That's why it is important for us to take a walk through the Bible each day. Psalm 48:12, 13 says: *"Walk about Zion, and go round about her: tell the towers thereof. Mark ye well her bulwarks, consider her palaces; that ye may tell it to the generation following.*" We must know the land well, not only so we can walk in all that we have been given ourselves, but so we can tell it to our children.

We have a responsibility to inform our children. Joshua told the scouts to write down a description of the land as they walked through. That's why I like to write down the most significant Scripture that I read in the Word each day. This way, I don't forget it myself, but I also have it written in my book to be able to share with family and with you!

As I walk through a new part of the land in my daily reading each day, I receive new revelation. As I receive new revelation, I can walk in a little more of the riches I have been given in Christ. I can tell my children about it so they can walk in it too. We must scout the land to bring back news for our children. We can be excited to tell them what we have found and what is available for them.

Proverbs 4:18 says, "*The path of the just is as the shining light, that shineth more and more unto the perfect day.*" Our walk in Christ is a "more and more" walk. We have a vast land before us. We dare not sit down and think we have it all. We have hardly started. Our minds have not comprehended all that is available to us in Christ. We must search for new territory and then possess it! I love to think that I can possess a little more every day.

A friend of mine shared with me a true story of how her brother in New Zealand purchased some land, but it was only enough for a hobby farm. Years later, he decided to sell the land and only then found out that he actually owned another 10 acres that he didn't even know about. These acres were fertile, the best land on the property, and would have provided him a full income. But he missed out because he didn't know what he owned!

Will you become an adventurer, exploring the land that has been given to you? Bring back the news to your family. "Children, this is what God has given to us. This is how we possess it. Come on. Let's go in and take it!"

PRAYER:

"Thank you, God, for the vast land of blessings that you have provided for me. Give me a vision to discover them for myself and my family and to possess all our possessions. Amen."

AFFIRMATION:

My children and I are setting out on an adventure each day in God's Word.

49

Pure in a Perverse Generation

"And that repentance and remission of sins should be preached in His name among all nations, beginning at Jerusalem" (LUKE 24:47).

We don't use the word "remission" very much in our society today, do we? The understanding of this Greek word, *aphesis,* means "to send away, the deliverance from the power of sin although not from the presence of sin."

For what reason did Jesus suffer, die upon the cross, and rise again? To deliver us from the power of sin! He has not chosen to deliver us out of this sin-sick world, but through the blood of Jesus that was poured out for us, He has given us the power to live sanctified lives in the presence of this sinful world. God forbid that we should limit the power of the blood of Jesus to keep us clean and pure in the midst of this evil world. Thank God morning and evening that He has forgiven your sins and for the power of the blood that keeps you cleansed from sin.

We need to also teach our children that Jesus came to bring remission of sins. It is our responsibility as parents to protect our precious "olive plants" and keep them from the wiles of the enemy. We protect them from evil people, we protect them from the lustful garbage on TV, and from humanistic and ungodly education.

We do not do this to hide them away forever. We do it to establish them on a strong foundation in the ways of the Lord. We do this to prepare them for their future. We train our children in the sanctuary of our homes in order to one day send them out into this sinful world to be lights in the midst of the darkness, to wave the banner of God's truth in the midst of deception, and to bring justice in the midst of perverted judgment.

This world is desperate for truth-upholding, sin-exposing, salvation-preaching, holy, and uncompromising believers, who will not hide away, but who will come forth, filled with God's Holy Spirit, and shine His light into the midst of the darkness.

Jesus said, "*The world . . . hates me because I testify of it that its works are evil*" (John 7:7, NKJV). Jesus did not compromise with the spirit of the world but testified against its evil. You, and even your children, will never be hooked into the world when you stand against it. Instead, you will be hated by the world. Again, Jesus said in John 15:18, 19 (NKJV): "*If the world hates you, you know that it hated me before it hated you. If you were of the world, the world would love its own. Yet because you are not of the world, but I chose you out of the world, therefore the world hates you.*" God has chosen us out of this world system to go back into it with His love and truth.

You don't have to live in a house in the country, away from civilization, to raise godly children. You can do it in the midst of your city street with evil all around you. God promises in Deuteronomy 28:3 that He will bless you in the city and in the country, and He mentions the city first!

Most of our children were in their teens when we moved from the little country of New Zealand to pioneer and pastor a church on the Gold Coast, the tourist mecca of Australia. Our church was opposite the Jupiter's Casino, and from the windows of our home, we looked out upon it. I cried out to God that He would keep our children in the midst of this materialistic and evil environment where most people walk the streets scantily clothed and topless sunbathers line the beach.

God answered, and they came out on the offensive. The older children started open-air preaching in Cavil Mall. Rocklyn was only 13 years old. In bare feet and jeans, he gathered crowds around as he preached like a fiery evangelist. Even Pearl preached in her little 11-year-old squeaky voice!

After most of our children were married, I remember one time lamenting to Howard, Evangeline's husband, that I pined for the days when all the children were still home and we sat around the family meal table together. His reply came as a rebuke to me: "Mother, didn't you train them to send them forth as arrows into the harvest field?"

I am also thinking of David's words in Psalm 23: "*You prepare a table before me in the presence of my enemies.*" We live in the midst of enemies. But in the midst of evil enemies all around us, God prepares a table for us. It is His divine presence. As we keep daily cleansed from sin and live in the presence of the Lord, we can live purely even in the presence of evil!

PRAYER:

"I thank you, Lord, for shedding your pure, precious blood to cleanse me from my sin. I thank you that you died to save and deliver me from sin. I thank you for your keeping power in the midst of this crooked and perverse generation. Amen."

AFFIRMATION:

Because I am delivered from the power of sin, I can take God's salvation and healing into the presence of sin.

50

Parents Have Honor

"Ye shall fear every man his mother, and his father . . .
I am the Lord your God"
(LEVITICUS 19:3).

God has given honor to the status of parenthood. God is a Father and He wants His children fathered in the anointing of His fatherhood. God also has a maternal heart and He has ordained that mothers should mother with the anointing of His maternal heart.

Because parents are parenting on God's behalf, He wants them to be treated with the same attitude as He is treated. He specifically commands that parents are to be obeyed, honored, and feared.

PARENTS MUST BE OBEYED

Ephesians 6:1 says, *"Children, obey your parents in the Lord: for this is right."*

Colossians 3:20 says, *"Children, obey your parents in all things: for this is well pleasing unto the Lord."*

PARENTS MUST BE HONORED

Exodus 20:12 says, *"Honor thy father and thy mother; that thy days may be long upon the land."*

Deuteronomy 5:16 says, *"Honor thy father and thy mother, as the Lord thy God hath commanded thee; that thy days may be prolonged, and that it may go well with thee."*

So that we do not forget, this command is repeated in the New Testament in Matthew 15:4; 19:19; Mark 7:10; 10:19; Luke 18:20; and Ephesians 6:2, 3.

PARENTS MUST BE FEARED

I am always astounded by Leviticus 19:3. Not only are children commanded to obey and honor their parents, but to fear them. The word "fear" that is used here is the same word that is used to fear God. Another astounding thing is that this time the mother is mentioned first. Children often have a healthy respect for their father's authority but fail to honor their mother's authority. This is not God's intention. He wants children to have reverence for their mothers, too.

How can we experience this? I believe we must be reminded of the truth that God has given honor to parents (including mothers), and because He has given us this honor, we must walk in the anointing of it. Perhaps you feel as though you have no honor. You feel like a total failure. You feel overwhelmed. You feel you can't make it. You feel hopeless as a mother. It's certainly easy to feel like this, isn't it?

However, God doesn't see you like this. He has put honor upon you as a mother. The role of mother is a high status in God's eyes. In Ezekiel 19:10, 11, God states that it is an exalted career, to be honored and revered.

Jeremiah 22:5 (Knox) talks about God bringing judgment upon Israel because of its sin: *"Disobey, the Lord says, and my own honor is engaged to make, of this palace, a ruin."* God was bound by His own honor to bring judgment because of their sin. Because God is holy, He had to judge them, or He would no longer be a God of honor. He has to honor who He is, a God of righteousness and holiness who cannot tolerate sin. Of course, He is also a merciful God who forgives and forgets the moment we repent.

We too, who parent in the likeness of God, must not give into disobedience and rebellion in our children. We must discipline because of the honor we have as parents. We cannot fail the honor that has been given to us. It is our right for our children to obey us. Of course, as with God, forgiveness and mercy are coupled with judgment.

Each morning, acknowledge the honor God has given to you as mother. See yourself with God's honor upon you and mother your children accordingly.

PRAYER:

"Dear Father, thank you for reminding me that you have given honor to me as a mother. Help me to walk in the anointing of this honor as I mother my children. Amen."

AFFIRMATION:

I am upholding the honor God has given to me as a mother.

51

Resolute for God
Part 1

"But you must be resolute, and observe jealously all the terms of that law which Moses committed to writing, never swerve from them to right or to left"
(Joshua 23:6, Knox).

Satan's first temptation was to deceive. It is still his greatest weapon today. Ever so subtly, he woos God's people to his deceptive ways. They sound so nice, so plausible, and so right. But, they are opposite to the ways of God. I believe it is time for us to become resolute in our souls, a resoluteness that will not give in to the humanistic thinking of this world, and that will not turn to the right or the left.

Many times God reveals truth to us and we are excited to walk in it—until persecution comes, or the way gets really tough. We may then be tempted to turn back. This is where we need to be resolute. We need to teach this character to our children also. The following are 10 affirmations for you, and your children, that will help you stand resolute for God and His truth.

1. I WILL NOT RETREAT!

Job 23:11-12: *"My foot has held fast to his steps; I have kept his way and not turned aside. I have not departed from the commandment of his lips."*

Luke 9:62: *"No one, having put his hand to the plough, and looking back, is fit for the kingdom of God."* Read also Genesis 19:17, 26.

Hebrews 10:38, 39: *"Now the just shall live by faith; but if anyone draws back, my soul shall have no pleasure in him. But we are not of those who draw back to perdition, but of those who believe to the saving of the soul."*

2. I WILL NOT BE OVERTAKEN BY THIS WORLD SYSTEM!

We live in an age that is twisted out of its true pattern. It is no longer functioning the way God designed it in the very beginning. We have turned far away from His original design. We must constantly come back to the Word of God. It should be the plumbline for all we believe, rather than what society, or even the church, is doing.

1 John 2:15-17: *"Do not love the world or the things in the world. If anyone loves the world, the love of the Father is not in him. For all that is in the world—the lust of the flesh, the lust of the eyes, and the pride of life—is not of the Father but is of the world. And the world is passing away, and the lust of it; but he who does the will of God abides for ever."*

James 4:4: *"Do you not know that friendship with the world is enmity with God? Whoever therefore wants to be a friend of the world makes himself an enemy of God."* Read also 2 Timothy 2:3, 4.

3. I WILL NOT YIELD MY BODY TO SIN!

Romans 6:12-14: *"Do not let sin reign in your mortal body, that you should obey it in its lusts. And do not present your members as instruments of unrighteousness to sin, but present yourselves to God as being alive from the dead, and your members as instruments of righteousness to God. For sin shall not have dominion over you."*

1 Corinthians 6:18: *"Flee immorality. Every other sin that a man commits is outside the body, but the immoral man (or woman) sins against his own body."*

Ephesians 5:3: *"But fornication and all uncleanness or covetousness, let it not even be named among you, as is fitting for saints."*

4. I WILL NOT SUBMIT TO DECEPTION!

Romans 3:4 challenges me: *"Indeed, let God be true but every man a liar."* I constantly ask myself the question, "Am I willing to walk in God's truth even if no one else in the world is following?"

5. I WILL NOT BE MOVED!

I will not be moved by fear. I will not be moved by what people say against me. I will not be moved by scoffing and ridicule. I will not be moved by persecution.

Isaiah 50:7, *"I have set my face like a flint, and I know that I will not be ashamed."*

Psalm 16:8: *"I have set the Lord always before me; because he is at my right hand I shall not be moved."*

In Acts 20:22-24, Paul confesses as he sets his face toward Jerusalem: *"The Holy Spirit testifies in every city, saying that chains and tribulations await me. But none of these things move me."*

1 Corinthians 15:58: *"Therefore, my beloved brethren, be steadfast, immovable, always abounding in the work of the Lord, knowing that your labor is not in vain in the Lord."*

1 Corinthians 16:13 (NKJV): *"Watch, stand fast in the faith, be brave, be strong."* Read also Philippians 4:1; 1 Thessalonians 3:8; and 2 Thessalonians 2:15.

Ephesians 6:13, 14: *"Therefore take up the whole armor of God, that you may be able to withstand in the evil day, and having done all, to stand."*

PRAYER:

"Lord, I ask that you will put resoluteness in my soul. Help me not to be moved from my trust in you, no matter what happens around me. Amen."

AFFIRMATION:

I have set my course for God. I will not turn aside to the right or the left!

52

Resolute for God
Part 2

"The root of the righteous cannot be moved"
(Proverbs 12:3 and Psalm 55:22).

Yesterday we read five affirmations to be resolute. Here are five more for you today. You may want to read these Scriptures to your children and encourage them to confess these affirmations also.

6. I WILL NOT SELL MY BIRTHRIGHT!

Proverbs 23:23: *"Buy the truth, and do not sell it."*

Hebrews 12:16, 17: *"Lest there be any fornicator or profane person like Esau, who for one morsel of food sold his birthright. For you know that afterwards, when he wanted to inherit the blessing, he was rejected, for he found no place for repentance, though he sought it diligently with tears."* Read also Mark 8:36, 37.

Revelation 3:11: *"Hold fast what you have, that no one may take your crown."* Read also Revelation 2:25.

7. I WILL NOT LOOK UPON EVIL!

Job 27:6: *"My righteousness I hold fast, and will not let it go."*

Psalm 101:3: *"I will set nothing wicked before my eyes."* This is a good Scripture to write above your TV.

Psalm 97:10: *"You who love the Lord, hate evil!"* Read also Psalm 34:14, 45:7; and Amos 5:15.

Romans 12:9: *"Abhor that which is evil; cleave to that which is good."*

How true are the words that one generation is a generation away from degeneration. I think back to my childhood, when it was unheard of for a Christian to enter a movie theater. Now, we live in a day where many "Christians" go to most movies that come to the theaters. Even worse, they watch movies condoning adultery and evil in their own homes! How can we expect the blessing of God upon our homes and upon our nation while we love evil instead of hating it?

8. I WILL NOT FEAR!

What do we fear most? Is it the opinions of our family, friends, and church members? Or is it God Himself? Many times we fear to walk in the truth that God has revealed to us because it is different from what the majority are doing. Forget worrying about what people think. It's what God thinks that matters! Lift your head high and walk in God's truth.

Do people ridicule you because you are having another baby? Do not be intimidated by your adversaries. Do not be governed by the deception of those around you. You are on God's side. You are on the side of life. You are in the perfect will of God.

Psalm 3:6: *"I will not be afraid of ten thousands of people who have set themselves against me all around."* Read also Psalm 112:7.

Psalm 11:1: *"In the Lord I put my trust; how can you say to my soul, 'Flee as a bird to your mountain?'"*

Psalm 56:11: *"In God I have put my trust; I will not be afraid. What can man do to me?"*

Acts 4:19, 20: *"Whether it is right in the sight of God to listen to you more than to God, you judge. For we cannot but speak the things which we have seen and heard."*

Hebrews 13:5, 6: *"I will never leave thee, nor forsake thee. So that we may boldly say, The Lord is my helper, and I will not fear what man shall do unto me."*

9. I WILL NOT CONFESS NEGATIVE THOUGHTS AND FEELINGS!

Proverbs 13:3: *"He who guards his mouth preserves his life, but he who opens wide his lips shall have destruction."*

Proverbs 18:21: *"Death and life are in the power of the tongue."*

Proverbs 21:23: *"Whoever guards his mouth and tongue keeps his soul from troubles."*

2 Corinthians 10:4, 5: *"For the weapons of our warfare are not carnal but mighty in God for pulling down strongholds, casting down arguments and every high thing that exalts itself against the knowledge of God, bringing every thought into captivity to the obedience of Christ."*

When negative thoughts come to your mind, as they invariably will, resist them in the name of Jesus. Never confess them. When you speak them out, they will take root in your life. Instead of confessing your negative thoughts, confess who you are in Christ.

10. I WILL NOT TEMPT GOD WITH UNBELIEF!

The children of Israel tempted God in the wilderness by complaining about their difficult circumstances and not believing that God could provide for them. We are no better today. How often do we complain? Every day? How often do we fail to trust God?

Exodus 17:1-7: "*There was not water for the people to drink. Therefore the people contended with Moses, and said, 'Give us water, that we may drink.' And Moses said to them, 'Why do you contend with me? Why do you tempt the Lord?'" . . . So he called the name of the place Meribah, because of the contention of the children of Israel, and because they tempted the Lord, saying, 'Is the Lord among us or not?'*" Read also Numbers 14:22-24; Deuteronomy 6:16; Matthew 4:7; and 1 Corinthians 10:8-10.

May God help us to be unyielding in our stand for righteousness and truth.

PRAYER:

"Father God, help me to stand strong against all evil and deception. Help me to be unmoved by the opinions and dictates of this society. Amen."

AFFIRMATION:

I will stand—and keep on standing! ~ Ephesians 6:13

53

Resolute for God
Part 3

"God putting such a resolve into my heart. . ."
(NEHEMIAH 7:5, KNOX).

What does it mean to be resolute? The dictionary says, "having a fixed purpose, determined." Let's be one who is resolute, true to God's Word, and not swayed by the humanistic reasonings of our society.

You have now discovered 10 affirmations about being Resolute for God, each one affirming, "I WILL NOT!" We will now learn to confess 10 affirmations of "I WILL!" There are many "I wills" in the Word of God. David the Psalmist constantly affirmed his commitment to the Lord. It is a good thing to do. It is important to affirm what we believe. It is even more important to confess it out loud! I love the Scripture in 2 Corinthians 4:13: *"I believe, therefore have I spoken."*

Now for our affirmations about being resolute for God:

1. I WILL OVERCOME IN JESUS' NAME!

Revelation 12:11: *"And they overcame him by the blood of the Lamb, and by the word of their testimony; and they loved not their lives unto the death."*

Revelation 2:7: *"To him that overcometh will I give to eat of the tree of life."*

Revelation 2:17: *"To him that overcometh will I give to eat of the hidden manna, and will give him a white stone, and in the stone a new name written, which no man knoweth saving he that receiveth it."*

Revelation 3:21: *"To him that overcometh will I grant to sit with me in my throne, even as I also overcame, and am set down with my Father in his throne."*

Are you going through obstacles and difficulties? Don't despair! You are given these to overcome in the name of Jesus Christ. God's rewards are to the overcomers. If you have nothing to overcome, how can you receive a reward?

2. I WILL RESIST THE DEVIL!

James 4:7: *"Resist the devil and he will flee from you."*

1 Peter 5:8, 9: *"Be sober, be vigilant; because your adversary the devil walks about like a roaring lion, seeking whom he may devour. Resist him, steadfast in the faith."* Instead of giving in to the temptations of the enemy, be on the offensive and resist him.

3. I WILL TRUST IN THE NAME OF THE LORD!

Psalm 55:23: *"I will trust in you."* Read also Psalm 9:10; 18:2; and 143:8.

David was going through many troubles—enemies coming against him, violence and strife all around him, and even his closest friends maligning him. His heart was *"severely pained within him,"* but what was his response? "I will trust in the Lord." It is very easy to let the pressures and difficulties of life overwhelm you. But you do not have to be swamped by them. Instead, confess your trust in the Lord. Take the example of David and confess out loud, "I will trust the Lord!"

Psalm 56:3: *"Whenever I am afraid, I will trust in you."* Do you have concerns and fears? Fear will debilitate and strangle you. Instead of dwelling on your concerns and fears, say, "I will trust you, Lord."

Psalm 61:4: *"I will trust in the shelter of your wings."*

Psalm 62:8: *"Trust in him at all times."*

Psalm 125:1: *"Those who trust in the Lord are like Mount Zion, which cannot be moved, but abides for ever."*

Isaiah 50:10: *"Who walks in darkness and has no light? Let him trust in the name of the Lord and rely upon his God."*

Are you walking through a dark time in your life? You can't see any light at the end of the tunnel? You know what to do, don't you? Trust in the Lord. He is faithful. He will never forsake you. The blind person implicitly trusts his dog to lead him. You have the Almighty God leading you. The God who is light! He sees the way clearly even when you can't.

I love to sing the chorus of Louisa Stead's hymn, which she wrote in 1882 after witnessing her husband drown while trying to save a drowning boy.

Jesus, Jesus, how I trust Him!
How I've proved Him o'er and o'er
Jesus, Jesus, precious Jesus!
O for grace to trust Him more!

4. I WILL PRAY AND SEEK THE LORD!

Psalm 27:8: "*When you said, 'Seek my face', my heart said to you, 'Your face, Lord,* ***I will seek****.'*" Read also Psalm 18:3; 28:1; 61:2; 86:3; 141:1, 2; 1 Thessalonians 5:17; and 1 Timothy 2:8.

Psalm 5:2, 3: "*Give heed to the voice of my cry, my King and my God, for to you* ***I will pray****. My voice you shall hear in the morning, O Lord; in the morning I will direct it to you, and I will look up.*"

Psalm 55:17: "*Evening and morning and at noon* ***I will pray****, and cry aloud, and he shall hear my voice.*"

Psalm 57:2: "***I will cry*** *out to God Most High, to God who performs all things for me.*"

This is an affirmation that we must become more resolute about. God's people should be known as the people who cry unto the Lord. Our children should know us as people of prayer. Our homes should be known in our neighborhoods as homes of prayer. Do the people on your street know you as people of prayer? Do they ask you to pray for them because they see the power of prayer in your lives? Let's be resolute to pray for our nation, for it is a command (1 Timothy 2:1, 2).

5. I WILL GLORY IN TRIBULATION!

It's pretty hard to accept this one, isn't it? We would rather run from tribulation. I know I would. But, the apostle Paul constantly affirmed the blessing and joy of tribulations. May the Lord help us to experience this truth in our lives.

Matthew 5:11, 12: "*Blessed are you when they revile and persecute you, and say all kinds of evil against you falsely for my sake. Rejoice and be exceedingly glad, for great is your reward in heaven.*"

2 Corinthians 12:9, 10: "*He said to me, 'My grace is sufficient for you, for my strength is made perfect in weakness.' Therefore most gladly I will rather boast in my infirmities, that the power of Christ may rest upon me.*" Read also 2 Corinthians 4:16-18.

1 Peter 4:12-14 (NKJV): "*Beloved, do not think it strange concerning the fiery trial which is to try you, as though some strange thing happened to you;*

but rejoice to the extent that you partake of Christ's sufferings, that when his glory is revealed, you may also be glad with exceeding joy. If you are reproached for the name of Christ, blessed are you, for the Spirit of glory and of God rests upon you."

PRAYER:

"Father God, please put resolve in my heart that nothing will move me from my commitment to your truth. Amen."

AFFIRMATION:

I am resolved to follow God's ways.

54

Resolute for God

Part 4

"He only is my rock and my salvation; He is my defense; I shall not be moved"
(Psalm 62:6).
Read also Psalms 15:1-5; 16:8; 62:2; Acts 2:25 and 20:24.

Today we will look at the last five affirmations of "I will!"

6. I WILL PRAISE THE LORD!

Psalm 34:1: *"I will bless the Lord at all times; His praise shall continually be in my mouth."* You also may like to read Psalm 9:1, 2; 16:7; 30:1, 12; 31:7; 52:9; 54:6; 55:16, 17; 56:12; 63:4; 71:14; 86:12; 109:30; 111:1; 118:21, 28; 138:1; 139:14; and 145:1, 2.

Psalm 69:30: *"I will praise the name of God with a song, and will magnify him with thanksgiving."*

Psalm 57:9: *"I will praise you, O Lord, I will sing to you."* Read also Psalm 7:17; 13:6 and 28:7; 59:16, 17; 71:16; 75:9; 89:1; 104:33; 108:1; 144:9; and 146:1, 2. Philippians 4:4: *"Rejoice in the Lord always, and again I say, Rejoice."* It's easy to praise the Lord when everything is going fine, isn't it? It's not so easy when everything is going wrong. But God wants us to bless Him at all times, when things are good and when things are bad! I am sure that David didn't feel like praising the Lord when he was in the pit of despair, as he often was. But no matter what he was going through, he continually acknowledged, "I will praise the Lord at all times."

The Holy Spirit who lives within us can work with a resolute will that is set for God and His purposes. If our will is weak, we can easily give in to the pressures and temptations of the devil, and the Holy Spirit has a harder time keeping us hot for God.

7. I WILL WALK IN INTEGRITY!

Job 27:5: *"Till I die I will not put away my integrity from me."*

Psalm 26:1, 11: *"But as for me, I will walk in my integrity."*

Psalm 86:11: *"I will walk in your truth."*

Proverbs 20:7: *"The righteous man walks in his integrity; his children are blessed after him."*

There are constant opportunities to slightly deceive or tell half-truths. Make it your confession to always have integrity and do that which is right, even though no one else may know.

8. I WILL WALK IN THE STRENGTH OF THE LORD!

Psalm 71:16: *"I will go in the strength of the Lord God."*

1 Samuel 17:45: *"Then said David to the Philistine. . . I come to thee in the name of the Lord of hosts, the God of the armies of Israel, whom thou hast defied."*

2 Chronicles 14:11: *"Asa cried unto the Lord his God, and said, Lord, it is nothing with thee to help, whether with many, or with them that have no power: help us, O Lord our God; for we rest on thee, and in thy name we go against this multitude. O Lord, thou art our God; let not man prevail against thee."*

Many times we go in our own strength, and don't realize it. Get into the habit of walking in God's strength.

9. I WILL LOOK UP!

Psalm 5:3: *"I will look up."*

What a wonderful confession of the sweet psalmist of Israel. Make this your daily affirmation, too. Start the day by looking up to the Lord. Keep your eyes fixed on Him. It is easy to be discouraged when you look at your difficulties. It is easy to be overwhelmed when you look at all you have to face. But, when you look up, something happens. Your burdens lighten. Your stress turns to peace. Your churned-up stomach turns to rest. Every time you face something that causes you to be distressed, immediately confess, "I will look up." Make it the habit of your life.

10. I WILL ENDURE TO THE END!

Matthew 24:13: *"He that endures to the end shall be saved."*

2 Timothy 4:5: *"Endure afflictions."*

James 1:12: *"Blessed is the man who endures temptation; for when he has been proved, he will receive the crown of life which the Lord has promised to those who love him."*

James 5:11: *"Behold, we count them happy which endure."*

It's the end of the race that counts. When everything seems too hard, make your affirmation, "I will endure to the end."

PRAYER:

"Father in Heaven, I look up to you. I praise you. I trust in your promises. I do not trust in my own resources but in your unfailing strength. Thank you, Lord. Amen."

AFFIRMATION:

I will not be moved by trials.

I will not be moved by doubt.

I will not be moved by those who would steer me away from God's ultimate truth!

55

When to Keep Silent
Part 1

"It is the Lord that will do battle for you; your part is silence"
(Exodus 14:14, Knox).

God blessed us with a voice to communicate and fellowship with Him, and to communicate with one another. However, there are certain times when we need to keep silent! Let's look at some examples in Scripture.

IN TIMES OF UNBELIEF

After God delivered the Israelites from their slavery in Egypt, they camped by the Red Sea. But soon the Egyptian army pursued them! Now they were hedged in with no way of escape—the sea in front of them, the Egyptians after them. Their song of victory soon turned to doubt and fear and they turned against Moses with bitter complainings. Isn't that what we often do when things are going wrong? We complain and grumble!

But what did Moses say? *"It is the Lord that will do battle for you; your part is silence"* (Exodus 14:14, Knox). If only we could take these words to heart in the situations that we face! I grew up with the saying, "If you can't say anything nice, don't say anything at all!" I think we should add this adage too: "When faced with insurmountable problems, if you can't speak faith and trust in God, don't say anything at all!"

I am also reminded of the battle of Jericho. The strategy God gave Joshua was for all the men of war to compass the city every day for seven days and seven times on the seventh day. Joshua commanded the people, *"You shall not shout, nor make any noise with your voice, neither shall any word proceed out of your mouth, until the day I bid you shout; then shall you shout"* (Joshua 6:10).

God had a good reason for this. If He had allowed them to talk, they would have doubted and complained. "How can we take a city by just walking around it? How dumb! We'll be defeated. This is madness!" God did not allow one doubt to come forth from their mouths until the moment of victory! And this was the shout of deliverance!

Let's go to the New Testament to that startling day when an angel suddenly appeared to Zacharias the priest as he burned incense at the altar. The angel told him that he and Elisabeth (barren all her life) would have a son and to call his name John. This news was too amazing for Zacharias to comprehend. He wondered how it could happen. Therefore the angel said, *"Behold thou shalt be dumb, and not able to speak, until the day that these things shall be performed, because thou believest not my words"* (Luke 1:20). God did not want Zacharias speaking words of doubt to his wife or to anyone else, and therefore closed his mouth until the time the word was performed.

Proverbs 30:32 (NIV) says, *"If you . . . have planned evil, clap your hand over your mouth!"* Sometimes your mind may be filled with negativity and doubt, but at least do not confess it. When you give voice to it, it intensifies. When you shut your mouth and refrain from speaking unbelief, you are on the way to victory.

Do you think you could make this a precedent in your life? When you face a situation where there is no hope unless God breaks through, instead of speaking negativity, fear, and hopelessness, keep silent! Clap your hand over your mouth! Your part is to stand still, keep quiet, and see the salvation of the Lord.

PRAYER:

"Father, please strengthen my trust in you to know that you are the Sovereign Lord and nothing is out of your control. Take away all arguments from my mouth and please save me from speaking negative and complaining words that only bring destruction. Amen."

AFFIRMATION:

I will clap my hand over my mouth to stifle all unbelieving words!

56

When to Keep Silent
Part 2

"I will lay mine hand upon my mouth"
(Job 40:4).

We continue to look at when God wants us to keep silent!

IN TIMES WHEN YOU THINK IT IS NOT FAIR

One terrible day, two of Aaron's sons, Nadab and Abihu, offered strange fire before the Lord. God suddenly blazed forth fire from Heaven and consumed them! Aaron was stunned! He could not understand God's severity of punishment on his sons whom he loved. In his agonizing grief, Aaron must have resented God's punishment on his sons, but Moses spoke to him the words of the Lord, *"By those who come near Me I will be treated as holy, and before all the people I will be honored. So Aaron, therefore, kept silent"* (Leviticus 10:3, NASB).

When God revealed His holiness, Aaron was reduced to silence. Many times things happen in our lives that we do not think are fair, and we complain and argue with God. We must be careful that we do not reduce God down to our level and our puny understanding. God sees things from eternity. He is the Sovereign God. If we cannot agree with God, then we should be silent!

I am sure Job did not think it was fair that he had to suffer in the way that he did. In one day his ten children were killed, and all his sheep, oxen, and camels were taken away. Then he was covered with boils, living in pain and misery. He had many arguments with his three friends and with God!

Eventually, Job got the message that God is in control and that He holds us in the palm of His hand. God said to Job: *"Do you still want to argue with the Almighty? . . . Then Job replied to the Lord, 'I am nothing—how could I ever find the answers? I will put my hand over my mouth in silence. I have said too much already. I have nothing more to say'"* (Job 40:1-4, NLT). It was when he became silent, instead of putting up his ideas and arguments, that God revealed Himself to him. Soon he was healed and God blessed the latter days of Job even more than his beginning.

David cried: *"Lord, where do I put my hope? My only hope is in you. Rescue me from my rebellion . . . I am silent before you; I won't say a word. For my punishment is from you"* (Psalm 39:7-9, NLT).

Arguing with God will never get us anywhere. We will do better when we see things from an eternal perspective rather than an earthly perspective. When we see things from God's perspective, we will have no more arguments.

IN TIMES OF PERSECUTION AND RIDICULE

When we are persecuted, or people say unkind things to us or behind our backs, we want to answer back. We want to defend ourselves. This is the natural way. But God has a better way. Silence! "What? You mean to say that I can't even defend myself? Do you mean to say I have to shut my mouth when my husband or someone else accuses me?"

Jesus showed us what to do when he was accused.

Isaiah 53:7 says, *"He was oppressed, and he was afflicted, yet he opened not his mouth."*

Matthew 26:62, 63 (NLT) says: *"The high priest stood up and said to Jesus, 'Well, aren't you going to answer these charges? What do you have to say for yourself?' But Jesus remained silent."*

Matthew 27:12 (NLT) says, *"When the leading priests and other leaders made their accusations against him, Jesus remained silent."*

1 Peter 2:23 says, *"Who, when he was reviled, reviled not again; when he suffered, he threatened not; but committed himself to him that judgeth righteously."*

David also shut his mouth in the face of accusers.

Psalm 38:12-15 says, *"They that seek my hurt speak mischievous things, and imagine deceits all the day long. But . . . I was as a dumb man that opens not his mouth."*

Remember, there is a time to speak and a time to keep silent!

PRAYER:

"Lord God, please help me to keep my mouth shut instead of spouting off foolish words. Lord, I thank you that I can trust you to deal with those who falsely accuse me. I do not need to say a word. Amen."

AFFIRMATION:

I will lay down all my arguments in the face of God's sovereignty.

57

Second Milers

"Whoever forces you to go one mile, go with him two" (MATTHEW 5:41).

As we prepared to update the address labels to send out a new issue of *Above Rubies*, we encountered a problem. We had to manually verify a thousand of our addresses right when we needed to print labels! It is a lengthy task to locate the address, go to the USPS webpage, verify it, and then change it on our database. Knowing the urgency of the task, my *Above Rubies* helper smilingly started to work. She didn't only work from 9 a.m. to 5:00 pm as we do each day in the office. She worked through her lunch hour. She shifted into a new gear—the "second mile" anointing! She kept on with the job in the evenings. She worked all through the weekend and continued the same pattern the following week. She didn't stop until the last address was verified! I called her "Second Mile Haley."

What a joy to see a "second miler" in action! Going beyond what was asked of her. My heart was encouraged and I know God looked down upon her with a smile. God is a second miler and He gives far beyond what we deserve. And He looks for second milers. There are so few of them around today. Most times people only do what is required, and you can't squeeze another inch out of them.

When we send out each issue of *Above Rubies*, I call for reinforcements. Folks lovingly and willingly come and help to get this massive job accomplished. I love it when Penny Raine arrives with her children. She doesn't come for a few hours. She and her family come for the whole day and they work from morning until dark! It was delightful to see Penny's nine-year-old daughter, Mercy, helping too. Children love to help with counting and little jobs. They work for awhile, get tired of it and go off to play, and I am happy for them to do that. But not Mercy! Happy and smiling, never stopping, she worked all day. When other children stopped, she kept going. I thought to myself, *She's being trained well. She's going to be a second miler!*

Today was a lovely warm winter day, a perfect day to get outside and winterize my garden. I asked Cedar, my nine-year-old grandson, to help me. We got stuck in, shoveling manure and compost onto each bed and then covering them with straw. Later in the day, grandsons converged on our lawn to play soccer. I counted twelve of them! As they all enjoyed playing together, I said to Cedar, "You're welcome to go and play too." "No," he replied, "I want to keep working." And he kept working until it was dark! He didn't have to keep working. He did it of his own volition. Another second miler!

What kind of lifestyle are you teaching your children? Do you teach them to do only what's necessary? Do you allow them to give only a token of their time or their ability? Or do you show them by your lifestyle how to go the second mile? It is the second milers who will go far in this life. It is the second milers who will accomplish mighty exploits for God. Young people who do not stop when it is "time" to stop, but keep going until the job is finished! Young people who keep serving, even at inconvenience to themselves.

1 Corinthians 15:58 tells us to *"abound"* in the work of the Lord. The word "abound" means to go the second mile, to go above and beyond, to do more than is necessary. This is how we are to work in our homes each day. Not grudgingly, but aboundingly! Doing more than is necessary. This is how we teach our children to work.

PRAYER:

"Dear Father God, I thank you for salvation, a gift beyond what I deserved. Thank you for giving me more than is necessary. Help me to also have this attitude and to always give more than is necessary. Help me to teach my children to live this lifestyle. Amen."

AFFIRMATION:

I am raising second milers for God!

58

Antidote to Depression

"Now the God of hope fill you with all joy and peace in believing, that ye may abound in hope, through the power of the Holy Ghost"
(Romans 15:13).

Dr. Northoff, a medical researcher and psychiatrist, is researching the neurochemistry of hopelessness and why so many young people turn to suicide. One survey revealed that 20 percent of 140,000 Chinese high school students have considered suicide. Most of these victims have no hope because they cannot see into the future. They cannot see the end of the tunnel, only a dark hole. Northoff believes this is due to a dysfunction in part of the brain.

This may be so, but God, who created us in the beginning, knows what is necessary for us to live in victory and joy. The antidote to depression is hope, and our God is the God of hope. Our hope is found in Him. Hopelessness can trigger problems in the brain, but the brain can also be made whole as we learn to trust in the God of hope (Proverbs 13:12).

Myriads of people take comfort in the words of Jeremiah 29:11: *"For I know the thoughts that I think toward you, saith the Lord, thoughts of peace, and not of evil, to give you an expected end."* The Hebrew word for "expected" is *tikvah,* which means "hope," and many translations say, *"To give you a future and a hope."*

It is hope that gives us a good outlook on life, and often, it is what keeps us alive. I think of the Jewish people, who, for nearly 2,000 years, were scattered to the four corners of the earth, enduring persecution, pogroms, herded into ghettos in the countries where they lived, and eventually suffering Hitler's holocaust. Through all these years, they never ever gave up hope for their land of Israel. There were times in history when Jerusalem was called by other names, but they never forgot their city even though they had never set their eyes upon it. Every year at Passover they recited in hope, "Next year in Jerusalem."

In 1886, Naftali Hertz Imber from Bohemia wrote a poem which in 1948 became the Israeli national anthem. It is called *HaTikvah,* meaning "The Hope." The translated Hebrew words are . . .

As long as the Jewish spirit is yearning deep in the heart,
With eyes turned toward the East, looking toward Zion,
Then our hope, the two-thousand-year-old hope, will not be lost:
To be a free people in our land, The land of Zion and Jerusalem.

These words were written before there was any dream of Israel becoming a nation again, but hope kept the nation of Israel alive as they waited for the promise. Many years ago, while walking through the bush in Australia, Colin and I met a Jewish couple. Colin immediately began witnessing to them about Jesus and they became very dear friends. The guy was a Russian Jew and the wife a Persian Jew, both having made aliyah to Israel. The gentleman shared with us that although living in Communist Russia and never having heard of the land of Israel, he always longed and hoped for his homeland that he didn't even know existed.

Hebrews 6:11 (NASB) inspires us *"to realize the full assurance of hope until the end, so that you will not be sluggish."* The word "sluggish" is *nothros* and means "a sluggishness which makes a person unfit for activities of the mind or spirit." That's a picture of depression! What saves us from this kind of state? Hope!

Psalm 31:24 tells us that when we put our hope in the Lord, He puts courage and strength into our very soul! Teach your children from a young age how to put their hope in the Lord rather than getting into the habit of dwelling on their problems. David's mother must have instilled this into her son. David confesses in Psalm 71:5, *"For thou art my hope, O Lord God: thou art my trust from my youth."* Read also Psalm 78:4-7.

I can't let you miss out on this Scripture: Psalm 146:5 says, *"HAPPY is he that hath the God of Jacob for his help, whose hope is in the Lord his God."* We are reminded again that hope is the antidote to despair. When we put our hope in the Lord we will be happy. This particular "happy" in the Hebrew is *esher* and is only ever used in the plural. It means "doubly happy!" Don't you love that? Proverbs 10:28 says, *"The hope of the righteous is GLADNESS"* and Proverbs 16:20 reminds us that *"Whoso trusteth (hopeth) in the Lord, HAPPY is he."*

Hope literally means to be constantly looking, waiting, and expecting something good to happen. This is the way God created us to live. This is what keeps us in health and happiness.

PRAYER:

"I thank you, Father, that you have destined me to live a life of hope. Help me to get into the habit of knowing that you are working out everything for my good, even if it isn't to my liking. Fill me daily with your Holy Spirit so that I will go around my home ABOUNDING IN HOPE. Amen."

AFFIRMATION:

I am ABOUNDING in hope today!

FURTHER STUDY:

To be encouraged in your soul, read the Scriptures listed on page 279.

59

In the Kitchen Again?

*"Well reported of for **good works**; if she have brought up children, if she have lodged strangers, if she have washed the saints feet, if she have relieved the afflicted, if she have diligently followed every **good work**"*
(1 Timothy 5:10).

Do you feel like doing something good today? How about making your husband his favorite meal? Or, make some healthy cookies or an extra special meal for your children. Or, you may like to bake a cake or some homemade bread and a big pot of soup for someone you know who is sick, pregnant, or recently had a new baby.

"Goodness, you don't want me to get into the kitchen again, do you?" I hear you say. Yes! And you will be doing the *"good works"* God planned for you.

There are two particular passages in the New Testament that give a description of God's plan for women. As I read them again recently I noticed that they bring us back to the kitchen! God is very practical. And He wants us to be heavenly practical! That means doing the *"good works"* He planned in Heaven for us to do on earth!

The first passage is in 1 Timothy 5:10, where it gives a beautiful description of a godly woman. The second passage is Titus 2:3-5, where we have the list of what God wants the older women to teach the younger women. Let's look at what God has commissioned us to do.

1. NOURISH CHILDREN

The word in the Greek is *teknotropheo* and means "to cherish, nourish, and give food to children; it is also used of a mother nursing a baby at her breast." This is all about food! It starts with nursing our baby at the breast and then feeding them every day of their lives until they leave home! This means spending a lot of time in the kitchen! But it is not a waste of time. It is all part of our nurturing/mothering anointing. What does she do next?

2. SHOW HOSPITALITY TO STRANGERS

Hospitality is also about food. The more people you invite to your table and to stay in your home, the more you'll be in the kitchen! It's a wonderful ministry and God looks upon it with favor. He says it is a good work!

3. WASH THE SAINTS' FEET

In biblical times they washed the feet of their guests when they arrived at the home and before they sat them down to a meal. It speaks of serving. Once again, it is all about food. Washing feet is preparing to serve them food.

4. RELIEVE THOSE WHO ARE IN DISTRESS

Most of the time this will mean feeding those who are hungry and bringing into your home those who have nowhere to stay (which once again means feeding them)!

Do you notice how these *"good works"* are all to do with food?

But, we haven't finished yet. The other passage is in Titus 2:3-5, where it tells the older women to teach the younger women *"good things."* The Greek word is *kalodidaskalos* which means she is teaching them things that are valuable and beautiful to behold. The JBP translation says that these things are *"a good advertisement for the Christian faith."* Of the good things that are mentioned, most of them refer to food. Let's have a look.

5. LOVE YOUR HUSBAND

You can't love your husband without feeding him. The old saying is true that "the way to a man's heart is through his stomach." One of the good things you can do for your husband is to make sure that you have a nutritious, attractive, and aroma-filled meal ready for him when he gets home. Not an hour after he gets home, but as soon as he gets home! You abundantly bless him when he arrives home to a beautifully set table, a lovely meal, and the family waiting for him to take his place at the head of the table.

6. LOVE YOUR CHILDREN

You certainly show your love to your children by preparing wholesome meals for them, not with resignation, but with excitement and joy. They know you love them when you delight to cook for them and make special things for them. And as you cook, you will encourage them to help you, showing the way for the next generation.

7. BE SENSIBLE

This is translated "discreet" in the KJV. The Greek word is *sophron* and means "a person who limits his own freedom and ability with proper thinking, demonstrating self-control with the proper restraints on all the passions and desires, one who voluntarily places limitations on his freedom." To prepare meals for our husband and family, day after day, week after week, year after year (I have now been doing it for more than 50 years!), takes sacrifice and limiting your own freedom. We happily stop doing "our own thing" when it's time to prepare meals.

8. BE A KEEPER AT HOME

This speaks of running our home efficiently. To competently manage a home we need to plant a garden to provide fresh food for our family, shop, order food from afar, plan, preserve, and prepare wholesome and delicious meals. It's all about food again!

9. BE GOOD

Remember, cooking and preparing meals is a *"good thing"* and God is watching!

10. BE OBEDIENT TO YOUR HUSBAND

Having a meal ready for our husband shows our deference and submission to him. What does the virtuous woman do to her husband? *"She will do him **good** and not evil all the days of her life"* (Proverbs 31:12).

Have fun cooking! Now you can do it with revelation rather than resignation!

PRAYER:

"Thank you, Father for showing me that preparing food is not an inferior task, but high on the list of your agenda for mothers. Help me to remember that it is one of the good works you have chosen for me to accomplish."

AFFIRMATION:

Look out, family—mother is cooking up a storm!

FURTHER STUDY:

Scriptures about hospitality: Luke 14:23; Acts 2:44-47; Romans 12:13; 1 Corinthians 16:15; and 1 Peter 4:7-9.

60

Care for One Another
Part 1

"And let us consider and give attentive, continuous care to watching over one another, studying how we may stir up (stimulate and incite) to love and helpful deeds and noble activities"
(HEBREWS 10:24, AMP).

How grateful we are that God cares for us (1 Peter 5:7). He tangibly wants to show His loving care to us, but the only way He can do it is through His people. To encourage us to fulfill these words of Scripture, let's look at different ways we can show care to one another, beginning in our homes, and then reaching out to those around us. There are 31 points, one for every day of the month.

The inspiration for these caring ideas came from a dear friend of mine in New Zealand, June Louis, who has now gone to be with the Lord. I cannot think of a greater example of a godly woman who walked with God, loved His Word, never compromised, and constantly cared for people with "good works." June came to know Jesus soon after she was married and prayed continually for her husband's salvation, but never saw the answer to her prayers while she was alive, even though she passed away in her eighties. This did not stop her from unwaveringly serving the Lord and being totally committed to her marriage.

Don't forget to look up the Scriptures. They are the best part.

1. **Comfort.** Comfort the lonely, hurting, sad, and the depressed (Acts 20:35; Romans 15:1-2; 2 Corinthians 1:3, 4; 7:6, 7; and 1 Thessalonians 5:11, 14). And don't forget to comfort Israel and God's chosen people (Isaiah 40:1-2).
2. **Chat.** Take time to visit with someone who is sick or lonely (Matthew 25:31-46 and Philippians 4:14).
3. **Chores.** Do laundry or housework for a mother with a new baby or

someone who is sick (Philippians 2:4).

4. **Cook.** Invite a single mother, a widow, or a family to your home for a meal. Pursue hospitality (Acts 2:46; Romans 12:13; and 1 Peter 4:9).
5. **Child-Minding.** Relieve a busy mom for a few hours (1 Corinthians 10:24 and Galatians 6:2).
6. **Cheerful.** Keep a cheerful spirit in your home. Smile at your husband and your children constantly. Keep a cheerful countenance when you meet people so they will be uplifted by your presence rather than depressed (Proverbs 15:13, 15; 17:22; 18:21; and Isaiah 3:9).
7. **Convert.** Take every opportunity to tell others about Jesus and the good news of the Gospel (Mark 8:36; 1 Corinthians 1:18; and 9:16).
8. **Call.** Call your husband at work to remind him that you love him. When the Holy Spirit lays someone on your heart, call to encourage them. Your words can change their whole day. *"Anxiety in a person's heart weighs him down, but an encouraging word brings him joy"* (Proverbs 12:25, NET).
9. **Compassion.** Words are often not enough. Show love in your actions, too (Proverbs 31:20; James 2:15, 16; and 1 John 3:16-18).
10. **Cookies.** Bake some wholesome cookies for a family in need or a mother who has a new baby (Proverbs 31:20 and Luke 6:38).
11. **Cards.** Keep a stack of encouraging cards. Look for them when you are out shopping. When the Holy Spirit brings someone to your mind, write an encouraging word and send it to them (1 John 1:4).
12. **Customs.** Look out for folks from other countries and take an interest in them and their customs. Invite them for a meal (Acts 2:9-11).
13. **Clucky*.** Never say "No" to a baby from God. And take notice of all babies, even when shopping or in the street. Encourage every young mother with a new baby (Psalm 127:3).
14. **Concern.** Show concern for all, especially the elderly (Leviticus 19:32 and 1 Timothy 5:1).
15. **Consideration.** Take time to think about the needs of others. God cannot reveal to you the needs of others if you are always thinking about yourself (Mark 8:35 and Hebrews 10:24).

PRAYER:

"Oh Father, please give me the same spirit of caring that you have. Save me from being self-centered. I want to give room in my heart and my thoughts for you to tell me about people who are hurting. Amen."

AFFIRMATION:

"Rescue the perishing, care for the dying,
Snatch them in pity from sin and the grave;
Weep o'er the erring one, lift up the fallen,
Tell them of Jesus, the mighty to save."
~ Fanny Crosby, 1870

**I have been informed that American readers are not familiar with the word "clucky." In New Zealand we call someone "clucky" who gets excited about babies. They love to hold a baby and wish they could have one of their own.*

61

Care for One Another
Part 2

"But whoso hath this world's good, and seeth his brother have need, and shutteth up his bowels of compassion from him, how dwelleth the love of God in him? My little children, let us not love in word, neither in tongue; but in deed and in truth"
(1 JOHN 3:17, 18).

Today we continue the rest of the 31 points about caring for one another—in our homes and out of the home.

16. **Car.** Offer a lift to someone who doesn't have a vehicle so they can do their shopping, go to church, or visit (Romans 12:11).
17. **Children.** Make a point of encouraging each one of your own children every day. When visiting with families, take time to talk to the children as well as the adults (Proverbs 10:21a).
18. **Courtesy.** Good manners show that you care for people (Proverbs 11:16; Luke 4:22; and 1 Corinthians 13:4, 5).
19. **Correspondence.** Always be ready to write and encourage someone. Write a card, letter, email, or Facebook message. Don't forget family members (especially grandparents) who live in a different city or country. And don't forget those on the mission field (Proverbs 25:25).
20. **Creativity.** If you have a talent or hobby, use it to bless others (Matthew 25:14-30; Acts 9:36-42; and Romans 12:4-8).
21. **Cuddle.** Hugs do wonders for husbands and children, and other ladies you meet (Romans 12:10).
22. **Captivity.** Remember to pray for our Christian brothers and sisters who are being persecuted (Hebrews 13:3). Two hundred million Christians across the world are currently suffering from some form of persecution and over 100,000 Christians are murdered each year

for their faith. If we were being persecuted, we would certainly like to know others were praying for us, wouldn't we? We like to use the book, *Praying Through the 100 Gateway Cities of the 10/40 Window* at our Family Devotions each evening. It gives information of the most needy cities in the world and how to pray for them (available from www.aboverubies.org).

23. **Constant Prayer.** Prayer will accomplish what nothing else can. Don't give up praying (Luke 11:6-10; 1 Timothy 2:1-4; and James 5:16).
24. **Commitment.** Be committed to your husband, your family, and to the saints of God—today, and in the weeks and months ahead (Psalm 16:2, 3).
25. **Co-Opt.** Call upon others to help you when you minister to needy situations. Enlist your family. Don't try to do it all by yourself (Romans 16:3-5, 7; Philippians 1:5; 2:25; 4:3; 1 Thessalonians 3:2; and Philemon 1, 23, 24).
26. **Charity.** Charity begins at home, but doesn't end there. Pour out God's love on your husband and children, but take His love to hurting people outside your home, too (John 3:16; 13:34-35; 1 Corinthians 10:33; 1 John 3:14-18; and 4:20, 21).
27. **Continue.** Keep loving, serving, and blessing people, even when you receive nothing in return. Don't get weary in well-doing (Galatians 6:9 and 2 Thessalonians 3:13).
28. **Check.** At the end of each day, check to see if you have spoken words of encouragement to your husband, your children, or to someone God has put upon your heart (Hebrews 3:13, 14).
29. **Conciliate.** Try to be a peacemaker, rather than having a reactionary spirit (Psalm 34:14; Matthew 5:9; 2 Corinthians 13:11; Hebrews 12:14; and 1 Peter 3:8-11).
30. **Contentment.** Give thanks for all things, but don't expect thanks for all that you do. Your reward is in Heaven (Ephesians 6:5, 6 and Colossians 3:22-24).
31. **Courier.** Take an *Above Rubies* magazine to a friend, a neighbor, or keep some in a plastic bag in your handbag to give to mothers when you go shopping. Be a courier that spreads the good news (Psalm 60:4).

After you have looked up the Scriptures for each point for the last two devotions, you may like to share them with your children, too. I am sure you will find it a great blessing to use these life-changing Scriptures at your Family Devotions. It is important for your children to embrace this vision of caring for one another and to make it your family lifestyle. You will become a caring family with a vision for caring for the world around you, too.

PRAYER:

"Dear Father God, please save me from thinking about myself all the time. Please bring to my mind those you want me to bless and encourage. Even in my prayers, help me to be thinking of others and pouring out my heart for them, rather than for myself. Amen."

AFFIRMATION:

Instead of selfish, I want to be caring,
A life outpoured, and never sparing.

62

Winter Beauty

"To appoint unto them that mourn in Zion, to give unto them beauty for ashes, the oil of joy for mourning, the garment of praise for the spirit of heaviness; that they might be called trees of righteousness, the planting of the Lord, that he might be glorified"
(Isaiah 61:3).

I looked up from reading God's Word in my morning quiet time. Oh what a glorious sight met my eyes. A beautiful sunrise of brilliant salmon pink glowed through the bare, leafless branches of the winter trees. It was glorious. I was awe-inspired. Why hadn't I seen these beautiful skies before? I realize that I hadn't noticed them before because they were hidden from my view by the thick foliage of the tall trees that surround us here in the Tennessee woods.

Wintertime is stark and barren, but it is in these bare times that we see beauty that we don't normally see. As I drive the country roads in the winter, I often exclaim, "Oh, I haven't noticed that home before." Or,"I've never seen that barn before." The lovely leafy-laden trees had blocked them from view.

Perhaps you are going through a winter season in your life. Your heart is cold. The outlook seems ugly. You feel stripped of all that you hold dear. Can I remind you to lift up your head? Look up. As you do, you will see things in a new light. You will see God in a new way. You will see different facets of His beauty that you hadn't noticed before. You will see things that God has been waiting to show you that He couldn't reveal to you with all the foliage around your life.

Often God has to strip us of all our trappings and the things we daily rely upon so He can reveal Himself to us. We don't see Him clearly when our sights and senses are filled with other things.

I used to think the bare trees of winter were rather ugly, but I have now come to appreciate their own special attractiveness. I love their intriguing beauty as they silhouette against the differing moods of the sky. I love seeing the tiny thin branches of the trees which show up like lace in the sun-setting sky. There is nothing more striking than the moon shining down through the bare trees. What could bring more pleasure to the eyes than seeing the hoar frost or a fresh snowfall balancing on their bare, outstretched limbs? And, of course, I now see the sunrises that I don't see in the other seasons.

There was also a time in my life when I didn't like going through hard times. I'd rather not face them at all. But I have learned to find beauty in these times, too. This is when God does His deepest work in our hearts. This is when we really grow. This is when God is able to conform us to the image of His Son.

Don't despise the winter seasons. Don't let your heart get bitter. Fling off that self-pity. Don't cower in the dungeon of despair. Open your spiritual eyes and look up. Unless I had looked up from my reading to see the sunrise, I would have missed it. You won't see unless you look up. There are beautiful things to behold that you haven't seen before, which you cannot see in any other season. You will see a new sunrise in your life.

PRAYER:

"Father, I have been shivering in this winter experience. I feel bare and stripped of everything. Lord, I am sorry that I have been looking at the ugliness of it all. I have been consumed with self-pity. Lord, I will look up, for I want to behold your beauty. I look to see your goodness in the land of the living. Show me glimpses of the good work you are doing in me in this winter season. Amen."

AFFIRMATION:

Looking at my ugly problems doesn't work; I'm looking up to God who has the answers!

63

How to Please Your Husband
Part 1

"Love is patient and kind; love does not envy or boast; it is not arrogant or rude. It does not insist on its own way. It is not irritable or resentful" (1 Corinthians 13:4, 5, ESV).

Who are you pleasing today? Although we have our husband and the constant needs of our children to attend to all day, we would like to have some time to please ourselves, wouldn't we? However, Romans 15:1-3 tells us that we are *"not to please ourselves. . . For even Christ pleased not himself."* Jesus *"came not to be served but to serve, and to give his life"* (Matthew 20:28) and He gave us His example so we *"should follow his steps"* (1 Peter 2:21 and Philippians 2:3-8).

It really gets to the "nitty gritty" when Paul talks about marriage in 1 Corinthians 7:32-35. Paul says that the unmarried woman is free to please the Lord, but the married woman is to give first priority to pleasing her husband. However, it's not meant to be a duty. The word "please" not only means to seek to please, but it involves exciting the emotions! What are some of the ways you can please your husband today and in the coming days?

1. DELIGHT TO BE YOUR HUSBAND'S HELPER

The first description of a wife is a "helper" (Genesis 2:18). Really? Maybe you are thinking you are the one who needs help! You have little children around you all day who constantly draw on your resources. Don't despair, mother. The word "helper" is the same word that is used to describe God who is "our help" (Psalm 33:20 and 70:5). As a helper, you reveal the likeness of God, who is always available to come to our aid. You are also a helper to your husband as you care for your home and your children. Together you are building a godly home and godly children.

2. DAILY ENCOURAGE YOUR HUSBAND

Men are like little puppy dogs waiting for recognition and encouragement. As you encourage your husband, he will grow into all that God wants him to be. Not by nagging, but by encouraging! Take time to think about his good points and affirm them. Be big enough to overlook the negatives—you didn't notice them when you fell in love.

Proverbs 12:25 (TLB) says, *"A word of encouragement does wonders."* It will do wonders in your husband, too. Is your husband bowed down by worry, financial pressures, and the burden of providing for you all? Proverbs 12:25 (NET) says, *"Anxiety in a person's heart weighs him down, but an encouraging word brings him joy."*

Write more love notes to him than "Honey Do" lists. Leave them on his pillow. Put them in his socks when folding them. Text "surprise" notes to him and call him to tell him nothing else except that he is amazing. Take time to laugh together. Laugh at the little things. Laugh together as you watch the children.

3. BE AFFECTIONATE TO YOUR HUSBAND

In Titus 2:4 the older women are commissioned to encourage the young women *"to love their husbands."* The word "love" in this passage is *philandros* which means "to be affectionate." In other words, we are to be touchy, kissy, and cuddly! When we were a young couple, an older man told us that he never passed his wife in the home without stopping to cuddle and kiss her.

The way to please your husband is to do the same things you did before you were married, the little things that made him fall in love with you. Keep doing those things and he'll keep falling in love with you over and over again. When your husband speaks to you, look at him adoringly. I am sure you did this before you married.

How often do you smile at your husband? Or do you give him more frowns than smiles? Start a new habit of smiling at him each time you look at him. Even when you don't feel like smiling, do it. Your action will change your attitude. Not only smile at your husband, but smile affectionately at your children. The whole atmosphere of your home will change.

4. KEEP A HUMBLE, SOFT, AND TENDER-HEARTED ATTITUDE TOWARD YOUR HUSBAND

Stubbornness and pride kill a marriage. Don't ever let your heart get hard toward your husband. A hard heart is the foundation of divorce (Matthew 19:7-9). God has given us many principles in the Scriptures to show us how to have a blessed marriage. However, I think that if we only had one Scripture in the whole of the Bible to help us understand the secret of a successful marriage, it would be Philippians 2:5-8: *"Let this mind (or this attitude) be in you, which was also in Christ Jesus: Who being in the form of God, thought it not robbery to be equal with God: But made himself of no reputation, and took upon him the form of a servant, and was made in the likeness of men: And being found in fashion as a man he humbled himself and became obedient unto death, even the death of the cross."*

How is it that we hang on to our stubborn attitude (which is usually quite ridiculous) when Jesus was prepared to give up Heaven and His Godhead to die for our sins? How is it that we can't even humble ourselves when Jesus, who was used to the glory of Heaven, was willing to humble Himself to become a man for us?

5. HAVE A HEARTY AND NUTRITIOUS MEAL READY FOR YOUR HUSBAND WHEN HE ARRIVES HOME

Remember, the way to a man's heart is through his stomach! You tell your husband you are thinking of him when you have a lovely meal ready for him as he walks in the door at the end of the day. Set the table attractively with candles and music playing.

It is your responsibility to serve food to your husband. Bless him by serving him a healthy breakfast. If you leave it to him, he'll be sure to eat some junk! Can you send him off with a healthy lunch, too?

PRAYER:

"Oh God, please help me to understand that I only hurt myself when I don't love and bless my husband. Even when I don't feel loved, give me the strength to love and encourage. Amen."

AFFIRMATION:

I am going to be more delightful to my husband than when he first met me!

64

How to Please Your Husband
Part 2

"Sweetness of the lips increases learning"
(PROVERBS 16:21).

Here are the last five ways to shower your husband with blessings.

6. SPEAK SWEETLY, KINDLY, AND LOVINGLY TO YOUR HUSBAND

Your husband can't take your criticism. He can't take your harshness. He can't take your retorts. He can't take your indifference. He will run from it. Do you want to draw him closer to you? Talk sweetly to him. And never forget to say "I love you" every day. You are allowed to say it more than once a day. In fact, I give you permission to say it ten times a day if you would like!

7. KEEP TO YOUR OWN ROLE

Keep to the task God has given you. You are the nurturer and nestbuilder of the home. Your husband is your provider and protector. You take away the anointing God has given him when you take his role of providing. You already have a huge career of General Manager of your home and garden (1 Timothy 5:14).

8. RESPECT AND HONOR YOUR HUSBAND

There is more than submitting to your husband and obeying him, although this is required of us (Ephesians 5:22-24; Colossians 3:18; and Titus 2:5). God wants you to honor your husband. The greatest way you can please your husband is to respect and honor him.

As women, we long for love and security. However, more than anything else, a man longs for RESPECT AND HONOR from his wife. It is a God-given instinct that we as wives need to understand. He will never be truly happy until he has it, but when he does, look out world! He will feel that he can face anything.

We can love our husband, and yet not show the respect and honor that he instinctively needs. The Amplified Version of Ephesians 5:33 explains the Greek word very clearly: *"Let the wife see that she respects and reverences her husband (that she notices him, regards him, honors him, prefers him, venerates, and esteems him; and that she defers to him, praises him, and loves and admires him exceedingly)."*

Honor your husband with the way you speak to him and the way you look at him. Does your husband sit at the head of the table? Does he have his special chair? We show our honor in little practical things, too.

9. BE INTOXICATING TO YOUR HUSBAND

Do not deprive your husband sexually. 1 Corinthians 7:2-5 says that we are to fulfill each other's sexual needs. The KJV calls it giving one another *"due benevolence."* The full understanding of these words means, "we owe it to one another, we are under obligation to one another, we have a debt to one another, we have a duty to one another, and we are bound to do it."

Proverbs 5:19 tells husbands *"to be always intoxicated with her love."* Whose love? The wife's love. That means you. You are to be ravishing, captivating, and intoxicating to your husband. The Hebrew word actually means "to lead astray." Do you like that? Don't wait for your husband to initiate lovemaking. Surprise him. Lead him astray from the worries and burdens of his day and intoxicate him. You'll forget your worries, too.

1 Corinthians 7:5 (ESV) says, *"Do not deprive one another, except perhaps by agreement for a limited time, that you may devote yourselves to prayer; but then come together again, so that Satan may not tempt you."* Are you currently doing a season of fasting and prayer? If not, you know what you should be doing!

10. BE PASSIONATE ABOUT YOUR MARRIAGE

Jesus said in John 10:10 that He came to give us life MORE ABUNDANTLY. The word "abundantly" is *perissos* and means "superabundant, excessive, exceedingly abundantly above the normal, beyond measure, over the top, above and beyond." This is the way God wants us to live life in every area, including mothering in our home and as a wife to our husband.

I am sure you have a good marriage, but even a good marriage can get into a rut! God does not intend for you to have a normal marriage. Good is not good enough. He desires for you to have a marriage that is exceedingly above the normal!

What are the good things you are doing in your marriage? Do them *more* abundantly, *more* frequently, *more* joyfully, *more* smilingly, *more* adoringly, *more* sweetly, and *more* passionately. Get out of the rut into a new realm.

You know the old saying, "The grass is greener on the other side of the fence." This applies to marriage, too. Satan would like to destroy your marriage. He loves to bring deceiving and dissatisfying thoughts to your mind. Don't listen to his lies! Instead, water, feed, and fertilize your marriage. It will grow so luscious and green that you'll never want to take another look anywhere else.

PRAYER:

"Oh God, please save me from thinking about myself all the time. Bring ideas to my mind on how to love and please my husband, for in doing this I please you. Amen."

AFFIRMATION:

Instead of dull, I will be desirable;
Instead of insipid, I will be intoxicating;
Instead of staying in the rut, I will be ravishing.

65

Where Is Your Heart?

"Your wife shall be a like a fruitful vine in the very heart of your house, your children like olive plants all around your table"
(Psalm 128:3, NKJV).

Where is your heart focused, dear mother? Is it in your home? Or do other interests captivate your heart? Even if you are a stay-at-home mother, your heart can still be focused in other directions.

God wants us to be physically in our homes, but He wants our hearts to be there too. The most accurate translation of Psalm 128:3 says, *"Your wife shall be like a prolific vine in the recesses of your dwelling."* The Hebrew word for *"by the sides of thine house"* (KJV) is *yrekah* and it means "the rear or the recess."

In plain English, God wants mothers to be in the very heart of their homes and He wants home to be in their hearts. The heart is the most important organ in a person's body. If it stops beating, the person will die. In the same way, the mother is the heartthrob of her home. If her heart beats faintingly, the home will falter. If her mother heart stops beating, the home will disintegrate. It is the mother who keeps the home and her family together.

Many mothers are on the periphery of their home, rather than in the recesses. I think we can all relate to the bumper sticker, "If a mother's place is in the home, why am I always in the car?" It's so easy to get caught up in the rat race of society, even with children's activities. We end up running around the city, taking our children to this and that, and the home is vacated.

Many times mothers are still out on the road in the early evening, the time when they should be at home to prepare the evening meal and make their home a sanctuary for their husband to return to. They drop by for some fast food on the way and the children miss out on a wholesome meal. They miss the precious atmosphere of sitting around the table together in the sanctuary of their own home. Children's childhood memories will consist of sitting in a car and rushing here and there, rather than the warmth and joy of their home.

Is this God's pattern? No. When God paints the picture of a home that is blessed of the Lord, He shows us the wife and mother in the very heart of the home, with her children all sitting around the table (Psalm 128:3).

THE GOOD IS THE ENEMY OF THE BEST

"But, it is necessary for my children to be involved in all these activities," you say. Mother, did you know that you don't have to do what everyone else is doing? You don't have to conform to society. Of course, there will be certain things that are important for your child or children to be involved in. But, take stock. Eliminate the unnecessary. Remember the old adage, "The good is the enemy of the best!" I know that everything your children are involved in is good, but is it the very best?

Who do you think knows best? God, or what society promotes? God says that His blessing is upon the mother and children who are in the heart of the home. When your heart is in the home, you can make your home an exciting place—a place to create, learn, and dream; a place of potential and possibility; a place of love, joy, peace, and contentment.

Recently a friend joined my husband and I for our early morning walk. We enjoyed rapport together, but I especially loved one statement he shared with us, "Wherever you are, be there!"

Mother, you are physically in your home. Make sure your heart and mind are there too. Don't waste your time dreaming of being somewhere else. You are right in the place where God wants you. You are in His perfect will.

It takes time to make a house a home. It takes thought. It takes your heartbeat. It takes prayer. It takes vision. And most of all, it takes being there. Glory in your home and make it a sanctuary for the living God.

Will you be forgotten and waste away if you spend most of your time in the recesses of your home? No. You may be hidden according to the world's standard. However, while others are out fulfilling their own aspirations or careers for rewards that will pass away, you are training God's children for rewards that will last forever. You are the winner! Often your days may seem like drudgery and toil, tedium and frustration, but lift up your heart. You are working for God. You are working for an eternal reward. You are determining the course of this nation.

One day, out from the recesses of your home, will come "arrows" whom you have sharpened and polished and who are ready to be shot from the bow—young warriors who will go forth to hold up the truth of God's Word in the nation. These arrows will be shining and bright lights in the midst of this dark world. What could be more powerful?

The home is God's chosen plan for the blessing, preservation, and continuance of the family. Put your heart, soul, and physical body into strengthening your home.

PRAYER:

"Dear Father, You have chosen my home to be my sphere of influence. Give me a love for being in my home. Give me a love for mothering my children in my home. Give me a vision for my home. Help me to see the creative potential that I have in my home. Help me to make my home a place where my family loves to be and where you love to dwell. Amen."

AFFIRMATION:

Planted in the home, I am where God purposes me to be.

66

A Whispering Campaign

"And the men, which Moses sent to search the land, who returned, and made all the congregation to murmur against him, by bringing up a slander upon the land, even those men that did bring up the evil report upon the land, died by the plague before the Lord"
(NUMBERS 14:36, 37).

God loves the land of Israel because He chose it and it is in His plan. God loves the land of motherhood because it is the anointing He has chosen for us to live in. Because both lands are very close to the heart of God, Satan hates them. He hates Israel and wants to annihilate it from the face of the earth because the land of Israel proves the promises of God's Word and the existence of God. He wants to eliminate motherhood because it brings forth life (which Satan hates) and the image of God in the world.

When the spies came back from checking out the Promised Land, they came back *"bringing up a slander upon the land."* Yes, they told the other Israelites that it was a fruitful land, flowing with milk and honey. It took two strong men to carry one cluster of grapes! But, they also told them about the giants and the walled cities that would be impossible to overcome! They did not believe God was big enough to do what He promised. They slandered the land that God had searched out for them and given to them by divine covenant.

Just as the spies slandered the land of Israel, many times mothers slander the land that God has given to them. They do not believe that God will be with them in their pregnancies and births. They do not believe God can provide for the children He wants to give them. Often, they do not even believe they are meant to be in their homeland of motherhood and would prefer to live "out of the land." They talk disparagingly against motherhood. They laugh with contempt about having another baby. They are doing exactly what the spies did—"spreading lies" (GWT) about the land!

God calls it "*slander*" and "*an evil report*" when we do not believe that He is able to provide for us. Psalm 78:19-22 says: "*Yea, they spake against God; they said, Can God furnish a table in the wilderness? . . . Can he give bread also? Can he provide flesh for his people? Therefore the Lord heard this, and was wroth; so a fire was kindled against Jacob, and anger also came up against Israel; because they believed not in God, and trusted not in his salvation.*"

Who were the spies that gave this evil report to the children of Israel? They were not the ordinary rank and file. Each one was a ruler among their tribes! They had been carefully chosen. Once again we see a parallel. It is often the leaders in the churches and the "older women" who slander the land of motherhood. Many pastors counsel newly married couples to delay childbearing. They encourage couples to limit having children as they may not be able to afford to send them to college. Even some pastors' wives give a wrong example by limiting their families and leaving their homes to pursue careers.

The older women of this generation have turned this new generation of mothers away from the land. They give them an evil report. I know older women who have a mission to stop mothers having more babies. They have a "*whispering campaign*" going on. The MLB translation calls it a "*whispering campaign against the land.*" This whisper of unbelief about motherhood has spread across the land, even in the church, until now we live in a society that rejects the highest purpose God has for women. Are these "older mothers" aware that they have turned a generation away from God's truth and are responsible for eliminating God's children in the earth?

Do you belong to the "*whispering campaign,*" or do you have a different spirit like Caleb and Joshua?

God dealt fatally with the spies who slandered the land. It is not something we can take lightly. God says that "*he that uttereth slander is a fool*" (Proverbs 10:18). Titus 2:3-5 is very strong when it says that those who slander the land are "*blaspheming the Word of God.*"

Am I guilty? Yes, I am often tempted to speak unbelieving words regarding God's provision. May God save me from this sin of unbelief (Romans 14:23). May God help us to have a positive confession about the good land of motherhood. May we always confess that God will carry us through and that He will provide.

PRAYER:

"Oh Lord God, please help me to see the good things in the land of motherhood and not to be overcome with unbelief and doubt. Amen."

AFFIRMATION:

I will confess five positive things about my land of motherhood each new morning!

67

Stretching Your Faith

"Jesus said to Philip, 'Where shall we buy bread for these people to eat?' He asked this only to test him, for he already had in mind what he was going to do"
(John 6:5, 6, NIV).

The crowds gathered to hear Jesus' words of life and to be healed of their sicknesses. Soon there were thousands—five thousand men besides women and children. Jesus was filled with compassion toward these people. He not only wanted to feed their souls, but feed their bodies. And so He turned to Philip to ask him where they could buy food for all these people.

Philip was dumbfounded! "It would take a small fortune!" he spluttered in unbelief. Actually, different translations give different amounts. The NIV says *"eight months' wages would not buy enough bread."* The CEV translation says that *"it would take almost a year's wages."* The situation looked impossible to Philip. He couldn't see past the thousands of people and the impossibility of feeding them all. His faith could not go beyond his sight.

But Jesus had asked him this question to test and stretch his faith. Jesus knew all along what He would do. And we now know the outcome of the story and how Jesus fed this huge crowd from five small barley loaves and two small fish!

Let's put ourselves in Philip's place. What would you have answered? I'm sure my response would have been the same as Philip's! I pray that my faith will be stretched. I want to see beyond the looming difficulties in front of me. I want to see beyond the impossible situations. I want to look to God, to whom nothing is impossible.

God wants us to believe Him. He wants us to trust in His mighty right arm. He wants to lift us up from our earthly-sighted view to see Him. Our God is not a man. We must not bring him down to our level and to what we see. We must come up to where He is and see things as He sees them.

He sees far beyond the circumstances that we see. He knows how He will deliver us. He knows the final outcome. All we have to do is trust.

Next time you face an impossible situation, do you think you could change your response? Instead of confessing it is impossible, confess your trust in God. "Lord, I know that you are bigger than this situation. I can't see a way out, but I know that you know the way out. I trust you to lead me. I trust you to do what is impossible."

There are times when God will put you in situations, just as He did Philip, in order for your faith to stretch and grow. Don't waste these situations.

Remember that all along God knows what He will do. He has the answer. He has everything in control. Absolutely nothing is impossible to Him.

PRAYER:

"Oh God, I thank you that nothing is impossible to you. Help me to increase my faith. Help me to get into the habit of always looking to you instead of the problems I face around me. Amen."

AFFIRMATION:

Nothing is too difficult for God!

68

Sweet Strength

"Out of the strong came forth sweetness"
(Judges 14:14).

I am often amazed to see women shouting down men they are debating. It does not become them as women. In fact, it spoils them.

Are we then meant to be weak as women? No. I believe God wants us to be strong, but it is a different kind of strength than that of men. The "*virtuous*" woman in Proverbs 31:10 was a strong woman. The word in the Hebrew is *chayil* and means "valiant, strong, the strength of an army." We are to be strong in standing for truth, strong in our convictions, strong in faithfulness to our marriage and motherhood, strong in commitment, strong in purity and morality, strong in faith, strong in sacrifice, and strong in endurance. It is strength of character rather than dominance and dogmatism that should epitomize a woman. It takes a strong woman of faith to believe for her marriage when her husband is not walking in God's ways. It takes strength to endure in difficult circumstances.

How do we demonstrate this strength? Is it by loudness and harshness? Is it by demanding our own way? Is it by stubbornness, which is actually inverted strength? No. It is revealed by a sweet, serving spirit.

Let me tell you the story of today's Scripture. Samson wanted to marry a Philistine woman (even though this was against the Hebrew law). On the way down to Timnah to visit her, a lion attacked him, but the Spirit of the Lord came upon him and he ripped the lion's jaws apart with his bare hands. Some time later when he returned to Timnah for the wedding, he turned off the path to look at the carcass of the lion and noticed a swarm of bees inside the lion. It was filled with honey and he enjoyed eating the special treat.

It was the custom to tell riddles at weddings and so Samson put forth his riddle. *"Out of the eater came forth food, and out of the strong came forth sweetness."* Nobody could guess the riddle until Samson's wife nagged him day after day to tell her.

Where did the sweetness come from? It came from strength. Sweetness without strength can be weak and sickly. Strength without sweetness can be harsh and hurtful. We need both. To demand our own way is weakness. Any three-year-old can do that! Unyielding stubbornness can be weakness. However, it takes strength to speak kind and sweet words when you'd rather "fly off the handle." It's easy to react with sharp words. We need God's strength to be loving and sweet.

I love the picture the bridegroom paints of his bride in Song of Songs 4:11: *"Your lips, O my spouse, drip as the honeycomb; honey and milk are under your tongue."* What does honey taste like? Sweet. What does milk speak of? Nourishment. What kinds of words drip from your mouth? Sweet, nourishing, and life-giving words come forth from the strong woman because she is concerned for others rather than herself.

We see another picture of the strong and meek together in the picture of Jesus in Revelation 5:1-8. John wept because there was no one worthy to open and read the book until one of the elders proclaimed, *"Do not weep. Behold, the Lion of the tribe of Judah has prevailed to open the scroll. . . And I looked, and behold, in the midst of the throne . . . stood a Lamb as though it had been slain. . ."* The heavenly elder announced Jesus as the Lion of the tribe of Judah, but when John looked, it was a Lamb!

Strength and meekness flow together. A mother also reveals these two aspects—sweet tenderness, but also a strong, protecting spirit that guards her children with her life.

Nobody could guess Samson's riddle. Maybe people cannot guess where your love and sweetness comes from when you are in the midst of a difficult marriage. They cannot understand your quiet endurance in the midst of trial and tribulation. They don't know that it comes from the strength of your inner man as you trust unwaveringly in the Lord. They don't understand that true love comes from strength that *"bears all things, believes all things, hopes all things and endures all things"* (1 Corinthians 13:7). This is the true strength of a woman. A sweet spirit will nourish and build up a marriage. A strong spirit that is not tempered with sweetness can destroy family life.

When Samson found the honey, he also took some to his parents and they enjoyed the sweetness too. Can others feed from the sweetness you offer from your life?

PRAYER:

"Oh Lord God, I cannot be strong of myself. I cannot be sweet by myself either. My flesh has no sweetness in it. Please work in my heart by your Holy Spirit and pour into me your gentle, sweet spirit. Let it flow out from me at all times, in all situations, and especially in my home toward my husband and family. Thank you, Lord. Amen."

AFFIRMATION:

In the strength of the Lord I will be sweet and loving.

69

Storing Up Treasure

"Laying up in store for themselves a good foundation against the time to come, that they may lay hold on eternal life"
(1 TIMOTHY 6:19).

The above Scripture encourages us to lay up in store for the time to come. In the context, it speaks to those who have riches in this world, exhorting them to be rich in good works and generous to the needy. However, I believe this message is for us, too. I think it is one of the greatest exhortations we can have, don't you?

Every moment of our lives we should be *"laying up in store"* for the eternal kingdom. We cannot take any material possessions out of this world. It is all vanity. 1 Timothy 6:7 says, *"For we brought nothing into this world, and it is certain we can carry nothing out."* We will only take what we lay up in Heaven.

We need to remind ourselves again of Matthew 6:19-21: *"Lay not up for yourselves treasures upon earth, where moth and rust doth corrupt, and where thieves break through and steal: but lay up for yourselves treasures in heaven, where neither moth nor rust doth corrupt, and where thieves do not break through nor steal: for where your treasure is, there will your heart be also."*

I have always been challenged by the statement, "Life is a dressing room for eternity." Everything we do and say either builds for this world, or for the eternal world.

I think we will have a lot of surprises in Heaven. I remember reading about a man of God who had a vision of the eternal realm. He saw that the people who were closest to the throne of God were the mothers and intercessors. Our liberal society does not have time for these ministries. Even the Christian world does not always affirm them. They don't receive the limelight, but they are powerful in God's eyes.

Dear mother, I want to remind you that as you sacrificially pour out your life for your children, as you mother and nurture them in the ways of God, as you pour out your heart in prayer for them—you are laying up treasure for eternity! Your mothering is never wasted. It builds for eternity. You are preparing your children for the heavenly realm. And you lay up heavenly treasure for yourself as you do it.

You may feel inferior because you think you are wasting your education as you lay down your career for motherhood. You may feel sorry for yourself because you are not making money like your neighbor, who is choosing her career over motherhood. You may feel insecure because you don't feel that you are accomplishing great things in your home.

Don't listen to these deceptions and negatives. As you mother your children, you are in the perfect will of God. You are building for eternity. You are laying up store for the time to come.

You are building a big mansion for yourself up there! This is certainly not a waste of time!

PRAYER:

"Lord, please help me to put value on the eternal things, on the things that you put value on. Help me to remember each day that motherhood is building for eternity."

AFFIRMATION:

I have given up hoarding for this world; I am hoarding up treasure for the heavenly kingdom.

70

Are You Ready for Battle?

"For mine Angel shall go before thee, and bring thee in unto the Amorites, and the Hittites, and the Perizzites, and the Canaanites, the Hivites and the Jebusites: and I will cut them off"
(Exodus 23:23).

Do you like battles? I am sure that you would rather avoid them if you could. We often think that battles just come upon us, or the enemy of our souls instigates them. However, the above Scripture tells us that it is God who leads us into battle. It was God who brought the children of Israel face to face with their enemies. Before they could enjoy the promises of God they had to face their battles and win the fight!

Do not think that you are out of the will of God because you are facing trials and battles. God wants you to learn how to fight. He wants to reveal His power to you. He wants to prove to you that He is the Lord of Hosts, the God of the armies of Heaven.

God led His people into battle, but He did not leave them on their own. He stayed with them and fought with them. As they learned to trust God and not their own resources He showed His mighty right arm. They won every battle when they listened to God's advice and were obedient to Him (Joshua 24:8, 11).

Are you facing a battle in your life right now? God has brought you to this place and He is with you. He has not left you! He will fight for you. Listen to Him. Learn to use the weapons He has given you—the power of the precious blood of Christ, the power of the name of Jesus (Yeshua), and the power of the living Word of God. Revelation 12:11 says, *"And they overcame him by the blood of the Lamb, and by the word of their testimony; and they loved not their lives unto the death."*

Jesus Himself won his battles by confessing the Word of God and telling the devil, *"It is written"* (Matthew 4:1-11). Wield these weapons with the authority that He has given you as a child of God.

The children of Israel did not straggle out of Egypt in whatever manner they felt like. Exodus 13:18 (Knox) tells us they *"left Egypt in war-like array."* The margin of my Bible says that they marched out five in a rank, as an army. You are also part of an army. As such you will continually face battles. When you realize this, you can put on your armor, rise up, and fight in the power of God. Don't waste your time feeling sorry for yourself any longer.

Not only do you have to learn to fight, but you must teach your children how to fight. You must teach them how to fight against the enemy, how to fight against the temptations of the flesh, moods, and evil. Our children dare not go out to face this world without being experts in fighting the enemy.

Judges 3:1, 2 (NLT) tells us: *"The Lord left certain nations in the land to test those Israelites who had not participated in the wars of Canaan. He did this to teach warfare to generations of Israelites who had no experience in battle."* Each new generation had to be trained in the art of war.

They did not train them half-heartedly. They trained skilful warriors (1 Chronicles 5:18), valiant warriors (1 Chronicles 7:2, 11), and they trained them to be expert in war (1 Chronicles 12:24). Hebrews 11:34 (the great faith chapter) tells us of those who, although weak, were made strong in the battle and became mighty in war. They were not great fighters at the beginning, but learned with each battle. The more battles we face, the stronger we become.

Are you afraid of the battle? Do not give in to your fears. Fear comes from the enemy. God will never leave you alone in your battle. Let me encourage you today:" *"Fight the good fight of faith"* (1 Timothy 6:12) and *"war a good warfare"* (1 Timothy 1:18).

PRAYER:

"Father God, I thank you that you are with me in every battle I face. I thank you for the powerful weapons you have given me. Help me to continually confess the power of your name and the precious blood of Jesus. Amen."

AFFIRMATION:

I am training my children to be expert in war.

71

Out of . . . Into
Part 1

"He brought us out . . . that he might bring us in"
(Deuteronomy 6:23).

God brought the children of Israel out of bondage, out of slavery, out of affliction, out of servitude, and out of the iron furnace to bring them into a land that He had chosen for them. It was a good land, a land overflowing with milk and honey.

God also brings us out to bring us in! He doesn't deliver us out of the kingdom of darkness and leave us dangling. He brings us out to lead us on. He brings us into good things. He brings us . . .

1. OUT OF DARKNESS INTO LIGHT

1 Peter 2:9 says, *"Proclaim the praises of him who called you out of darkness into his marvelous light."*

God has brought us out of darkness into light. Marvelous light. Amazing light. Wonderful light. Pure light. Penetrating light.

Come out from the shadows. Come out from hiding. Come out from the darkness. God is waiting for you to live in His light. His life is light and His light is life. They are inseparable. Light is one of God's garments, and He wants to clothe you with it too.

This light exposes all sin and everything that grieves the Holy Spirit. This light shines upon our way and guides our paths. This light saves us from stumbling. This light brings revelation to our soul. This light is our life.

Don't hide from it. Live in it. It is yours. As you live in the light, your light will expose the darkness around you.

And in God's kingdom there is always more light to be revealed. Proverbs 4:18 says, *"The path of the just is as the shining light, that shineth MORE*

AND MORE unto the perfect day."

2. OUT OF THE PIT INTO SAFETY

Psalm 40:1, 2 says: *"I waited patiently for the Lord; and he inclined unto me, and heard my cry. He brought me up also out of a horrible pit, out of the miry clay, and set my feet upon a rock, and established my goings."* What is the horrible pit you are in today? The pit of self-pity, helplessness, despair, despondency, or even desperation? Cry out to Him and His mighty arm will reach down and pull you out. He will place you on the dry land, safe and secure in His arms, where you can trust in His precious promises.

3. OUT OF DEATH INTO LIFE

Ephesians 2:4-6 says, *"But God, who is rich in mercy, because of his great love with which he loved us, even when we were dead in sins, made us alive together with Christ . . . and raised us up together, and made us sit together in the heavenly places in Christ Jesus."*

God has brought us out of death into an abundant life (John 10:10 and Galatians 2:20). It is an overflowing life. Life to the full. Life with hope. Life with purpose. Christ's life living in us. This is the life we were born to live.

Ephesians 4:22-24 (The Message) says: *"Everything—and I do mean everything—connected with that old way of life has to go. It's rotten through and through. Get rid of it! And then take on an entirely new way of life—a God-fashioned life, a life renewed from the inside and working itself into your conduct as God accurately reproduces his character in you."*

PRAYER:

"Oh Father in Heaven, I thank you that you are my light and my salvation. Thank you for bringing me into your world of life and light. Help me to live in it and shine for your glory in this dark world. Amen."

AFFIRMATION:

"Out of my shameful failure and loss,
Jesus, I come! Jesus, I come!
Into the glorious gain of Thy cross,
Jesus, I come to Thee!"
~ William T. Sleeper (1887)

72

Out of . . . Into
Part 2

"The Lord sent Jerubbaal, and Bedan, and Jephthah, and Samuel, and delivered you out of the hand of your enemies on every side, and ye dwelled safe"
(1 SAMUEL 12:11).

Isn't it wonderful that we do not have to stay in the state we are in? God brings us out to a higher place.

4. OUT OF BONDAGE INTO FREEDOM

Galatians 5:1 says, *"Stand fast therefore in the liberty wherewith Christ has made us free and be not entangled again with the yoke of bondage."* Now that you have experienced the cleansing of the blood of Jesus making you clean and have Christ's life living in you, Satan has no more power over you. He can no longer keep you in chains and bondage, unless you allow him. You no longer belong to Satan. You belong to God. You are His child. You are a free woman. You are not a child of the slave woman, but of the free woman. You are Sarah's daughter, and she was the free woman (Galatians 4:30, 31).

Just as the Jews recline in a manner of free people at Passover to remember their great deliverance from the bondage of Egypt, so we too should live like free people. Jesus died to set us free and deliver us from the power of the enemy. When we stay in bondage to fears, habits, and sin, we spurn the power of the blood of Jesus Christ that has power to free us from the tyranny of the enemy.

Leviticus 26:13 (AMP) says, *"I am the Lord your God, who brought you forth out of the land of Egypt, that you should no more be slaves; and I have broken the bars of your yoke and made you walk erect as free men."* Your chains are broken. Confess this truth. Live in your freedom that has been won for you. Walk in your freedom.

Galatians 5:16-18 (The Message) says: *"Live freely, animated and motivated by God's Spirit . . . Why don't you choose to be led by the Spirit and so escape the erratic compulsions of a law-dominated existence?"*

"Out of my bondage, sorrow and night, Jesus I come, Jesus I come; Into Thy freedom, gladness and light, Jesus I come to Thee." ~ William T. Sleeper (1887)

5. OUT OF DECEPTION INTO TRUTH

The Bible tells us that the whole world is under the power and control of the evil one. The NKJV says that it *"lies under the sway of the wicked one"* (1 John 5:19).We cannot believe what the world says. It is based on deception and wickedness, master-minded by Satan, the father of lies.

We need to be reminded that we have been delivered from the power of this present evil age. Yes we have. This is truth—truth that is greater than your feelings and greater than your enemies! Galatians1:4 tells us that *"Jesus Christ gave himself for our sins that he might deliver us from this present evil world."* We have been delivered out of deception and wickedness and we have been positioned in Christ who is the Truth. We must walk in the promised land that God has brought us into—the land of truth and the authority of God's Word.

Don't let the world suck you back into its deceitful mold. Because we live in this world, it is very easy to absorb its values and think it is normal. It's way of living is foreign to our new life in Christ. What man thinks is wisdom is foolishness to God. We must constantly align our thinking with God's Word and His truth. Read John 8:32; Romans 12:2; 1 Corinthians 1:18-31 and 1 John 2:15-17.

PRAYER:

"Oh God, I thank you that you have delivered me from the clutches of this present evil world through the power of your death upon the cross. I claim the victory you have won for me. Help me to live daily in this victory. Amen."

AFFIRMATION:

I am walking in the power of the cross of Jesus which is greater than my feelings, greater than my circumstances, and greater than the temptations of this world.

73

Out of . . . Into
Part 3

"The Lord has taken you and brought you out of the iron furnace, out of Egypt, to be his people"
(Deuteronomy 4:20).

Praise God that we have been delivered out of the devil's kingdom to be one of God's own children.

6. OUT OF BITTERNESS INTO LOVE

1 John 4:7, 8 says: "*Beloved, let us love one another: for love is of God; and every one that loveth is born of God, and knoweth God. He that loveth not knoweth not God; for God is love.*"

God is love. He loves you with an everlasting love. He has called you into love. The life of Christ in you is a life of love. Live it. Share it. Give it, even when it is against every inclination within you to do so. Love extravagantly.

This love forgives over and over again. This love is patient. It is kind. It is not jealous. It is not proud. It is not rude. It does not demand its own way. It is not irritable. It keeps no record of when it has been wronged. It rejoices in the truth, but not evil. It never gives up. It never loses faith. It always hopes. It endures through every circumstance. This love is your life because it is Christ's love in you (1 Corinthians 13 and Romans 5:5).

It is not dependant on your love, which runs out easily. It's easy to love when people love you. It's only Christ's love in you that can continue loving when you are hurt, scoffed at, and rejected.

Ephesians 3:17-19 (The Message) says: "*I ask Him that with both feet planted firmly on love, you'll be able to take in with all Christians the extravagant dimensions of Christ's love. Reach out and experience the breadth! Test its length! Plumb the depths! Rise to the heights! Live full lives, full in the fullness of God."*

Ephesians 5:2 MSG says, *"Mostly what God does is love you. Keep company with him and learn a life of love. Observe how Christ loved us. His love was not cautious but extravagant. He didn't love in order to get something from us but to give everything of himself to us. Love like that."*

7. OUT OF DESPAIR INTO JOY

Isaiah 61:3 says, *"To appoint unto them that mourn in Zion, to give unto them beauty for ashes, the oil of joy for mourning, the garment of praise for the spirit of heaviness: that they might be called trees of righteousness, the planting of the Lord, that he might be glorified."*

You no longer have to get your joy from doing special things or being entertained as you did in the old life. Now you have joy continually residing in you.

Once again, this joy is not dependant on circumstances. It is separate from circumstances. This joy does not rely on having to feel happy. Anyone can feel happy when everything is going great. But life is not always great. Life can be hard, difficult, and hurtful. This joy is Christ Himself. It is His joy in you. He is exceeding joy. This joy is unspeakable and full of glory. No man, no circumstance, no hardship, or even suffering can take it from you.

Habakkuk 3:17, 18 says: *"Though the fig tree may not blossom, nor fruit be on the vines; though the labour of the olive may fail, and the fields yield no food; though the flock be cut off from the fold, and there be no herd in the stalls—yet I will rejoice in the Lord, I will joy in the God of my salvation."*

Live joy. Smile with joy. Laugh with joy. Bubble over with joy. Give joy to your family. Give joy to all you meet.

Romans 14:17 says, *"For the kingdom of God is not meat and drink; but righteousness, and peace, and joy in the Holy Ghost."*

PRAYER:

"Dear Father, I thank you that I am not dependent upon my joy, which fades quickly. I thank you for your life of love and joy, which is shed abroad in my heart by the Holy Spirit. Amen."

AFFIRMATION:

"Out of earth's sorrows into Thy balm,
Out of life's storms and into Thy calm,
Out of distress to jubilant psalm,
Jesus I come to Thee."
~ William T. Sleeper (1887)

FURTHER STUDY:

Living a life of joy:

Deuteronomy 26:11; Nehemiah 8:10; Psalm 5:11; 16:11; 28:7; 30:5; 32:11; 33:21; 35:9; 32:11; 40:16; 43:4; 51:12; 68:3, 4; 70:4; 89:15, 16; 90:14; 97:12; 105:3, 43; 113:9; 118:15, 24; 126:5, 6; 132:9, 16; 149:2; Ecclesiastes 2:26; Isaiah 12:3; 25:9; 29:19; 35:10; 51:11; 55:12; 61:10; 65:14, 18; Jeremiah 31:13; Habakkuk 3:17, 18; Luke 10:20; John 15:11; 16:20, 22, 24; 17:13; Acts 2:28; 13:52; 20:23, 24; Romans 15:13; 2 Corinthians 6:10; 7:4; Galatians 5:22; Philippians 3:3; 4:4; Colossians 1:10-11; 1 Thessalonians 5:16; Hebrews 3:6; 12:2; James 1:2; 1 Peter 1:6; and 4:12-14.

74

Out of . . . Into
Part 4

"He brought you out of Egypt with his Presence, with his mighty power driving out from before you nations greater and mightier than you, to bring you in, to give you their land as an inheritance"
(DEUTERONOMY 4:37, 38).

What a wonderful promise. God brings us out of the clutches of Satan with His Presence and mighty power. He brings us into His land, filled with all His precious promises.

8. OUT OF WORRY INTO PRAYER

"Did I read correctly?" you answer. Yes, it is true. Worry does not belong to the kingdom of God. Worry belongs to the old kingdom from which you have been delivered by God's mighty power.

Unfortunately, worry has become such a habit of our lives that it is hard to break. "What can I do if I can't worry? I've got to do something!" you say. As someone has said, "Worry is like a rocking chair: it gives you something to do but doesn't get you anywhere."

God has provided a wonderful weapon for us in the gift of prayer. Prayer is a gift. It is God's gift to you. He has put the incredible privilege of prayer into your hands. He has given you this tool, not only to fellowship with Him, but to turn His heart. He brings deliverance through prayer. He turns people, circumstances, and even nations upside down through prayer. He changes our own hearts through prayer.

The confession of the old kingdom is, "Why pray when I can worry?" The confession in God's kingdom is, "Why worry when I can pray?"We are to live in a world of prayer for we belong to a kingdom of prayer! Philippians 4:6 (NLT) says, *"Don't worry about anything; instead, pray about everything."*

Worry brings us into despair. Prayer brings us in touch with the supernatural power of God. You either pray or worry. You choose.

9. OUT OF FEAR INTO FAITH

Fear is crippling. It is a tormenting enemy. It is Satan's tool and belongs to his kingdom of darkness. But, are you getting the message? God has delivered you out of Satan's kingdom into His glorious kingdom. He has delivered you out of the power of fear into the realm of faith. When fears begin to overpower your mind and soul, rebuke them in the name of Jesus. They do not belong to you. Jesus has already died to deliver you from them.

2 Timothy 1:7 explicitly tells us that "*God has not given us the spirit of fear: but of power, and of love, and of a sound mind.*"

David confesses in Psalm 34:4, "*I sought the Lord, and he heard me, and delivered me from **all my fears**.*" Not just some fears, but all fears!

I know that fears can seem overwhelming. But they are totally deceiving. Satan always uses deception to pull us down. Put on your shield of faith. Rebuke the fears. Claim the promises of God. Thank God for delivering you from all your fears. Thank Him for the victory. Thank Him for His presence in your life. Thanking Him will take you out of fear and into faith.

PRAYER:

"I thank you, Oh God, my Deliverer, that I no longer belong to the kingdom of darkness. You have delivered me through the power of your death upon the cross. You have delivered me from all my fears. I claim this truth and receive it in the name of Jesus. Amen."

AFFIRMATION:

"I will trust and obey, for there's no other way,
To be happy in Jesus, than to trust and obey."
~ John H. Sammis (1887)

75

Out of . . . Into
Part 5

"He brought me up also out of a horrible pit, out of the miry clay, and set my feet upon a rock, and established my goings. And he hath put a new song in my mouth, even praise unto our God: many shall see it, and fear, and shall trust in the Lord"
(Psalm 40:2, 3).

God brought me "up" and "out." This was David's testimony. He couldn't do it by Himself. You can't do it by yourself either. It is all His doing. No matter how big the hole you have dug for yourself, God is able to pull you out. No matter how deep the mire into which you have sunk, it is not too hard for God. No matter how impossible the way ahead seems, God will pull you "up" and "out" and set your feet upon the Rock.

Let's look at one more thing that God delivers us out of to bring us into His glorious life.

10. OUT OF SELF INTO GOD

2 Corinthians 5:15 says, *"And that he died for all, that they which live should not henceforth live unto themselves, but unto him which died for them, and rose again."* This is perhaps the greatest deliverance of all. Jesus Christ not only died for our sins and to deliver us from the seductive power of this evil age, but to save us from our inherent selfish nature.

To be a slave to self is the biggest bondage of all. The basis of all sin is the middle letter of that word, I. How wonderful that Jesus died to free us from the slavery of self and bring us into His freeing life.

There is only one place to be free of self, and that is at the cross. At the cross Jesus gave up His Godhead, His life, and His desire to have His own way. It is at the cross that we die to self. In Luke 22:42 Jesus cried out, *"Father, if thou be willing, remove this cup from me; nevertheless, **not my will,***

but thine, be done. Can we learn to say these words when we are trying to have our own way? These are the words that bring us the victory. NEVERTHELESS! "I want my way, but NEVERTHELESS, I yield to your will, Father." Say it out loud: "Not my will, but thine, be done."

The Scriptures tell us that when Christ died, we died with Him. When He was buried, we were buried with Him. When He rose, we rose with Him to a new life in Christ. Our old life is dead and buried. We now have a new life. This is truth, but you have to acknowledge it and walk in it by faith. When "I" starts to take over, which it will try to do continually, confess these words: "I am dead and buried. I am no longer serving self. I serve the living God." The more you acknowledge this truth, the more it will become part of your life.

"Out of myself to dwell in Thy love,
Out of despair into raptures above,
Jesus, I come to Thee."

NEVER GO BACK AGAIN

Deuteronomy 26:8 says, *"The Lord brought us forth out of Egypt with a mighty hand, and with an outstretched arm, and with great terribleness, and with signs, and with wonders."*

God brought the children of Israel out of Egypt with a mighty and outstretched hand. He bared forth His mighty hand as he sent the plagues upon Egypt. He brought them through the Red Sea on dry land. He delivered them utterly from the ensuing Egyptians.

We have also been delivered by God's mighty hand. Jesus Christ not only died a painful death and shed His precious blood for our sins, but he broke the chains of death and hell. He delivered us from the clutches of the enemy. He did not suffer this death for us to go back to the old kingdom again (2 Corinthians 5:17).

Egypt speaks of the world and Satan's kingdom. God told the people of Israel, *"You must never return to Egypt"* (Deuteronomy 17:16, NLT). He did not even want them to remember Egypt any more. They were to forget about it completely. Sadly, when things got difficult, the children of Israel forgot the hardships they endured in Egypt and wanted to return. They started pining for the fish, cucumbers, melons, leeks, onions, and garlic of Egypt. And they despised the heavenly manna which was *"angels' food."* I guess we can't criticize them too much because we are guilty of grumbling and complaining us much as they did!

This grieved the heart of God (Exodus 13:17; Numbers 11:4-6; 14:2, 3; Psalm 78:17-25; and Ezekiel 23:27). God did not deliver them *"with great terribleness, and with signs and with wonders"* for them to go back again. Never! Jesus has also delivered us, never to go back to the old way of living again.

You have been brought "out of . . . into"! Live your new life. It is *"Christ in you, the hope of glory"* (Colossians 1:27).

PRAYER:

"Thank you, Lord, for delivering me from the power of self and the kingdom of darkness.Please save me from being tempted to ever go back to Egypt again. I now live in a new kingdom. Help me to live life to the full in your glorious kingdom. Amen."

AFFIRMATION:

I will not remember Egypt any more!

76

What Kind of Children?

"Has not the one God made and sustained for us the spirit of life? And what does he desire? Godly offspring. So take heed to yourselves and let none be faithless to the wife of his youth. For I hate divorce, says the Lord the God of Israel"
(MALACHI 2:15, 16, RSV).

God reveals His heart about marriage in the above Scripture. He wants the wife and husband to be one. He wants them to be faithful to one another. He does not want them to divorce. And He makes His reason very clear. The disruption of marriage tampers with the godly offspring. The thing that God looks for in marriage more than anything else is godly children. He looks eagerly for the coming children. This is His heart's desire.

It is the nature of God to want children in His image. And because we were made in the likeness and image of God, it is inherent for us to also want children in our image. We long to see who they will be like. And yet we now live in a distorted age. Couples have been so brainwashed by humanist deception that they often refuse to have children, or at least limit how many they have. They live counter-culture to God's kingdom and to their own instinctive design. While they live to their own desires, God waits with patience to see children born in His image. Grandparents wait to continue the godly dynasty.

But, even more challenging is that it is not just offspring that God looks for. It is *godly* offspring. The margin in my Bible says, *"the seed of God."* What kind of children are the seed of God? It is even more challenging again when we find that the Hebrew word is *elohim*. As you know, the name Elohim is one of the names of God, the first name that God uses to introduces Himself to us with, in Genesis 1:1, and it occurs 2,570 times in the Bible.

God's name, Elohim, is used 35 times in Genesis 1:1 to 2:4, revealing God's creative and governing power. He created this vast universe by His spoken word. Nathan Stone writes: "It is most appropriate that by this name God should reveal Himself—bringing cosmos out of chaos, light of darkness, habitation out of desolation, and life in His image.*"

Because we are created in His image, we also have the ability to create. God has put into our mouths the power of the spoken word. We can minister life or death by our tongue (Proverbs 18:21). God wants us (and each new babe that is born) to create and speak for His kingdom and His glory. He wants the godly offspring to fill the earth with His words, His truth, and His character.

The name of Elohim also reveals God as a covenant-keeping God. There are many Scriptures revealing this, but here are a few.

Genesis 17:7 says, *"I will establish **my covenant** between me and thee and thy seed after thee in their generations for an everlasting covenant, to be a God (Elohim) unto thee, and to thy seed after thee."*

Genesis 9:15-17 says, *"And I will remember **my covenant** . . . And the bow shall be in the cloud; and I will look upon it, that I may remember the **everlasting covenant** between God and every living creature. . ."*

On Joseph's deathbed he said, *"God will surely visit you, and bring you out of this land unto the land which **he sware** to Abraham, to Isaac, and to Jacob"* (Genesis 50:24).

When Solomon dedicated the temple he prayed, *"There is no God like thee, in heaven above, or on earth beneath, who keepest covenant and mercy with thy servants that walk before thee with all their heart"* (1 Kings 8:23).

Because Elohim is a covenant-keeping God, He wants us to also manifest covenant-keeping. This is how we reveal the image of Elohim. He wants each godly offspring to be a covenant-keeper. It is interesting that God talks about the godly seed coming forth in the context of a covenant-keeping marriage. Malachi 2:14 (RSV) says, *"The Lord was witness to the covenant between you and the wife of your youth, to whom you have been faithless, though she is your companion and your wife by covenant."*

It is not having lots of children that will solve the world's problems. It is having godly children who will impact the nations for God. May God enable us to welcome the godly seed and train them to truly reveal the character of Elohim. There is no career anywhere that can compare with the enormity and power of this vision.

* Nathan J. Stone, Names of God (Moody Press, 1944).

PRAYER:

"Dear Father God, please help me to be a faithful covenant-keeper and to train my children to also be covenant-keepers. Amen."

AFFIRMATION:

I have the awesome privilege to raise the "seed of God."

77

The Creeping Mold
Part 1

"It seems to me there is as it were a plague in the house" (LEVITICUS 14:35). READ THE WHOLE PASSAGE IN LEVITICUS 14:33-57.

Can plagues come to houses as well as people? Yes, and not only in ancient times, but in our modern society as well.

We have friends who had to move out of their home because of a creeping mold that began to take over. Their washing machine overflowed through faulty installation. They cleaned it up, yet silently the mold grew. After a few weeks, members of the family experienced rashes, nose bleeds, and bad headaches. They called in the experts, who ordered them to leave their home immediately.

Worse than molds that can infect your walls are leprous plagues that eat into the relationships of the home-dwellers—plagues that contaminate the joy and harmony of the home. They are the creeping molds of arguing, dissension, resentment, anger, bitterness, hate, jealousy, unforgiveness, the "silent treatment" and non-communication, grumbling and complaining, impurity and adultery, pornography, and the invasion of the worldly spirit through TV and worldy literature and music.

What should we do when these plagues creep into our relationships? We must deal with them immediately or they will destroy the home. We cannot let the plague continue. We have to be serious about them. No wonder Ephesians 4:26 enjoins us to *"let not the sun go down upon your wrath."*

Life is not perfect. Difficult situations can arise in our marriage relationship and in dealing with our children. But, if we get mad or angry, we must not hold the grudge! We have to exterminate it immediately, at least before we go to sleep for the night! Isn't it wonderful that God has an answer for every challenge we face in our daily lives?

Natural molds, of which there are many variations, can develop within 24-48 hours from standing water if not thoroughly dried in that time. Very soon they multiply, and through the ventilation system put millions of spores into the air. Every spore has a toxin that produces poison. Just as it is in wood and brick, so it is in our daily relationships. We must deal with the infection before it spreads and causes more havoc. Sin is never stagnant; it always spreads.

1. TEAR OUT THE STONES

Even back in the Old Testament, God gives us the plan on how to deal with these plagues in our homes. Leviticus 14:40 tells us that we must *"tear out the stones with the plague in them and throw them away."*

2. THOROUGHLY SCRAPE

That's not all! Next, they had to "*thoroughly scrape*" all around to make sure every bit of the infection was eradicated (verse 41). Scraping? Oh, this hurts, doesn't it? It hurts our putrid pride. Even the noise of it grates on our nerves. But this is how we have to deal with this *"spreading mildew."* We have to scrape it clean, no matter how much is uncovered and leaves us bare and exposed. We have to humble ourselves and give up our own way. We cannot leave one tiny spore of contamination or it will grow again. I know this is hard, but there is no other way! It's the only way to save your marriage and home from destruction.

3. FILL UP THE EMPTY HOLE

But, we haven't finished yet. Once we have scraped every bit of the plague away, we then have to *"take **other** stones, and put them in the place of those stones*" (verse 42). We can't leave the space empty or more "wicked spirits" will fill the home (Luke 11:24-26). By God's power and grace, we must fill up the gap with "other" stones—stones of humility, meekness, forgiveness, love, blessing, kindness, longsuffering, and tolerance. These "other" stones will heal strained relationships. They will mend broken relationships. They will restore hurting marriages.

Do you have a plague eating away at your marriage relationship or in your home? God has given you the answer to eradicate it. Obey His principles and you will find healing and blessing.

PRAYER:

"Dear Father God, I confess my sin before you now (name it before the Lord). I repent of it. I lay down my pride and stubbornness at the foot of the cross and leave it there. Please give me strength to pull out all the infection and scrape it completely clean. Fill me with your Holy Spirit. Fill me to overflowing that I will overflow and pour into my home the beautiful stones of love, meekness, and forbearance. I thank you, Lord, for showing me the way. Amen."

AFFIRMATION:

"The dearest idol I have known,
Whate'er that idol be—
Help me to tear it from Thy throne
And worship only Thee."
~ William Cowper

78

The Cleansing
Part 2

"And he shall take the cedar wood, and the hyssop, and the scarlet, and the living bird, and dip them in the blood of the slain bird, and in the running water, and sprinkle the house seven times; and he shall cleanse the house with the blood of the bird, and with the running water"
(Leviticus 14:51, 52).

Yesterday we learned the principles of how to eradicate an infectious plague from our homes. Once we have destroyed these creeping molds, we must then receive by faith the cleansing of the blood of Jesus. Our homes must be cleansed by the power of the blood of Jesus and the "running water" of the living Word of God. These are the two most powerful cleansing agents in the world. We need them in our hearts. We need them in our homes. They bring salvation, healing, protection, and deliverance. Through them we conquer the enemy! Revelations 12:11 says, *"They overcame him by the blood of the Lamb and by the word of their testimony."*

THE BLOOD AND THE WORD

If you have been going through a purging in your home, make sure you plead the precious blood of Jesus over every member and every room in your home. Honor the blood of Jesus in your home. Sing songs and hymns about the blood of Jesus. The blood of Jesus is your only access into the presence of God.

And don't forget the cleansing water of God's Word. Speak it out loud in your home. Read it personally. Read it together as a family when you sit at your family meal table. Memorize Scriptures and confess them in every situation. The blood and the Word of God will keep your home washed clean (John 15:3; 2 Corinthians 7:1; and Ephesians 5:26). They will deter all future contaminating molds that would try to take over your home again.

However, you cannot use the precious blood of Jesus flippantly. It is holy. It will not cover unconfessed sin. It will not cover unrepentant anger, maliciousness, uncleanness, adultery, or any other contamination. Leviticus 14:33-53 tells us that the house could not be cleansed until the leprosy was totally scraped out. However, once we have confessed, repented, and dealt with the sin, we can receive total healing through the blood of Christ.

TWO BIRDS AND TWO GOATS

After the home was healed, the priest had to take two birds. The first one he killed and the blood was shed. He then dipped the living bird, plus the cedar wood, the hyssop branch, and scarlet in the blood of the slain bird and sprinkled the house seven times. After this, he took the living bird (that had been dipped in the blood) outside the city and let it go into the open fields.

Was this just for fun? No, everything that God ordained in the old covenant has a type for us today. It was written for our learning and admonition.

Letting the bird fly away is similar to what happened on the Day of Atonement, which you can read about in Leviticus 16. On that day, God commanded them to bring two goats to the door of the tabernacle and cast lots. One received the Lord's lot and the other the lot of the scapegoat. The Lord's goat was slain and Aaron took the blood of this goat into the Holy of Holies and sprinkled it seven times upon the mercy seat to atone for the sins of the people.

By the way, do you know how many times the High Priest went into the Holy of Holies on the Day of Atonement? It was three times. First of all, he went in wearing his linen clothes (speaking of the righteousness of Christ) and carrying a censer of burning coals in his right hand and fragrant incense in his left. The incense filled the Most Holy Place and covered the Mercy Seat to protect Aaron in the holy presence of God. He then returned for the blood from the bullock, which he sprinkled on the Mercy Seat to atone for his own sins and the sins of his own household. He then entered the third time with the blood of the goat to atone for the sins of the nation.

After this he came forth, laid both his hands upon the scapegoat, confessed over it all the sins of the children of Israel, and then like the bird that was let go, the goat was sent away. God commanded in Leviticus 16:21, 22 to *"send it away into the wilderness by the hand of a suitable man . . . to an uninhabited land, and he shall release the goat in the wilderness."*

This goat represents the efficacy of the blood of Jesus in taking our sins away. This goat was taken into an uninhabited wilderness and lost, never to be seen or heard of again! This is what the power of Jesus does with our sins. He takes them out of sight! Because Jesus bore our sins upon His own body, we go free, like the bird that flew into the open fields. Isn't that amazing?

CEDARS ARE RESISTANT

The cedar, hyssop, and scarlet were also used in the cleansing. Scarlet represents the blood of Jesus. The hyssop was used to sprinkle blood on the home (as they also did at the time of Passover, Exodus 12:22). What about the cedar? The cedars of Lebanon are strong, firmly rooted, evergreen trees. The wood is reddish color and they are fragrant. Most interesting of all, insects will not attack them! When you are cleansed by the blood of Jesus, and live by faith under the covering of His blood, the insects of evil will not be able to eat into your home. Instead, you will emanate the sweet fragrance of Jesus to your husband and children.

PRAYER:

"Dear heavenly Father, I thank you for the power of the blood of Jesus and the power of your living Word to cleanse my heart and home. I thank you that your blood avails for me in every circumstance. I thank you in Jesus' name. Amen."

AFFIRMATION:

"Precious blood, by this we conquer
In the fiercest fight,
Sin and Satan overcoming
By its might."
~ Frances Ridley Havergal

79

The Forgiving
Part 3

"The blood of Jesus Christ his Son cleanses us from all sin . . . If we confess our sins, he is faithful and just to forgive us our sins, and to cleanse us from all unrighteousness"
(1 JOHN 1:7, 9).

Are you tormented with guilt? Is there some sin in your life you feel God can't forgive? Or, perhaps you can't even forgive yourself? I want to remind you that there is no sin that God cannot forgive. Jesus shed His powerful, precious, pure blood to atone for all sin. He is the Scapegoat who bore all your iniquities so you could go free (Leviticus 16:22). Not some sins, but all of them. There is nothing too wicked for the blood of Jesus. His life-giving blood has power to wash away all sin.

I think God must have known we would have trouble believing this truth. Therefore, He gives us different pictures in the Bible to show us how the blood of Jesus completely eradicates our sins when we repent and confess it to Him. Shall we look at what happens to them? They are . . .

WASHED CLEAN!

Revelation 1:5 says, *"Unto Him that loved us, and washed us from our sins in his own blood."* Read also 1 Corinthians 6:11 and Titus 3:5.

WHITE AS SNOW!

Isaiah 1:18 says, *"Come now, and let us reason together, saith the Lord; though your sins be as scarlet, they shall be as white as snow; though they be red like crimson, they shall be as wool."*

Psalm 51:7 says, *"Purge me with hyssop . . . and I shall be whiter than snow."* Although this Scripture does not mention the blood, it refers to it because it was the hyssop that was used to sprinkle the blood (Revelation

7:13, 14).

CLEANSED!

1 John 1:7 says, *"The blood of Jesus Christ his Son cleanses us from all sin."* Read also Jeremiah 33:8 and Hebrews 9:14. In the New Testament, the Greek word for "cleansed" and "purged" is the same. It means "to purify from the pollution and guilt of sin."

PARDONED!

Micah 7:18 says, *"Who is a God like unto thee, who pardons iniquity, and passes by the transgression of the remnant of his heritage? He retains not his anger forever, because he delights in mercy."*

FORGIVEN!

Ephesians 1:7 says, *"In Him we have redemption through His blood, the forgiveness of sins, according to the riches of His grace."* Read also Colossians 1:14.

TAKEN AWAY!

When John the Baptist saw Jesus, He called out, *"Behold the Lamb of God who takes away the sin of the world"* (John 1:29). God not only forgives, but He takes our sins away, out of sight.

We have already looked at two examples—the bird that flew away into the open fields, and the scapegoat that was taken into an uninhabited wilderness. Other translations of the Bible use different descriptions such as *"a land of separation," "a desolate region," "a land where no one lives," "a solitary land," "a barren waste,"* and *"an isolated place."* They are taken away where we can't see them any more—into oblivion. The Hebrew word for scapegoat is *azazel* and means "an entire and utter removal" (Leviticus 16:22).

Don't keep looking at your sin and groveling over it. God has taken it out of sight, so why try to retrieve it back again? It is out of sight, beyond the track of man, unseen and forgotten. Because Jesus paid your price, you are now as free as a bird (Romans 11:27).

AS FAR AS THE EAST IS FROM THE WEST!

Psalm 103:12 says, *"As far as the east is from the west, so far has he removed our transgressions from us."* As we move farther and farther to the west, the horizon keeps shifting. We never come to the end. It's the same if we go east. Our sins have been taken so far away that we cannot find the end.

BEHIND GOD'S BACK!

Isaiah 38:17 says, "*You have cast all my sins behind your back.*" God can't see them when they are behind His back.

REMEMBERED NO MORE!

Jeremiah 31:34 says, "*I will forgive their iniquity, and I will remember their sin no more.*" Read also Isaiah 43:25 and Hebrews 10:17. God remembers everything, except our sins. One writer says, "Faith transfers them; Christ removes them; God forgets them."

BLOTTED OUT!

Isaiah 44:22 says, "*I have blotted out, like a thick cloud, your transgressions, and like a cloud, your sins.*" Read also Isaiah 43:25.

LOST! CAN'T BE FOUND!

Jeremiah 50:20 says, "*In those days, and in that time, saith the Lord, the iniquity of Israel shall be sought for, and there shall be none; and the sins of Judah, and they shall not be found.*" Once they are under the blood of Jesus, there is no way of finding them again. No matter who looks for them, or how long they look, they will never find them. They are lost forever!

BURIED IN THE DEPTHS OF THE SEA!

Micah 7:19 says, "*You will cast all our sins into the depths of the sea.*" They have been buried too deep to recover.

Oh the power of the blood of Jesus! It is too wonderful. By faith, live in the blessings of His precious blood that was shed for you.

PRAYER:

"Dear precious Jesus, thank you so much for your blood that you shed for my sins. I thank you for the power of your blood that totally cleanses me from all sin and all guilt. Help me to have a repentant heart and to daily confess the sins that tarnish my heart. I want to keep washed clean, pure, and white by the power of your blood. Thank you in Jesus' name. Amen."

AFFIRMATION:

"I hear the accuser roar
Of ills that I have done,
I know them well and thousands more—
Jehovah findeth none!"
~ Samuel Grandy

80

The Covering
Part 4

"When I see the blood, I will pass over you"
(Exodus 12:13).

It is imperative that we live under the covering of the blood of Jesus. The word for "atonement" in the Hebrew is *kaphar* and it means "to cover." It is only blood that can cover sins. Under the old covenant, they shed the blood of animals. Now, it is the blood of Jesus Christ, the spotless Son of God that covers our sins.

In the old covenant, not only was the blood sprinkled on the people, but also the tabernacle, and their homes. The writer of Hebrews reminds us of this in Hebrews 9:18-22: *"Moses . . . took the blood of calves and of goats, with water, and scarlet wool, and hyssop, and sprinkled both the book, and all the people, saying, This is the blood of the testament which God has enjoined unto you. Moreover he sprinkled with blood both the tabernacle, and all the vessels of the ministry."* Do you notice? He sprinkled the people, and the tabernacle, which was God's house, the place where God dwelt between the cherubims in the Holy of Holies!

God gives us another picture in Exodus 26:14 where He told Moses to *"make a covering for the tent of rams' skins dyed red."* They were commanded to die sheepskins red, which is a picture of the blood, and cover the tabernacle with them. Over this they had to place another covering of badgers' skins, which protected the red sheepskins from being bleached by the sun.

If God wanted His dwelling sprinkled with blood, shouldn't we need it over our dwellings? If God wanted a covering of red sheepskins, which was a type of the blood, over His tabernacle, shouldn't it also be important for us?

We no longer sprinkle literal blood, but by faith, we sprinkle the blood of Jesus Christ (which continually avails for us today) over our homes. The blood of Jesus delivers us and protects us. We all know the story of Passover where they had to kill a lamb and apply the blood to the two doorposts and the lintel above the door. God said, "*The blood shall be to you for a token upon the houses where you are: and when I see the blood, I will pass over you . . . and will not suffer the destroyer to come in unto your houses to smite you*" (Exodus 12:13, 22, 23).

The blood was a sign to the Destroyer that the home was protected by the power of God. The Avenger could not get through the power of the blood. The enemy hates the blood. He cannot break through the power of the blood of Jesus. It is our weapon against Satan in our personal lives. It is our protection over our homes.

Do you remember the story of Rahab? What protected her home from being destroyed when every other house was desecrated? It was the token of the blood! The spies told Rahab to bind a line of scarlet thread in the window, and she and all that were in her home would be spared. God miraculously caused the walls of Jericho to crumble, including all the homes that were built into the wall. But not Rahab's. Her home was left standing and she and all her family were rescued. Read the story in Joshua chapters 2 and 6.

Live under the protection of the blood. By faith, daily sprinkle the blood of Jesus over your own life, the lives of each member of your family, and your home.

PRAYER:

"Dear Father, thank you for the precious blood of Jesus Christ that was poured forth on the cross for me. I thank you that the blood of Jesus is now sprinkled on the mercy seat in the heavenly tabernacle and is miraculously available for me today. By faith, I sprinkle the blood of Jesus Christ over my home, my husband, and each one of our children. Amen."

AFFIRMATION:

"There is a fountain filled with blood
Drawn from Emmanuel's veins;
And sinners, plunged beneath that flood,
Lose all their guilty stains."
~ William Cowper

81

Your Lot in Life

"Cast thy burden upon the Lord, and he shall sustain thee: he shall never suffer the righteous to be moved" (Psalm 55:22).

I was surprised to discover that the word "burden" in the above Scripture is not exactly what I had previously thought—worries, cares, and heartaches. It is the Hebrew word *yhab* which means, "gift, what is given by Providence, that which has been assigned to you, your lot in life."

Your lot in life—your circumstances, your marriage, your lot in your home, and even your hardships—may not be what you had planned! But, it is the lot that has been given to you. Instead of resisting your lot in life, why not give it back to the Lord and trust Him to do His work in you? He has given you your circumstances to refine you as gold, to change you into the image of His dear Son, to make you the beautiful person that He has destined you to be, and to prepare you for His eternal kingdom.

If you were to choose your own way, I know you would choose the easy road. That's what most of us are inclined to do, aren't we? But the easy road will never lead you closer to the Lord, it will never deepen your understanding of the ways of God, and it will never allow you to be changed into the image of Christ.

This Scripture does not tell you to wallow in your miserable lot. It does not tell you to spoil your days with self-pity. Instead, it tells you to throw your lot upon the Lord. When you do, He will not only carry it for you, but He will carry you, too. He has promised to sustain you in the lot He has given to you.

The word "cast" in the Hebrew means "to throw away, to hurl, an adventure." I like the sound of "adventure," don't you? The dictionary meaning of "adventure" is "a hazardous or exciting experience, a bold and difficult undertaking, encountering risks, somewhat dangerous." This gets exciting, doesn't it?

When you try to order your own life and make it work the way you want it to, you miss out on all God has planned for you. When you cast your lot upon the Lord, it will be an adventure! You will face challenges. You will have to overcome many obstacles. You may even face hardship and suffering. But this is the adventure of life. It prepares you for the eternal world. 2 Corinthians 4:17, 18 says: *"For our light affliction, which is but for a moment, is working for us a far more exceeding and eternal weight of glory, while we do not look at the things which are seen, but at the things which are not seen. For the things which are seen are temporary, but the things which are not seen are eternal."*

Many try to run from their circumstances, from their responsibilities in the home, or even their marriage. Imagine standing at the Judgment Seat of Christ and God says to you, "Why did you run from your situation? I wanted it to lead you closer to me, to work my character into you, and change you into my image."

One writer says, "What God lays upon you, lay it upon the Lord."

Are you ready for an adventure?

PRAYER:

"I thank you, Father, that you know far better than I do what is best for me. I trust my life and my circumstances to you and know that you will sustain me. Thank you, Father. Amen."

AFFIRMATION:

I am ready for any adventure that God has planned for me.

82

You Don't Have to Stay Dry

"I give waters in the wilderness, and rivers in the desert, to give drink to my people, my chosen" (Isaiah 43:20).

Are you going through a desert place in your life? Do you feel dry, empty, and with nothing left to give? Don't despair, dear one. You are in the very place for God to pour into your life.

The children of Israel experienced the desert, not just for a day, but for 40 years! And they didn't just land there. God led them into the wilderness to test them and to see what was in their hearts (Deuteronomy 8:2). But, even in the desert wilderness, when there was no sign of water, when they thought God had deserted them, and when they were ready to go back to Egypt, God was still with them. He did not let them thirst. He wanted to show His people that they couldn't do it without totally relying upon Him.

We can't walk through the wilderness of this earth on our own resources either. They don't last. They run out quickly. What joy to know that in the heart of our everlasting Father are inexhaustible wells that never run dry.

Our love wanes. We think we have no love left, but there is a well of love that never runs dry.

Our patience dries up quickly. We become frustrated and quick-tempered, but there is a well of long-suffering that is inexhaustible.

Our joy runs out. We become cranky and irritable, but there is a well of joy, a well of victory, and a well of salvation that is everlasting.

Draw from these wells. Drink deeply. There is everything you need in the heart of the Father. Isaiah 12:3 says, *"Therefore with joy shall ye draw water from the wells of salvation."*

When we came out to the land where we now live, we had to drill a well. They drilled to more than 400 feet and still found no water! And every foot cost money. We were not very happy. We sought advice from the geological experts and started drilling another well. They drilled to 250 feet and still no water! I have never seen my husband depressed in his whole life until this moment! The next morning the drillers came to take away their equipment, but first checked the second well. Praise the Lord. We had water. We rejoiced. They put down the pump and we thought we were set. We enjoyed water for about three weeks until one day no water came from the tap!

What were we to do? How could we live without water? My husband threw a stone down the first well and could hear some water that had gathered. In faith he asked the drillers to put the pump down that well. They resisted, saying it was useless, but grumblingly did what he asked. My father arrived from New Zealand at that time and prayed over the well. God did a miracle and we continued to receive water from this well for three years, until we eventually found another source from a spring about a mile away. However, it was not an overabundant supply, and we had to conserve our water very carefully.

We had a survival well, but God has a bottomless well. You can draw until you overflow. You can drink until you are satiated. God does not give you a trickle of water. He pours it out. He promises in Isaiah 44:3, *"I will pour water upon him that is thirsty, and floods upon the dry ground: I will pour my spirit upon thy seed, and my blessing upon thine offspring."*

God gushed the waters out for His people. *"And they thirsted not when he led them through the deserts: he caused the waters to flow out of the rock for them, he cleaved the rock also, and the waters gushed out"* (Isaiah 48:21). And, *"He opened the rock, and the waters gushed out; they ran in the dry places like a river"* (Psalm 105:41).

There is no excuse to stay dry and empty. Draw from the never-ending wells that are daily available to you.

PRAYER:

"Dear Father, I run out of my resources so quickly, but I thank you that I can draw from your inexhaustible resources. I drink from your living well today. I draw from your unlimited wells of love, peace, strength, and joy. Amen."

AFFIRMATION:

I am drawing from God's inexhaustible well that never runs dry!

83

Training Children to Speak
Part 1

"And now, Lord, behold their threatenings; and grant unto thy servants, that will all boldness they may speak thy word"
(ACTS 4:29).

Many times we forget the purpose of our parenting, don't we? We plod along from day to day with what has to be done and we don't see the future picture. It is good to come back to God's Word and be reminded of what we are supposed to be doing.

God calls our children "arrows," which is in the context of war (Psalm 127:4, 5). This life is a battle between the kingdom of God and the kingdom of Satan. We are raising our children to be warriors for God's kingdom, to know how to face the battle, and to stand strong for God.

However, Psalm 127:5 says that we are to train our children to speak! Have you noticed that before? Check out the Scripture again. We are to raise children who will speak with the enemies in the gates. In Bible times, the gates of the city were more than an entranceway. They were the busiest place in the city. It was here that the elders sat to rule and direct the affairs of the city. It was here the judges and officers judged the daily matters of the people. It was at the gates the soldiers stood sentinel to guard and protect the city.

And this is where God wants our children to speak—in the important places of the city, the state, and the nation. He wants us to raise children who will be able to proclaim His truth in the gates—in the high places where decisions and laws are made. We are living in an era where *"Justice is turned back, and righteousness stands afar off; for truth is fallen in the street and equity cannot enter"* (Isaiah 59:14). In this hour of history, we need children who know more than a few Sunday school stories. We need to raise children who know and understand God's truth, who have discernment, and know how to execute justice. We need to raise children who are not afraid to speak God's truth, even in the face of opposition and persecution. The psalmist said, *"I will speak of thy testimonies also before kings, and will not be ashamed"* (Psalm 119:46). I love the Knox translation, which says, *"Fearlessly will I talk of thy decrees in the presence of kings, and be never abashed."*

Truth is not always easy to make known. People often compromise the truth because they are scared of the repercussions. But we are not raising wimps, we are raising warriors. We are raising children who are not afraid to face the enemy. C. T. Studd, the great missionary, prayed for real soldiers, not "chocolate soldiers." He wrote. . .

"Lord, send us lion-hearted men
With good courageous habits,
Who ne'er will run from the devil's gun
Like hares and bunny rabbits!"

Some translations of Psalm 127:5 say, *"Contend with the enemies in the gate."* Our "arrows" must know how to contend for their faith and the truth.

"How do we train our children to speak?" you may ask. Perhaps Apologetics should be part of every homeschooling curriculum. Our children must learn how to give an answer for the faith that is in them (1 Peter 3:15). Of course, it will be difficult to prepare children to be truth-bearers if we are not heralding the truth ourselves. We must not be afraid to speak God's eternal truths, even when they are counter-culture. The ideologies of our society regarding family are not working. There is so much heartache in marriages and family life. It is only God's way, although different to man's way, that is the way to blessing. We can speak with confidence for we know the way that works!

We should be like the apostle Paul, who spoke boldly in the synagogue and in the marketplace, testifying, reasoning, disputing, and persuading people in the truth. The psalmist and Paul both confessed, *"I believed, therefore have I spoken"* (Psalm 116:10 and 2 Corinthians 4:13). What do you believe? That's what you'll speak about. What are you teaching your children to believe? What is the passion of their hearts? That's what they'll speak about. Not clichés, but convictions!

Never forget—silence is surrender, but speaking the truth can change the culture of the nation.

Raise your children to be warriors for the Lord. Raise them to know and speak the truth—anointed, not-giving-in, not-backing-down words—in the marketplace and in high places.

PRAYER:

"Great God of the universe, please lift my vision for parenting my children. Help me to train them to know and understand the truth and be filled with zeal and boldness to speak your truth to all they meet. Help me to also be a truthbearer wherever I go and to never be ashamed of your timeless truths. Amen."

AFFIRMATION:

I am raising children to be truthbearers.

FURTHER STUDY:

Go to page 280.

84

Training Children to Speak
Part 2

"They were all filled with the Holy Ghost,
and they spake the word of God with boldness"
(ACTS 4:31).

The word "utterance" is the Greek word *logos*. It is also translated "speech" but means "the expression of thought." How wonderful that God enriches us in all speech and expression of His thoughts. God wants His thoughts and His ways made known and He uses us to do it. We must keep close to the Lord, listen obediently to Him, and fill our hearts with His Word. As we do, He will anoint us to be His oracle. Some will speak to individuals, some to people in high places, some to nations. But we must be available at all times to make God's truth known. If we don't, deception increases. Silence is surrender!

Paul encourages us in 2 Corinthians 8:7 to *"abound"* in speech. The word "abound" means "to superabound, to be in excess, to excel, to be over the top." That doesn't sound like being reticent, does it?

How do we prepare our children to speak the truth boldly? We must show by our own example and give them opportunity. Here are a few pointers to think about.

SPEAK DISTINCTLY

It is important to teach children to speak clearly and articulately from the time they learn to talk. I'll admit I am a little deaf and getting a bit older, but many times I cannot understand what some young people are saying. They talk so quickly and indistinctly that I don't know what they are talking about. I say, "I beg your pardon," and they still mumble away. I think we should teach children that it is selfish to speak so quickly that people have to ask them to repeat what they are saying.

How will they speak with those in high places if they cannot speak clearly?

BIRTHDAY SPEECHES

When our children were growing up, we always had birthday speeches. Each one in the family, and those who were invited, had to give a speech about the birthday person, expressing all the good things about them—their talents, character, and what they meant to them. The birthday person would be filled with encouragement, enough to last them a year! At the same time, our children learned to express themselves as they gave these speeches.

The children have now passed this tradition on to their own children. At each birthday among the grandchildren, they still do the same thing. The birthday child sits on a special chair while all the aunties, uncles, and cousins (and there are many of them) give a speech to this child. They sit with a big smile on their face and drink it all in. At the same time, the children, even the little ones, learn to give speeches.

TABLE DISCUSSIONS

I believe the table is a place to communicate. The family meal table can be boring or it can be full of life. It is also a place where we can increase in knowledge. One night (with twelve of us around the table), we got into a political discussion that continued so long that I burned my lovely sourdough bread in the oven! It cooked for two hours instead of one! In fact, I think that if my husband had not insisted we eventually stop for our Bible reading and prayer, we would have still been discussing until midnight.

When raising our children, my husband or I would either ask a question or bring a subject to the table to discuss. We still continue this today. I find that it is not enough to prepare the food for the meal; we need to prepare food for discussion, too. If you don't come with anything prepared, nothing happens, and often the conversation disintegrates. I like to think of new things to talk about at our table. I have also compiled a list so that if my mind goes blank when we sit down to the meal table, I can refer to the list.

When the children were little, we would ask basic questions such as, "What was the most interesting thing you did today?" or "What was something new you learned today?" Every person is expected to share, from oldest to youngest, including mom and dad. When each child speaks, all eyes are on them. They learn to speak and become more confident the more they do it.

As the children got older, we would bring subjects to discuss—biblical, spiritual, political, or general knowledge. Each child would be expected to share their views. This is a wonderful opportunity for them to learn to express their thoughts and articulate clearly.

Quite frequently I ask the girls living in our home to bring something to the table to read to us—a poem, a passage from a book they are currently reading, or a powerful quote. Recently I asked each one to share the book that has impacted their life the most, and why. We learned a lot that night and everyone wanted to read the book each one shared about. The other night I asked them to come prepared to speak about some person who has impacted this world. Some of the people we learned about were Annie Oakley, C. T. Studd, Eliezer Ben Yehuda, and John Newton. It keeps the table conversation lively and everyone learns to speak about something worthwhile.

PRAYER:

"Father God, please help me to remember that 'silence is surrender.' Help me not to be afraid to speak your truth in any situation, even if it is politically incorrect. Amen."

AFFIRMATION:

We are a family that proclaims God's truth.

85

Training Children to Speak
Part 3

"But ye shall receive power, after that the Holy Ghost is come upon you: and you shall be witnesses unto me both in Jerusalem, and in all Judea, and in Samaria, and unto the uttermost part of the earth"
(ACTS 1:8).

The word "witness" is *martus,* which means "one who knows or one who bears record to what he has seen or heard." We can't be a witness for the Lord unless we know what we are talking about. We must know His truth to communicate it. The English word "martyr" is derived from this word because he bears witness by his death. In many countries of the world believers are martyred for witnessing to the truth. In fact, 100,000 are martyred every year for their faith. A true witness will not back down in the face of persecution.

We continue to look at more ways to prepare our children to speak.

ASK QUESTIONS

When a child says, "God is the biggest God in the world!" ask another question. "Why do you think that?" or "How do you know that?" It will cause them to think a little more and give you an opportunity to add another precept of truth. Remember, this is not a lecture, just a question or two as they go their merry way. You can do this with many statements they make.

POEM NIGHTS/MEMORY VERSES

Every so often we have Poem Night with all the grandchildren. Each one has to memorize a poem and recite it to the audience of uncles, aunts, cousins, and grandparents. It is good practice for speaking and they grow more confident each time. You can do the same thing with Scripture memory verses. You may not have the audience on hand that we have, but you could do it by gathering a few families together.

You can also give opportunity for the children to read poems. Give each child a turn to bring a poem to the family meal table where they read it and share why they like this particular poem. Do this with Scriptures, too. Give each one a turn to bring a Scripture to the table, which they read and expound upon.

SPEECH NIGHTS

As we raised our children, we frequently enjoyed Speech Nights. Sometimes they had to prepare a speech on a given subject with time to study and prepare. Other times we wrote different subjects on paper and put them in a hat. After taking a subject from the hat, the children would have to give an impromptu three-minute speech on that subject.

We also did this with the Scriptures. Sometimes they had to prepare a talk on a certain Scripture or passage; other times we would put the Scripture in the hat and they would have to give an impromptu exhortation on it.

PREACHING NIGHTS

Our children were mostly in their teens when we lived on the Gold Coast of Australia. They loved to preach in the open air mall in Surfers Paradise. To prepare for this they had practice preaching nights where our children and their friends would practice. They would preach for a few minutes and then the next one would carry on. And this is how they did it in the open air mall. One would preach and, before they ran out of what to say, the next one would run out and continue the preaching. They could keep going like this for an hour or more and many crowded around to hear the gospel.

THE APOSTLES' CREED AND CATECHISMS

A good way to confess your faith is to recite the Apostles' Creed or other Scripture creeds. You could choose how often you would like to do this as a family (most probably at Family Devotions at the meal table). Perhaps once a week would be a good idea. You can also use catechisms where you ask questions and the children learn to recite the answers. Google to choose the ones you would like to use.

SHARING AT CHURCH OR HOME MEETINGS

Not many have this opportunity, although this was the premise of the early church. 1 Corinthians 14:26 says, *"How is it then, brethren, when ye come together, every one ofyou hath a psalm, hath a doctrine, hath a tongue, hath a revelation, hath an interpretation. Let all things be done unto edifying."* It is wonderful when young people, and even children, can share insights from the Word of God.

APOLOGETICS NIGHTS

Plan an Apologetics Night with your own family, or invite other families to join you. Prepare questions or subjects for your children to research, and come prepared to speak about or discuss.

Are you adequately training your children?

PRAYER:

"Lord, help me be to be constantly aware that I am preparing my children to speak for you and defend the faith. Amen."

AFFIRMATION:

I am a faith-defender and I am training my children to be the same.

86

Choice Young Men

"Our sons then are like plants, raised to full size in their youthful vigor" (Psalm 144:12, MLB).

What kind of young men does God want us to raise for Him? He wants our descendants to be mighty in the land.

THEY WERE CHAMPIONS!

These *"mighty"* offspring mentioned in Psalm 112:1, 2 are champions. The Hebrew word is *gibbor* meaning "valiant, warrior, champion." As we read through the books of Kings and Chronicles we see a picture of the kind of warriors they trained in Bible days. God hasn't lessened his standard for today, so let's see what they were like.

THEY WERE SKILLFUL!

1 Chronicles 5:18 says, *"The sons of Reuben, and the Gadites, and half the tribe of Manasseh, of valiant men, men able to bear buckler and sword, and to shoot with bow, and skillful in war, were four and forty thousand seven hundred and threescore, that went out to the war."*

The word "skillful" in war is *lamad*. It means to be "educated, taught, and trained." We cannot live with our heads in the sand, dear mother. We are in a battle. We are training our children for war. We must train them to fight against the enemy of their souls. We must train them to be warriors for God.

THEY WERE VALIANT!

1 Chronicles 7:2 says, *"The sons of Tola . . . were valiant men of might in their generations."*

This phrase *"in their generations"* is repeated over and over again. They did not raise one or two valiant men. They raised generations of them. This is what God is looking for—a whole generation of warriors who know how to overcome the enemy and take territory for God.

Now, what does this word "valiant" mean that we read over and over again? It is the Hebrew word *chayil* that means "an army, virtue, valor, military strength, great forces, noble, and strong." Here are just a few examples.

"Mighty men of valor . . . fit to go out for war and battle" (1 Chronicles 7:11).

"Very able men for the work of the service of the house of God" (1 Chronicles 9:13).

"And of the Gadites there separated themselves unto David into the hold to the wilderness men of might, and men of war fit for the battle, that could handle shield and buckler, whose faces were like the faces of lions, and were as swift as the roes upon the mountains" (1 Chronicles 12: 8).

"Of the children of Simeon, mighty men of valor for the war" (1 Chronicles 12:25).

"Zadok, a young man mighty of valor" (1 Chronicles 12:28).

"Men of valor . . . in the service of the king" (1 Chronicles 26:30).

"Men of valor . . . for every matter pertaining to God, and affairs of the king" (1 Chronicles 26:32).

THEY WERE READY!

1 Chronicles 12:24 says, *"The children of Judah that bare shield and spear were six thousand and eight hundred, ready armed to the war."* When our children are of the age to go out into the world, we must make sure that they are ready! Ready to stand against the foe. Ready to battle the enemy.

THEY WERE EXPERT!

1 Chronicles 12:33-36 talks about young men who were "*expert in war.*" We are not training mediocre warriors. We are training them to be expert. This is a full-time job. We can't take it lightly. We are responsible to the Lord of hosts for the quality of His arrows.

THEY WERE CHOICE!

1 Chronicles 7:40 talks about the children of Asher: *"All these were the children of Asher, heads of their father's house, CHOICE and mighty men of valor . . . And the number throughout the genealogy of them that were apt to the war and to battle was twenty and six thousand men."*

This word "choice" is a very special word. It is the Hebrew word *barar* and means "singled out, chosen, proved, cleansed, purified, and polished." What a vision! There is nothing greater you could do in the whole of the universe than raise young men who are singled out by God and who are cleansed, purified, proved, and polished!

PRAYER:

"Oh God, thank you for reminding me that you have enlisted me in your employment to train your task force in this end-time hour. Save me from taking this mission lightly. Fill me with your wisdom, your anointing, and your power to accomplish this mighty task. Thank you, Lord. Amen."

AFFIRMATION:

I am training valiant warriors, not wimps.

87

Virtuous Daughters

"Here is my description of a truly happy land where Jehovah is God: Sons vigorous and tall as growing plants. Daughters of graceful beauty like the pillars of a palace wall"
(Psalm 144:12, TLB).

Yesterday, we talked about raising valiant sons who are sharpened, polished, and ready for God's army. But what about our daughters? How are we to raise them? Are they to be part of the army too?

When you think of raising your daughters, I am sure your mind goes to Proverbs 31:10: "*Who can find a virtuous woman, for her price is far above rubies.*" You want your sons to be valiant, but you want your daughters to be virtuous. But what does "virtuous" mean? I think you will be surprised to know that it is the Hebrew word *chayil*, exactly the same word that is translated "valiant" for our sons!

WE RAISE THEM TO BE STRONG

Our daughters are also part of God's army. He wants us to raise them to be strong in character. He wants them to grow up to be strong in faith, truth, godly convictions, submission, strong and unbending in their commitment to virtue and purity, and standing strong against all deceptions of the enemy.

Our daughters also need to be strong physically. It is interesting that this psalm likens our daughters to pillars. We know that pillars have to be strong enough to hold up and bear the weight of a building. A palace is not a small building; it is usually a very large construction and therefore needs especially strong pillars. You would think that God would have likened our sons to pillars, but no, it is our daughters. He wants them to be trained and prepared to be strong enough to bear the weight of raising a family. This is no easy task. They have to be prepared mentally, emotionally, and physically. I believe the reason many mothers do not enjoy motherhood today is because they come into motherhood mentally unprepared. They are trained for a career in the workforce rather than motherhood and, therefore, are not mentally and emotionally conditioned for it.

As a young woman I read that it was important to nutritionally prepare your body three years before conceiving a baby. I thought that was good advice at the time, but now I have changed my opinion. I believe that we should start preparing our daughters for future childbearing and the physical commitment of raising a family from the moment they are born. We start by nursing them at the breast, giving them the life-giving food that God wondrously provides for them. As we introduce new foods, we continue to give them life-giving whole foods so their bodies grow strong. No serious or intelligent mother should ever allow her children to drink pop and eat the devitalized junk food that is prevalent today.

One springtime, as I walked around the sheep with my father in New Zealand, he remarked, "The ewes are so healthy this year, we have no problems with lambing." I pricked up my ears. "Yes," he continued, "if the ewes are on good grass, we have no still births and do not have to help birthing the lambs." This is exactly the same with us. We are what we eat. If we raise our children on living foods, their bodies will grow strong. If they eat dead, refined foods, they could well have physical problems later during pregnancy and childbirth.

Many parents like to start a bank account for their children when they are born to set them up in life when they grow older. We should also start a health bank for our children. Pregnancy and childbirth can draw quite a big chunk from their health savings. If it has been built up over the years with healthy, life-giving foods, there will be plenty to draw on. When the health bank is low, pregnancy and childbirth can be more difficult. Our bodies were created by God to bear children. It is a natural process, but physical problems in this area reveal a low or nonexistent health bank.

WE RAISE THEM TO BE BEAUTIFUL

Pillars not only bear weight, but the pillars of a palace are beautiful. They are a feature. God wants us to not only raise strong daughters, but beautiful daughters. Beautiful in spirit, soul, and body. Daughters who walk and act gracefully. Daughters who embrace their femininity and maternalness. Daughters who care about keeping their bodies fit and healthy.

The King James Version uses the word "cornerstones" in this Scripture.

This is also a wonderful meaning. The cornerstone is the most important and prominent stone of a building. The rest of the building takes its direction from the cornerstone. Without the cornerstone the building would be totally out of alignment. As we train our daughters for future mothering, we are the pivot on which the home is built. We are indispensable to the building of a strong home and determining the character of the home.

PRAYER:

"Father God, the Originator of parenting, please give me your vision for my daughters. Help me to train them for the purposes that you have destined for them, rather than being pressured by our modern society. Give me wisdom as I polish them and prepare them to be beautiful pillars in their homes. Amen."

AFFIRMATION:

I am raising caring but courageous daughters; daughters who will not be afraid to stand against the deceptions of our modern society!

88

The Suckling Mother

"And he (Jesus) answered and said unto them, Have ye not read, that he which made them at the beginning made them male and female" (Matthew 19:4).

God created a male and a female. He didn't make two Adams. He didn't make two Eves. He created an Adam and an Eve.

The most common Greek word for "woman" in the New Testament is *gune,* which simply means "woman, wife." However, Jesus used a more specific word when He answered the Pharisees who asked him about divorce. He used the word *thelus,* which comes from the root word *thele*. The noun means "the nipple of a woman's breast from which a baby sucks to find sustenance and to thrive" and the verb means,"to suckle at the breast." In other words, Jesus described the female as a "suckling mother." "This is how God made them in the beginning," He reminded them. And God has not yet made a new model!

This word would not have been offensive to those listening to Jesus at that time. Nursing mothers were a natural part of the lifestyle. Unfortunately, today there are many women who would not like to hear Jesus describing them in such a way. To be a suckling mother seems degrading to a career woman. And yet, this is who God created us to be. When we embrace children and suckle them at the breast we fulfill our highest destiny. We live in the glory of our femaleness. We find our greatest beauty. And we wield a mighty power.

The mother who embraces life and suckles a babe at her breast is not wasting her time. She nourishes a child who bears the image of God—a child who will come forth from her home one day to bring God's love and salvation to many. Maybe this child will be a mighty voice to turn a nation to God. And she nurtures a child for everlasting eternity. It is still true that "The hand that rocks the cradle rules the world."

When a mother nurses her baby she produces prolactin, which is known as the "mothering hormone." The more the mother suckles the baby, the more prolactin she produces and, consequently, the more motherly she becomes. God has divinely endowed the female with a maternal instinct, but when she suckles her baby at the breast her maternalness increases. She lives more in the anointing of who God created her to be—to reveal the maternal character of God to her children and those around her.

Some mothers say, "I'm only interested in quality, not quantity" and so they limit their children so they can supposedly give more to the one or two they choose to have. This is a false conception. As her two children grow and go off to school, she is mothering less and less and looks to find fulfillment elsewhere, often going out to work and establishing herself in a career. And her children receive less of her time. Whereas, when a mother has another baby and suckles the babe at her breast, prolactin kicks in and the motherly hormones charge through her system again. Not only does her baby benefit from this loving hormone, but her whole family does as well. The love and nurturing spreads out to all her children. This is how God keeps the mother protecting and delighting in her children in the home.

God also uses this description of the female as a suckling mother in Romans 1:26: *"For this cause God gave them up unto vile affections: for even their women (thelus) did change the natural use into that which is against nature."* This is a very challenging Scripture to all females because it states that when a woman turns away from the natural function of how God created the female body to function, with a womb to conceive and nurture life and breasts to suckle this life, God gives them up to vile affections.

Isn't it amazing that we have become such a deceived generation that women do not want to be who God originally created them to be? Please understand, I am not talking about mothers who are not able to conceive children, or even those who are not physically able to breastfeed. We don't live in a perfect world, and not everyone's bodies are functioning as God originally intended. God looks at our heart and our intentions.

He wants us to turn toward Him in our hearts, not turn away from the way He created us.

PRAYER:

"Dear God, my Creator, please help me to be truly female as you designed me to be. Amen."

AFFIRMATION:

"As I hold this baby in my arms
I'm like a picture of you,
To nurture with your love is what
You made me to do."
~ Serene Allison (El Shaddai, Creator of the Lullaby)

89

Who Was She?
Part 1

"But I your servant have feared the Lord from my youth" (1 Kings 18:12).

Who was the mother of this young man? Who were these godly parents who raised a son to walk in righteousness in the midst of an evil society? Obadiah lived and worked in the courts of the palace of Ahab and Jezebel, a wicked king and an even more wicked queen. Israel was no longer a God-fearing society at this time. Instead they worshipped Baal and golden calves. But, in the midst of this godless Baal-worshipping society, these parents raised a God-fearing young man. How did they do it?

1. THEY RAISED HIM TO FEAR THE LORD

Obadiah feared the Lord from his youth. This is why we know he had a God-fearing mother, a mother who had a vision to raise godly sons in the midst of godlessness. I know that you often look at the evils in our society today and wonder how you can raise godly children. Be encouraged. You can do it. God is behind you and backing you all the way. Keep this vision before you. This is His purpose for your children. You do not raise them to keep them forever behind closed doors but to go out as lights into this dark world.

Obadiah not only feared the Lord from his youth, but 1 Kings 18:3 tells us that *"Obadiah feared the Lord **greatly**."* This was the testimony over his life. He didn't have this testimony in church. He had this testimony in the midst of wickedness and idolatry.

I have to confess that I have never been able to get up and give an "exciting" story about how I came to Jesus Christ. All I can testify is that I have known and walked with Him all my life. It only takes one minute to give this testimony, but I know it is the greatest testimony I can give. Let us pray, as we build godly generations, that this will be the confession of all our children and grandchildren.

Timothy had this testimony. From a child he was taught the Holy Scriptures from his God-fearing mother, even though his father may not have been a believer. Paul, the apostle, acknowledges that Timothy's strong and genuine faith, which he walked in as an adult, was because of the input of his mother, Eunice, and his grandmother, Lois (2 Timothy 1:5 and 2 Timothy 3:15).

Samuel had this testimony. When Samuel was addressing the children of Israel, he said, *"I am old and gray-headed . . . and I have walked before you from my childhood unto this day."*

The aged man in Psalm 71:5, 17 had this testimony. He confesses, *"For You are my hope, O Lord God; You are my trust from my youth. . . O God, you have taught me from my youth and to this day I declare your wondrous works."*

How do we fear the Lord? If we fear the Lord, we will love God with all our heart, mind, soul, and strength; we will love His Word and obey it; we will obey God rather than man; and we will love to pray.

How do we teach our children to do this? We teach them in the spirit of life, not in legality. It is not so much what we say and teach, but what they see in our lives that will steer them in the right direction. We must pray and seek God that our children will come to know and experience God and His reality for themselves. We must pray that they will know God in such a way that they will be able to go out into the world and walk in the midst of evil and yet not be lured by it.

PRAYER:

"Dear Father, please anoint me to raise children who will fear you all their lives, children who will never walk away from you, even for one day. I pray that you will pour out your spirit upon my children and reveal yourself to them. Cause them to know your salvation and the reality of your powerful presence in their lives. Thank you Lord, Amen."

AFFIRMATION:

My mission in life is to raise God-fearing children!

90

Who Was She?
Part 2

"The fear of the Lord is the beginning of wisdom; and the knowledge of the holy is understanding" (1 Kings 18:3).

We continue to look at how Obadiah's parents prepared him for his life's destiny.

2. THEY RAISED HIM TO STAND FOR GOD AND FOR TRUTH, EVEN IF HE HAD TO STAND ALONE

Obadiah lived and worked in the midst of evil all around him. He lived in the midst of temptation. All of the king's court worshipped Baal. It was popular. It was the current trend. Obadiah was on his own as he gave his allegiance to the one true God. He had no encouragement, but he was not deterred. He was raised with an awe of God. He knew that God was the true I AM, even though he was the only one who continued to believe. To *"fear the Lord greatly"* in the midst of Jezebel's court, who sought to massacre all the prophets of the Lord, was certainly a great testimony.

Pray that God will empower you to raise children who will stand for God and His truth even if they have to stand alone, children who will confess, *"Let God be true but every man a liar"* (Romans 3:4).

3. THEY RAISED HIM TO WALK IN INTEGRITY AND TO DO A JOB WELL

Obadiah was the Lord High Chamberlain. I am sure that Jezebel hated Obadiah. She wanted to eradicate all those who served God, but she had to put up with Obadiah, because King Ahab could not do without him. The king's court ran smoothly under Obadiah's jurisdiction. No one else could do the job as well as he could. When we read 1 Kings 18:5, 6 we see that

Obadiah was next to the king in organizing the important matters of the land. Spurgeon comments that he "neither compromised his conscience nor jeopardized his position."

Don't accept mediocrity. Raise your children to excel in the gift that God has given them. Of course they don't have to excel in everything. God has made each one totally different. We must encourage them to be the very best in that which God has given them to do.

4. THEY RAISED HIM TO BE COURAGEOUS, EVEN IN THE FACE OF DEATH

When Jezebel ordered all the prophets of God to be massacred, Obadiah, at great risk to himself, hid 100 prophets in two caves. He went against the edict of the queen to do what was right. Obadiah's parents did not raise a weak jellyfish, but a warrior for God's army.

Pray that God will anoint you to raise sons and daughters who will be courageous men and women who will do what is right, even if they have to risk their lives. May they be young people who will answer God's call to David's cry: *"Who will rise up for me against the evildoers? Or who will stand up for me against the workers of iniquity?"* (Psalm 94:16).

5. THEY RAISED HIM TO BE GENEROUS

Obadiah not only hid the prophets, but he fed them bread and water from his own finances. This was in a time of severe famine when food was scarce and expensive.

Pray that God will help you to raise children who will not be interested in accumulating wealth for themselves but whose passion is to advance the kingdom of God.

6. THEY RAISED HIM FOR GREATNESS AND PREPARED HIM FOR HIS DESTINY

Obadiah may have been born and raised in a humble home, and yet he ended up in the king's court. His parents trained him thoroughly in every area of his life. They tutored him seriously. They prepared him to be ready for whatever destiny God had planned for him.

God has a destiny planned for each one of your children, and whether this task is large or small, it is great in the eyes of God. God has given you the awesome task of preparing each child for this purpose. You don't have to have a big, luxurious home to raise great children. You may only have a humble home. You may not even have all the things you think you need for teaching your children. Don't despair. You have enough when you have God. You have His power and His powerful Word.

I remember visiting the home in Kentucky where Abraham Lincoln was born. It was a tiny cabin, no bigger than many kitchens today. It had a dirt floor and an open fireplace to cook. But out of this humble abode, a home that would be condemned today, came a great president of the United States.

Lift your vision high. Raise your children for greatness. Encourage them to believe that they can do anything God gives them to do. They were born to fulfill the purposes of our mighty God. Raise them to believe that nothing is impossible. Give yourself totally to preparing them for their destiny and then stand back and watch what God will do. You will be amazed at where he will take your children to influence this world for God.

PRAYER:

"Oh God, I am aware of the mighty task you have given me to train and prepare my children for your purposes. I know I cannot do it on my own, but I thank you that you are with me. Please anoint me mightily for this task. Grant me your wisdom that you have promised to give liberally to those who ask for it. And let me never lose the vision of what I am doing. Amen."

AFFIRMATION:

I have the most important career in the nation. I am employed by God to prepare His children for the destiny He has planned for them.

91

Guarding All Fronts

"Appoint guards from the inhabitants of Jerusalem, each at his post, and each in front of his house" (Nehemiah 7:3).

God is very concerned about guarding. We don't have to wait long in the Bible to learn the principle. When God put Adam and Eve in the Garden of Eden, He told them to work in it and guard it (Genesis 2:15)! To guard a home is high on God's priority. We turn from the first book of the Bible to the last and find that God has twelve angels guarding the twelve gates of the New Jerusalem (Revelation 21:12). If it is important for God to have angels guarding each gate of His Holy City, then surely it is important to guard the gates of our homes.

We go to 1 Chronicles 9:17-27 and see the gatekeeping Levites guarding the house of the Lord in Solomon's time, just as their ancestors had guarded the tabernacle in the wilderness. They guarded *"the entrance" and they guarded "the four sides, to the east, west, north and south. . . And they spent the night around the house of God, because the watch was committed to them."* In Nehemiah we read that they appointed guards *"each in front of his house."*

GATEKEEPING MOTHERS

We are also gatekeepers, guarding on all fronts! We can never let down our guard. The enemy is subtle and he is out to destroy marriages and fragment godly homes. The biggest threat to his success is godly gatekeeping mothers who will not allow one opening for him to enter their homes. They watch at their entrance and they watch on every side. They watch what their children listen to, look at, read, and even what they speak! They check what is happening on their children's Facebook. They establish God's standard of righteousness in their home, not the world's standard. Consequently, when the enemy comes running to attack, he comes to a screeching halt at the gates of this righteous home! He has no access! No loopholes to get in! And he bows! Proverbs 14:19 says, *"The evil bow before the good: and the wicked at the gates of the righteous."* Don't you love that?

NEVER VIOLATE YOUR CONSCIENCE

One of the greatest ways we guard is by example. Your children see whether you have courage to act according to your conscience or whether you compromise. Sometimes on the weekend the extended family will come and we watch a family movie together. We have a big screen for our songs at church so we can play the movie on the big screen. It is sad that we sometimes find a scene that is not wholesome, even with family movies! What do we do? We immediately stop the movie.

That's the end, even though we could be tempted to see the ending! But, the children are watching. By our example they are going to learn to act according to their conscience, or compromise!

An *Above Rubies* helper asked our daughter Evangeline how she guards her 10 children. She replied, "We train them to be gatekeepers themselves. We train their conscience. We teach them righteous principles and train them to keep to them, not just when people are looking, but to be true to their own soul."

We cannot weaken in training our children. Proverbs 29:15 (NASB) says, *"The rod and reproof give wisdom, but a child who gets his own way brings shame to his mother."* You leave your children unguarded when you let them get their own way. That teaches them how to give into temptation. You are setting them up to be a prey to the enemy! You are preparing them to have a turbulent marriage. The diligent gatekeeping mother will teach her children how to say No to the temptations of the flesh.

THE DAILY RULE

We also guard our home by conducting Family Devotions with our family each morning and evening. It is hard for the enemy to take hold in our home when we read God's Word and pray together each day as a family. In 2 Chronicles 8:13, 14 (NASB) it tells us that, *"Solomon offered burnt offerings to the Lord on the altar of the Lord . . . and did so according to the daily rule . . . he appointed the Levites for their duties of praise and ministering before the priests according to* ***the daily rule*** *. . ."* This was a daily rule God expected of His people, morning and evening.

"What's all this business about a daily rule?" you argue. "Isn't that religiosity and legality? Shouldn't we do it when we feel the urge? I don't like the sound of duty." Yes, I am sure that it could become tedious if it is done without the anointing of the Holy Spirit who illumines the Word. 2 Corinthians 3:6 tells us that the *"letter kills but the Spirit gives life."*

LIFE-GIVING WORDS

However, how can a "daily rule" be legality when we are reading LIFE-GIVING WORDS? Jesus said, *"The words that I speak unto you, they are spirit, and they are life"* (John 6:63). God's life-giving words, anointed by the Holy Spirit, will guard your marriage and your children from the deceptions of the enemy. Read also Hebrews 4:12 and 2 Peter 1:3, 4. Sadly, many marriages are no longer together because they never established the daily rule of praying and reading God's Word together. Many families are in disarray because they have not gathered together daily around the Word of God, which is our manual for life.

May the enemy be scared of you as you guard the entrance to your home!

PRAYER:

"Father, please teach me how to be a diligent gatekeeper of my home. Please show me areas that are weak in my marriage and family life and please teach me how to build up the wall again. I want our family to be a bulwark against the enemy. In Jesus' name, Amen."

AFFIRMATION:

I am guarding my marriage and home on all fronts!

FURTHER SCRIPTURES ABOUT THE DAILY RULE:

Exodus 29:36, 38, 39; Numbers 28:3; 1 Chronicles 16:40; 23:30; 2 Chronicles 2:4; 13:11; 31:3; and Ezra 3:3, 4.

92

A Prudent Wife

Part 1

"A prudent wife is from the Lord"
(Proverbs 19:14).

I know you want to be a prudent wife, but what does it mean to walk it out in experience?

Different translations of the Bible translate "prudent" in different ways: *"a sensible wife"* (Moffat and many other translations), *"an intelligent wife"* (NEB), and *"an insightful wife"* (CEB).

The word "prudent" in this Scripture is the Hebrew word *sakal* and is translated by 25 different words in the King James Bible. We'll look at seven of these words, which teach us how to be prudent.

1. A CONSIDERING WIFE

A prudent wife **considers** what is right and how to act (Psalm 41:1 and Proverbs 21:12). My Lexical Aid describes a prudent wife as one who has "an intelligent knowledge of the reason for what she is doing." She is not walking in the dark. She knows who God created her to be as a wife and mother and walks in her role with pride and dignity.

2. AN INSTRUCTED WIFE

A prudent wife is an **instructed** wife. She comes to her marriage instructed and taught by the Holy Spirit, God's living and eternal Word, and by godly older women who are walking in truth. However, I acknowledge that many have not been taught this way and come into marriage completely clueless of what God expects of them. But, they are wives who want to learn and want to walk in the fullness of God's purpose for them.

It's never too late! So they set out to be instructed. They have a teachable heart to learn God's ways, rather than walking in their own ways. They search God's Word and seek out godly older women to teach them. They are open to reproof, instruction, and are willing to change.

Nehemiah 9:20 says, "*Thou gavest also thy good spirit to* ***instruct*** *them.*"

Psalm 32:8 says, "*I will* ***instruct*** *thee and teach thee in the way which thou shalt go: I will guide thee with mine eye.*"

Proverbs 21:11 says, "*When the wise is* ***instructed****, he receiveth knowledge.*"

3. A WISE-SPEAKING WIFE

A prudent wife teaches her mouth. She guards her lips knowing that her words will either build up and strengthen her marriage and family, or pull it down and destroy it.

Solomon confessed in Proverbs 10:19, "*In the multitude of words there wanteth not sin: but he that refraineth his lips is* ***wise****.*" The ESV translation says, "*When words are many, transgression is not lacking, but whosever restrains his lips is* ***prudent****.*" The prudent wife guards her mouth. She is not constantly blabbing, but chooses when to speak and what to say.

Proverbs 16:23 says, "*The heart of the wise teacheth his mouth, and addeth learning to his lips.*"

4. A SKILLFUL WIFE

The prudent wife seeks to be **skillful** in everything she does. She seeks to become an **expert** in mothering, teaching her children, and home management. She does not take her career lightly. She is never mediocre. She studies diligently how to feed her family healthily. She is the best cook in the neighborhood. She is always learning better ways to efficiently manage her home. She doesn't settle for the status quo, but searches out God's way for birthing, nursing babies, and natural God-given ways for healing.

This same word is used of a mighty warrior who is ***"expert"*** in shooting arrows (Jeremiah 50:9).

God gave Daniel and his three friends "*knowledge and* ***skill*** *in all learning and wisdom*" (Daniel 1:4, 17; 9:22).

5. AN UNDERSTANDING WIFE

The prudent wife has **understanding** (intellectual comprehension and insight) of God's ways. And she continually seeks for more and more understanding. She never stays in a rut. She is continually seeking and researching for God's understanding on every matter relating to her children and her home.

She understands that her marriage is a covenant for life and she does everything in her power to keep her marriage strong and healthy. She understands that her husband is her covering and that submitting to his leadership is for her blessing.

She understands that God has given her a unique role as a wife and mother to nurture and nourish her family. She is intelligent enough to know that this is her full-time career, appointed by God Himself. She does not compete for her husband's role as provider of the home. She understands that she is an Eve and not an Adam.

Daniel 11:33 says, "*They that* ***understand*** *among the people shall instruct many.*" The more we understand God's ways, the more opportunity we have to instruct people all around us. A prudent wife will drop seeds of truth wherever she goes and to whomever she speaks.

Also read these Scriptures where *sakal* is translated as understanding: Deuteronomy 32:29; 1 Chronicles 28:19; Nehemiah 8:13; Psalm 106:7; 119:99; Isaiah 41:20; Jeremiah 9:23, 24; and Daniel 9:13.

PRAYER:

"I thank you, Father, that I cannot make myself prudent. You remind me that a prudent wife comes from you. I yield myself to you to instruct me and lead me in your ways of wisdom and understanding. Please make me into the prudent wife you want me to be. Amen."

AFFIRMATION:

I am polishing the skills God has given me to be a prudent wife and mother.

93

A Prudent Wife

Part 2

"Many daughters have done virtuously, but thou excellest them all" (PROVERBS 31:29).

We continue our understanding on how to be a prudent wife.

6. A WISE WIFE

The prudent wife behaves **wisely**.

1 Samuel 18:30 tells us that *"David behaved himself more **wisely** than all the servants of Saul; so that his name was much set by."* Because of his prudence and wisdom, David's name was highly esteemed everywhere. The prudent wife also establishes a good name in the community, and even the nation. Proverbs 31:31 says, *"Give her of the fruit of her hands: and let her own works praise her in the gates."*

David confessed, *"I will behave myself **wisely** in a perfect way. . . I will walk within my house with a perfect heart"* (Psalm 101:2). Wisdom starts in the home before anywhere else.

Daniel wrote in Daniel 12:3, *"And they that be **wise** shall shine as the brightness of the firmament; and they that turn many to righteousness as the stars forever and ever."* The margin of my Bible and the AMP translate "wise" for "teachers." I believe that God has given mothers an inherent ability to teach. We begin teaching our children from the time they are born. We have an innate desire to teach our children in order for them to learn, and we do it naturally. We have the privilege of being "wisdom teachers" to our children and everyone around us. And, in doing so, we shine like the brightness of the sky above. Because mothers are teaching all day long, God sees them shining for Him. Does that make you happy?

Also read these Scriptures that translate *sakal* as wise: Job 22:2; Proverbs 1:3; 10:5; 15:24; 16:20; Daniel 12:10; and Amos 5:13.

7. A PROSPEROUS WIFE

The prudent wife makes everything in her home to **prosper**.

As a helpmeet to her husband, she cares for him, prepares healthy meals for him, prays for him, inspires him, builds him up, loves him, and encourages him daily. A husband who is respected and honored will ultimately prosper as a husband, father, and a man of God in all that he does.

As a mighty mother, she teaches, trains, and prepares her children to prosper. Of course, she knows that their greatest success is not the success of the world, but to walk in the destiny God has planned for them, to be strong in the Lord, to know how to stand against the wiles of the devil, to hate evil and love righteousness, and to walk in integrity and honesty. She knows her greatest task is to fill her children with God's Word as this is their secret to success.

Joshua 1:8 says, *"This book of the law shall not depart out of thy mouth; but thou shalt meditate therein day and night, that thou mayest observe to do according to all that is written therein: for then thou shalt make thy way prosperous, and then thou shall have good success."*

As a diligent manager of the home, she is frugal, she plants a garden, she doesn't waste her husband's hard-earned money, she looks well to the needs of her home, and she prepares for the future. Consequently her home prospers.

Ultimately, she knows that the secret of her success is in knowing God and walking in obedience to His Word and His ways. Deuteronomy 29:9 says, *"Keep therefore the words of this covenant, and do them, that ye may **prosper** in all that ye do."* Read also 1 Kings 2:3.

May you have a prosperous day.

PRAYER:

"Dear Father, I want to be a prudent wife. Please help me to be diligent in making my home to prosper, for the blessing of my husband, my children, and ultimately the world. Save me from being slovenly and foolish in all matters of the home. Amen."

AFFIRMATION:

I am no longer a halfhearted, but a wholehearted wife and mother.

94

Laid Bare
Part 1

"Now the purpose of the commandment is love from a pure heart, from a good conscience, and from sincere faith"
(1Timothy 1:5).

My friend, Val Stares (fellow-helper in the ministry of *Above Rubies* since its inception over 37 years ago and who was visiting with us from Australia), and Colin and I were driving home from town and exclaiming rapturously over the beautiful sight of the bare winter trees silhouetted in the twilight sky. The fine outer branches and twigs of the trees looked like intricate lace.

We could see every branch and every twig as the trees were laid bare for winter. God is a God of seasons—hot and cold, springtime and harvest. Just as it is necessary to have the "bare" winter in the physical realm, it is also part of the spiritual realm. It is good to have a season where we allow our hearts to be laid bare before the Lord.

We do not see the heart of the tree when it is covered with leaves. In the same way, we can cover up many things in our lives with "leaves." We can look good on the outside and yet have ugly habits or attitudes that we have not dealt with on the inside.

The bare branches and twigs speak of our inner thoughts, intents, and motives—motives that God alone sees, not even our husband. Why do we do what we are doing? What is our motive? Why do we speak the way we do? What is the underlying reason? In fact, it is a good idea to ask the Lord such questions. "Why am I angry?" "Why am I yelling at the children?" "Why am I always depressed?" If you come into God's presence and take time to listen, He will answer you and show you the answer so you can put it right.

Here and there we noticed birds' nests in the bare trees which we did not notice when they were covered with leaves. Often, too, we nest things in our hearts—good and bad. Sometimes we have a grudge and grow a nest all around it. Or, we harbor unforgiveness and make a nest of it, building up a foreign body in our hearts.

When you walk through a winter season, do you think you could lay your heart bare before the Lord? Can you let His pure light expose all your thoughts and motives? All the shadows? All the dark areas? Whatever He exposes, repent of it and deal with it.

Forget the façade. Let Him shine His light on all that hides in your heart.Throw away your nests of revenge, hurt, or self-pity that show up when your heart is exposed.

Make sure that your heart is pure and cleansed before the new season's leaves grow again.

PRAYER:

"Lord, I lay my heart bare before you. Expose everything in my heart that grieves your Holy Spirit. Please help me to get rid of all 'cover-ups.' I want a pure heart. Amen."

AFFIRMATION:

I am walking before the Lord and my family with a transparent heart.

95

The Upward Look
Part 2

"Thou art worthy, O Lord, to receive glory and honor and power: for thou hast created all things, and for thy pleasure they are and were created" (REVELATION 4: 11).

We are still enjoying this car ride and beholding the beauty of the winter trees. Now that I can see all their branches, I see they are stretching outward and mostly upward toward their Maker, reaching out in praise to the One who created them.

God created all things for His pleasure—all of His creation, and especially mankind, who is His highest creation. All creation was created to praise Him. Once again, we learn a lesson from the trees. We should always be looking up and stretching out our arms in praise to Him Who alone is worthy.

Recently, I was at my sister's home. Beautiful music played softly in the background. Suddenly, we recognized the *Hallelujah Chorus* of Handel's Messiah. We turned up the volume to the absolute maximum! Loud! The anointed music pulsated the room. We rose, and without thinking about it, automatically raised our arms in praise to the One who is the only Potentate, King of kings and Lord and lords, and who will reign for ever and ever.

May we be saved from looking downward and taking our eyes off the Lord. Every branch reaches upward to the Lord, the Sun of righteousness. Like the branches, keep looking up. Get into the habit of raising your heart and soul to the Lord. And yes, your arms too. Throw away all your inhibitions. You were born to praise Him. You were born to raise your arms toward Him. You were born to fix your heart and gaze upon Him.

Raise your hands to Him in praise. Raise your arms to Him when you are crying out for His mercy and for answers to your prayers. Not only the tree branches, but each tiny twig reaches upward to the Lord. Turn everything in your life to Him—your thoughts, yearnings, cries, hurts, sorrows, and your praise and thanks.

Reach out to the heavens. With upward look and lifted arms, your vision will enlarge. You will see things you have never seen before. You will view life from a different vantage point.

Join with David and cry out, *"Unto thee, O Lord, do I lift up my soul"* (Psalm 25:1). Again, *"I will lift up my hands in thy name"* (Psalm 63:4). And especially for your children: *"Lift up your hands to him in prayer, pleading for your children. . ."* (Lamentations 2:19, NET). Sometimes the concern for your children is such that a little prayer is not enough. You have to cry out to the Lord. In times like this it is instinctive to lift up your arms as you cry out to the Lord.

PRAYER:

"Thank you, Lord, that I can praise you along with all your creation. Help me to be like the trees that are always turned to you in praise and adoration. Amen."

AFFIRMATION:

I'm changing my downward look to the upward look!

FURTHER STUDY:

Nehemiah 8:6; Psalm 28:2; 86:4; 119:48; 121:1, 2; 123:1; 134:2; 141:2; 143:8; Isaiah 40:26; Lamentations 3:41; Luke 21:28; 1 Timothy 2:8; and Hebrews 12:2.

96

Plenty of Room
Part 3

"My people will no longer be ashamed. For when they see the surging birth rate and the expanding economy, then they will fear and rejoice in my name"
(Isaiah 29:22, 23, TLB).

As we drank in the beauty of the bare winter trees, we also noticed something very interesting. Every now and then we would see a bird's nest in a tree, and yet amazingly the trees were not *full* of bird's nests. And yet there are thousands and thousands of birds. We see birds all the time around our home here in the woods. Obviously there are plenty of trees for birds to choose to build their homes.

I think it is much the same way with people. The secularists and humanists frighten us with notions that the world is being overpopulated and we must limit having children. This is a lie. There is plenty of room for people, just as there are plenty of trees for the birds to build their homes. God has created a big world which He created to be inhabited. This is His purpose for the world He created.

If you have driven from Los Angeles to the East Coast across this great country of the USA, you will see that there is plenty of room in this land. You can drive for hours and hours and see no population at all. Suddenly, you drive through a big city and out again, once again driving through miles and miles of uninhabited land! And this is not only in the USA. I have traveled by bus and train through Malaysia, driving for miles between cities, seeing only a few homes here and there. The cities may be crowded, but the country is not.

Brian Carnell in *How Much Food is Available Now?* says, "The world currently produces more than enough food to provide every single man, woman and child alive today with an adequate diet."

Dr. Jacqueline R. Kasun in *Too Many People* states, "If you allotted 1,250 square feet to each person, all the people in the world would fit into the state of Texas."

Professor Budziszewski writes, "Fertility is already declining in every region of the world, and population growth has been slowing down since the late 1970s. In the developed countries, the net reproduction rate is 0.7 and dropping, which means that the next generation will be only 70 percent as large as this one. Nicholas Eberstadt of the *American Enterprise Institute* suggests that we may one day face not an explosion, but an 'implosion' of population."

"China, everyone's favorite supposed example, has fewer than 60 percent as many people per square mile as the United Kingdom (England, Scotland, Wales, and Northern Ireland). Obviously, then, China's problem is not overpopulation, but underdevelopment. Many people think that population growth prevents the economic growth of poor nations, but a number of economists now suggest the opposite: every new person brings not only another mouth to feed, but two hands with which to work. Misguided efforts to help poor countries by suppressing their natural population growth may actually hurt them."

Sean Lanahan states that the entire population of planet earth can lay down and take a nap inside the small state of Connecticut with some room to spare, leaving the remainder of the globe completely uninhabited.

We don't need these statistics as God, the Creator and Master of the universe, has everything in control. Isaiah 45:18 says, *"For thus saith the Lord that created the heavens; God himself that formed the earth and made it; he hath established it, he created it not in vain,* ***he formed it to be inhabited****: I am the Lord; and there is none else."* He gave us this earth to "subdue, and take dominion." As we look to Him, He will give the ingenuity and enablement to house and grow food for all the children God sends.

I think we should believe God rather than the pessimistic secularists, don't you? Isaiah 2:22 says, *"Cease ye from man, whose breath is in his nostrils: for wherein is he to be accounted of?"*

PRAYER:

"I thank you, Lord, that I can completely trust you. You have the whole universe in your command. You have everything in your control. You have created this world to be filled with your people. Amen."

AFFIRMATION:

The "foolishness" of God is wiser than human wisdom! I'm trusting God rather than man's ideas.

97

I Am Crowned!

"Bless the Lord, O my soul, and all that is within me, bless his holy name! Bless the Lord, O my soul, and forget not all his benefits: who forgives all your iniquities, who heals all your diseases, who redeems your life from destruction, who crowns you with lovingkindness and tender mercies"

(Psalm 103:1-4).

What a loving, tender-hearted, and compassionate God we have. Every day He crowns you and me with lovingkindnesses.

Do I hear you say, "When was the last time God crowned me?" Stop and think about it for a moment. God crowns you with His lovingkindnesses through people around you. When your baby or your little child smiles at you, in fact when anyone smiles at you, you are crowned with God's lovingkindness.

Every time your husband embraces you, you receive another one of God's lovingkindnesses. Every time he helps you with the dishes or bathes the children, it is God's blessing to you. When someone says an encouraging word to you, it is God's lovingkindness to you. He never forgets you. You are graven on the palms of His hands. He has forgiven your sins. He has healed you many times.

When you sit down at your table and eat the bountiful food God daily provides for you, it is His lovingkindness to you. When you reap the harvest from the garden you have planted, it is His blessing. When you look up at the clouds and are reminded of His faithfulness, you are crowned. You look at the mountains, the ocean, the undulating hills, and trees and you are blessed that He has given you all these things to freely enjoy. And you don't have to pay a cent. The world is yours to enjoy, no matter how little money you have in your pocket!

Start looking for God's lovingkindnesses. They are all around you. They are happening to you throughout the day. Instead of focusing on your problems and disappointments, look out for God's blessings. Learn to be aware of them. Do not forget one of His benefits. Not one! Gratefully, thank the Lord for every tiny one.

I am starting to do this more and more. In fact, when I read this Scripture about being crowned, I was very convicted. I realized that I had been taking God's blessings for granted. Now I seek to thank the Lord for crowning me every time I receive a blessing—a hug, a smile, a word of encouragement, the blessing of children around me, and the joy they give with their antics and funny things they say. The blessings of God's creation—the flowers, birds, butterflies, and the beautiful colors of the fall which I am beholding as I look out of my window now. It makes such a difference to your life when you become grateful for every little crowning from the Lord.

Because God crowns me through His people (and maybe even those who are not His people), am I letting Him use me to be His vehicle through which He can crown others? This is a challenge, isn't it?

Recently my daughter Serene faced a difficult trial, made a little more difficult because her husband was overseas fulfilling a contract with the military. In the middle of being weighed down by the problem, her car ran out of gas in the middle of a busy lane of traffic. She had all the children in the car and the car wouldn't budge another inch! She put on her blinkers and decided to call the police, but her phone suddenly went dead! She was stuck!

She cried out to the Lord. He nudged her to try the car again. Miraculously, it started and she managed, weaving through traffic, to get to the side of the road. She was still stranded, but God showed her His lovingkindness. People stopped their cars to help her. She had more help than she could use. Some were people she would normally be scared to talk to. One big burly guy with tattoos all over him drove to a service station and bought gas for her and filled up her car. She knew God was sending His angels to her. Not only did she get gas for her car, but the lovingkindness of strangers, including this big scary tattooed "angel," caused Serene to feel God's lovingkindness pouring all over her. She forgot all her problems and filled the van with praises the rest of her journey.

We can be used by the Lord to crown our husband, our children, and many others with the lovingkindness of the Lord. Let's be on the offensive to give love—hugs, smiles, affirmation, encouragement, and practical help wherever needed. What a blessing to be the instrument of God's lovingkindness.

PRAYER:

"Thank you, dear Father, for constantly crowning me with your lovingkindnesses. Help me to be aware of them and full of gratefulness to you. And please anoint me to be a messenger of your lovingkindnesses to others around me. Amen."

AFFIRMATION:

I will not forget a single blessing!

98

Hidden Jewels

"And they shall be mine, saith the Lord of hosts, in that day when I make up my jewels" (Malachi 3:17).

Every saint is a jewel of God. I am convicted by God to look at people (and also my children) in this light. Often we cannot see the jewel as it hides behind the rough exterior. All we see is unsightly hard rock, but God wants us to look beyond what we see on the surface.

We sometimes hear the phrase, "He's a rough diamond." This means that the person is pretty rough on the outside but inside they may have a heart of gold. We need to be reminded that there is a diamond, or perhaps a sapphire, an emerald, an opal, a ruby, or an amethyst in each person.

The jewel in every person is different. Each jewel will reveal different colors and lights of God's character. But we cannot see the beauty shining from the jewel until it has been cut and polished. And what a painful process this is. Much cutting has to be done to reveal the many-faceted hues and beauty of the gem. The cutting goes on and on. And when it is finished, the polishing starts. It hurts.

I know God has to do so much more cutting and polishing with me. May we let Him do His work and cut away all the roughness and hardness. May we also have patience with all God's saints, even those who are still rough and uncut, understanding that God is still working on them, as He is still working on us. One day we will see the finished product, the beautiful jewel.

May God give us patience with our children, too. God has given us the task of being a lapidary (a cutter and polisher of gems). It is the lapidary's art to reveal the gem. Sometimes we may feel it is a hopeless job, but we must never give up hope.

There is a jewel in every child of God. There is a precious jewel in every one of your children that waits to be revealed. We must see it by faith. We must pray it into being. We must have vision, patience, understanding, and diligence as we fulfill this great task. It does not happen overnight. It is painstaking and time-consuming.

There will come a day when God will make all His jewels into a crown. I am thinking of the hymn we used to sing as children . . .

When He cometh, when He cometh,
To make up His jewels,
All His jewels, precious jewels,
His loved and His own.

Like the stars of the morning,
His brightness adorning,
They shall shine in their beauty,
Bright gems for His crown.

Isaiah 62:3 says, "*Thou shalt also be a crown of glory in the hand of the Lord, and a royal diadem in the hand of thy God.*"

Zechariah 9:16 says, "*They shall be as the stones of a crown, lifted up as an ensign upon his land.*" The NLT says, "*They will sparkle in his land like jewels in a crown. How wonderful and beautiful they will be!*" God promises that there will be a day when Israel will sparkle like the jewels of a crown in their land. Although this literally talks about Israel, I believe that God wants all His redeemed people to shine in this world like glittering jewels in a crown.

It's time for all the roughness, hardness, mediocrity, worldliness, selfishness, and indifference to be cut away and for God's glory to be revealed in the land.

PRAYER:

"Dear Father, please cut away all the rough exterior that clouds your beauty from being revealed in me. I want to shine like a precious gem in this world for you. Help me to also see each one of my children as a precious jewel in your kingdom, waiting to shine with your glory. Amen."

AFFIRMATION:

I am a lapidary.

99

Emmanuel—God with Us

"Therefore the Lord himself shall give you a sign; Behold, a virgin shall conceive, and bear a son, and shall call his name Immanuel" (Isaiah 7:14).

The prophets revealed many different names as they foretold the birth of the Messiah who would come to deliver Israel and the world. Isaiah 9:6 reveals His name as Wonderful, Counselor, The Mighty God, The Everlasting Father, and The Prince of Peace. God revealed to both Joseph and Mary, at separate visitations, that His name would be called JESUS *"for he shall save his people from their sins"* (Matthew 1:21, 23 and Luke 1:31).

But it was also prophesied that He would be called Emmanuel—God with us. What love! What purpose God has for us in the gift of His son, Yeshua. He gave Him to be the Savior of the world—to save us from our sins and to deliver us from our selfishness and bondages so that we can live unto Him. But, He also gave Him to be with us. He wants to be close to us. He wants to fellowship with us. He wants to be present in every detail of our lives. There is no greater gift we could receive than Emmanuel.

Because Jesus died to take the punishment of our sin, we have cleansing and forgiveness, but also the infilling of the Holy Spirit, God with us.

This gets to the very nitty-gritty of our lives. Dear mother, God is with you in every moment of your mothering. He is with you when you feel overwhelmed and even when you feel you can't cope a minute longer. He is with you in all your frustrations. He is with you as you tackle another mound of dishes. He is with you as you scrub and clean. He is with you as you sort out squabbles and sibling rivalry. You are not doing all this on your own. Emmanuel is with you. Acknowledge that He is with you. Thank Him that He is with you. It makes all the difference (Revelation 21:3).

All these moments, the good and the difficult, are sacred moments because of Emmanuel. He is with you as you sit in your rocking chair and nurse your baby. He is with you as you read stories to your children and in the daily disciplines of teaching and training your children. Your attitude, and the atmosphere of your home, changes when you understand that God is powerfully with you in every mothering moment.

He is with you in the dark times. He is with you when you do not feel Him and think that He is far away. Your feelings have nothing to do with it. Your feelings do not change Emmanuel!

You may feel you are drowning in the waters, but in the midst of the deep waters, God says, *"I am with you . . . they shall not overflow you."* The waters of adversity may be swirling around you. They look fearful and you wonder how you will survive. But remember, you cannot drown when God is with you. It is impossible. Read Isaiah 43:2 again. Instead of talking about all that you are going through, thank God that He is with you in your trial.

Emmanuel is in command of the universe. I love the reference to Emmanuel in Isaiah 8:8, 10 that He is in charge and He owns the land! Yes, Emmanuel owns the land of Israel!

The greatest gift we have in this earthly life is that God is with us. We are not citizens of this world. We are only sojourners here, ambassadors for the King of kings on our way to eternity. He does not leave us here to grovel and exist on our own. He has sent Emmanuel to be with us, teaching us, guiding us, and filling us with His wisdom and His glorious presence as we fulfill our destiny.

PRAYER:

"Oh God, I thank you that you are Emmanuel. I thank you that you have promised to never leave me or forsake me. I thank you that you are with me even when I do not feel your presence. Amen."

AFFIRMATION:

I can face every situation in life because of Emmanuel!

100

The Humility of God

"Who, being in the form of God, thought it not robbery to be equal with God: but made himself of no reputation, and took upon him the form of a servant, and was made in the likeness of men: and being found in fashion as a man, he humbled himself, and became obedient unto death, even the death of the cross"
(PHILIPPIANS 2:6-8).

What is Christmas today? Christmas trees, decorations, lights, tinsel, parties, Santa Claus, and an overabundance of food. Total antipathy to the very first Christmas!

The first Christmas was celebrated in poverty. In fact, it was more than poverty. It was degradation. Today, if a couple were so poor that they had to have their baby in a dirty animal stable, the Social Services would take their baby away from them. But, 2,000 years down the line, it seems that the humility of Christmas has been forgotten.

I think it would be good to remind ourselves of the true reality of Christmas, don't you?

1. THE HUMILITY OF MARY

Mary was a humble maiden with a humble lineage. She was not a royal princess. She was not a High Priest's daughter. She was not rich. Mary herself confesses in her song: *"He hath regarded the low estate of his handmaiden. . . He hath put down the mighty from their seats, and exalted them of low degree"* (Luke 1:48-52). But God chose this unknown virgin to bring forth His precious Son. He chose her because she was a willing vessel. Often those who have everything materially are not willing vessels.

God is not looking for riches and material possessions. He is looking for women with obedient hearts—mothers who will welcome to their hearts the children God sends them. He is looking for those who have the same spirit Mary had when she said, *"Be it unto me according to thy Word"* (Luke

1:38). She was totally surrendered to the will of God. In the face of poverty, ridicule, rejection, and estrangement, she embraced this child who would be the Savior of the world.

2. THE HUMILITY OF JOSEPH

Joseph was a humble carpenter from a humble village. Do you remember that Nathanael said of Jesus, *"Can there any good thing come out of Nazareth?"* (John 1:46). Jesus was spurned by his fellow residents of Nazareth who asked, "Is not this the carpenter's son?" (Matthew 13:55).

3. THE HUMILITY OF HIS BIRTHPLACE

Jesus was born in a stable, most probably a cave, with the dirt, smells, and messes of the animals all around. He was then laid in a stone feeding trough, fit only for the animals. Jesus was born to be King, but God didn't provide a palace for His Son in which to be born. He didn't provide a doctor, nurses, and hospital. There was no cradle, beautifully draped with lace and frills. Only straw! Was there even that? No Christmas card paints the true reality of the scene.

Richard Crashaw writes . . .

> "That the Great Angel-blinding light should shrink
> His blaze, to shine in a poor Shepherd's eye;
> That the unmeasur'd God so low should sink
> As Pris'ner in a few poor rags to lie."

If this was the beginning of the Son of God, why do we, the sons and daughters of God, expect that we should have all the niceties of life? Of course, if God blesses us with them, we will receive them with joy, but should we expect them? Everything surrounding the birth of Jesus was humble. It is interesting that in the body of Christ we have the "Faith movement" and the "Discipleship movement" and so on. But, has anyone ever heard of the "Humility movement"? We don't take to this so well, do we? And yet this is how God planned for His beloved Son to be born, and this is how He lived all through His life. Shouldn't humility also be the hallmark of our Christian experience?

God reveals His heart to us in the place He chose for His Son to be born—the lowliest and humblest place possible. God loves the poor. He promises to raise up the poor. He watches over them. Even in the birth of

His Son, He relates to the poorest of the poor.

It is also amazing to think that God chose to bring forth His beloved Son through the process of birth. He could have sent him down from Heaven on a chariot of fire! He could have sent a legion of angels to escort Him from the majesty of Heaven. But no! He chose for His Son to be conceived and nurtured in a womb, to be born of a woman, the way that God planned for all human life to come into this world. Surely this raises birth to a high estate. What a privilege to give birth and give life to children, the very same way that Jesus came into the world. How blessed we are as women.

4. THE HUMILITY OF JESUS' DEDICATION

After the days of a mother's purification, the parents took the baby to the temple to be dedicated. They had to bring a lamb to be sacrificed for the dedication. However, if they could not afford a lamb, they brought two turtle doves or young pigeons (Leviticus 12:6-8). The account in Luke 2:22-24 tells us that Joseph and Mary brought doves or pigeons. They belonged to the poor class. They couldn't afford to bring a lamb. God chose the poorer class to bring forth the King of kings and Lord of lords.

We don't have to own our own home and have all the modern conveniences before we are ready to have a baby. All we have to have is willing and welcome hearts. God will always provide for the children He sends. The poor who have children are richer than the wealthy who reject children.

May God help us to keep humble hearts, for it is the humble God notices (Isaiah 66:2).

PRAYER:

"Dear Lord Jesus, thank you for leaving the glory of Heaven to come to this earth. Thank you for humbling yourself to become a little baby. Thank you that you came to die for my sin. How can I ever thank you adequately? With all my being I worship and love you. Amen."

AFFIRMATION:

God loves to bring His glory to humble circumstances.

Further Study

DAY 27

What is an abomination to God?

Leviticus 18:22-30; 20:13; Deuteronomy 7:25, 26; 18:9-13; 27:15; 1 Kings 14:24; 2 Kings 16:3; 21:2; 23:7, 24; Proverbs 3:32; 6:16-19; 11:1, 20; 12:22; 15: 9, 26; 16:5, 12; 17:15; 20:10, 23; 24:9; Jeremiah 4:1; 13:27; 44:22; Ezekiel 7:3-9; 11:21; Luke 16:15; Romans 1:25-32; 1 Corinthians 6:9, 10; 1 Timothy 1:9-11; and Revelation 21:8, 27.

Other Scriptures about the gates of the city for you to study:

Genesis 19:1; Deuteronomy 16:18; 17:2-5; 21:19-21; 22:15; 25:7-8; 28:52; Joshua 20:4; Judges 16:1-3; Ruth 4:1, 11; 2 Samuel 15:2; 19:8; 1 Kings 22:10; 1 Chronicles 9:19-23; 26:13; 2 Chronicles 8:5; 14:7; 32:6; 35:15; Nehemiah 3:1-32; 8:1-3; Esther 2:19-21; 3:2; Psalm 87:2; 147:13; Proverbs 1:21; 8:1-3; 31:31; Isaiah 29:21; Jeremiah 17:19, 20; 38:7; Ezekiel 44:1-3; 48:31-34; Daniel 2:49; Amos 5:10-15; Acts 3:1-10; and Revelation 21:12-21.

DAY 58

We have HOPE in God. (Sometimes the King James Version translates the Hebrew word for "hope" as "expectation" or "trust.") Psalm 4:5; 9:10; 13:5; 25:2; 26:1; 28:7; 31:6, 14, 24; 32:10; 33:18, 21-22; 37:3-5; 38:15; 39:7; 42:5, 11; 43:5; 52:8; 56:3-4, 11; 62:5-8; 71:5, 14; 84:12; 86:2; 91:2; 112:7; 115:9-11; 125:1; 130:7; 131:3; 143:8; 146:5; 147:11; Proverbs 3:5, 6; 28:25; 29:25; Isaiah 12:2; 26:3, 4; Jeremiah 17:7, 13, 17; Lamentations 3:22-26; and 1 Peter 3:5.

We have HOPE in God's "exceeding great and precious promises."

Psalm 119:42, 43, 49, 74, 81, 114, 116, 147, 165, 166; 130:5; Romans 15:4; and 2 Peter 1:4.

We have HOPE as we go through trials.

Job 13:15; Psalm 22:4, 5; Romans 5:3-5; 8:24, 25, 28; 1 Corinthians 13:13; 2 Corinthians 4:16-18; and Hebrews 12:2-3.

We have HOPE in a glorious future—eternal glory forever and ever.

1 Corinthians 15:19-22; Ephesians 1:18-20; Colossians 1:5; 2 Timothy 2:10; Titus 1:2; 2:12-14; 3:7; and 1 Peter 1:3-5, 13.

DAY 71

God brings us out to bring us in:

Deuteronomy 4:20, 34, 37, 38, 45, 46; 5:6, 15; 6:12, 21; 7:8, 19; 8:7, 14; 9:26, 29;11:10-12; 13:5, 10; 16:1, 3, 6; 20:1; and 26:8-9.

We have been called to live in light and show others the light.

2 Samuel 22:29; Psalm 18:28; 27:1; 34:5; 36:9; 43:3; 89:15; 90:8; 97:11; 104:2; 112:4; 118:27; Isaiah 2:5; 58:6-8, 10; 60:1, 2; Micah 7:8, 9; Matthew 4:16; 5:14-16; 6:22; Luke 1:79; 12:35; John 1:4, 9; 3:19-21; 5:35; 8:12; 9:5; 11:9, 10; 12:35, 36, 46; Acts 26:18, 23; Romans 13:12-14; 2 Corinthians 4:4-7; Ephesians 1:18; 5:8-11, 14; Philippians 2:14, 15; Colossians 1:12, 13; 2 Peter 1:19; 1 John 1:7; and 1 John 2:8-11.

DAY 83

Speaking boldly, disputing, and persuading:

Acts 4:13, 29-31; 9:27, 29; 13:43, 46; 14:3; 17:17; 18:4, 13, 26; 19:8, 26; 28:23; Ephesians 6:18, 19; Philippians 1:20; 2 Corinthians 5:11; and Proverbs 28:1.

Speaking before kings and rulers:

Psalm 119:46; Proverbs 22:29; Acts 4:8; 24:10-21, 24-27; and 26:1-32.

Always ready to speak, even to those who oppose:

Ezekiel 33:8, 9; Matthew 10:18-20, 32, 33; Colossians 4:6; 2 Timothy 2:25; 4:1, 2; and 1 Peter 3:15.